ChicaNerds in Chicana Young Adult Literature

ChicaNerds in Chicana Young Adult Literature analyzes novels by the acclaimed Chicana YA writers Jo Ann Yolanda Hernández, Isabel Quintero, Ashley Hope Pérez, Erika Sánchez, Guadalupe García McCall, and Patricia Santana. Combining the term "Chicana" with "nerd," Dr. Herrera coins the term "ChicaNerd" to argue how the young women protagonists in these novels voice astute observations of their identities as nonwhite teenagers, specifically through a lens of nerdiness—a reclamation of brown girl self-love for being a nerd. In analyzing these ChicaNerds, the volume examines the reclamation and powerful acceptance of one's nerdy Chicana self. While popular culture and mainstream media have shaped the well-known figure of the nerd as synonymous with white maleness, Chicana YA literature subverts the nerd stereotype through its negation of this identity as always white and male. These ChicaNerds unite their burgeoning sociopolitical consciousness as young nonwhite girls with their "nerdy" traits of bookishness, math and literary intelligence, poetic talents, and love of learning. Combining the sociopolitical consciousness of Chicanisma with one aligned to the well-known image of the "nerd," ChicaNerds learn to navigate the many complicated layers of coming to an empowered declaration of themselves as smart Chicanas.

Cristina Herrera holds a PhD in English from Claremont Graduate University and is currently Professor and Chair of the Department of Chicano and Latin American Studies at California State University, Fresno. She is the author of *Contemporary Chicana Literature: (Re)Writing the Maternal Script*. Cristina has also coedited multiple anthologies, including *Nerds, Goths, Geeks, and Freaks: Outsiders in Chicanx/Latinx Young Adult Literature* (with Trevor Boffone), and *Voices of Resistance: Essays on Chican@ Children's Literature* (coeditor with Laura Alamillo and Larissa M. Mercado-López). Journal publications include "Seeking Refuge Under the Mesquite: Nature Imagery in Guadalupe García McCall's Verse Novel" (*Children's Literature Association Quarterly*, Summer 2019), "Soy Brown y Nerdy: The ChicaNerd in Chicana Young Adult (YA) Literature" (*The Lion and the Unicorn: A Critical Journal of Children's Literature*, Fall 2017), and "Cinco Hermanitas: Myth and Sisterhood in Guadalupe García McCall's Summer of the Mariposas" (*Children's Literature*, 2016), among others.

Children's Literature and Culture
Jack Zipes, Founding Series Editor
Kenneth Kidd and Elizabeth Marshall,
Current Series Editors

Postcolonial Approaches to Latin American Children's Literature
Ann González

'The Right Thing to Read'
A History of Australian Girl-Readers, 1910–1960
Bronwyn Lowe

Battling Girlhood
Sympathy, Social Justice and the Tomboy Figure in American Literature
Kristen B. Proehl

Cyborg Saints
Religion and Posthumanism in Middle Grade and Young Adult Fiction
Carissa Turner Smith

Out of Reach
The Ideal Girl in American Girls' Serial Literature
Kate G. Harper

The Arctic in Literature for Children and Young Adults
Edited by Heidi Hansson, Maria Lindgren Leavenworth and Anka Ryall

Terror and Counter-Terror in Contemporary British Children's Literature
Blanka Grzegorczyk

ChicaNerds in Chicana Young Adult Literature
Brown and Nerdy
Cristina Herrera

For more information about this series, please visit: www.routledge.com/Childrens-Literature-and-Culture/book-series/SE0686

ChicaNerds in Chicana Young Adult Literature
Brown and Nerdy

Cristina Herrera

NEW YORK AND LONDON

First published 2021
by Routledge
52 Vanderbilt Avenue, New York, NY 10017

and by Routledge
2 Park Square, Milton Park, Abingdon, Oxon, OX14 4RN

Routledge is an imprint of the Taylor & Francis Group, an informa business

© 2021 Taylor & Francis

The right of Cristina Herrera to be identified as author of this work has been asserted by her in accordance with sections 77 and 78 of the Copyright, Designs and Patents Act 1988.

All rights reserved. No part of this book may be reprinted or reproduced or utilised in any form or by any electronic, mechanical, or other means, now known or hereafter invented, including photocopying and recording, or in any information storage or retrieval system, without permission in writing from the publishers.

Trademark notice: Product or corporate names may be trademarks or registered trademarks, and are used only for identification and explanation without intent to infringe.

Library of Congress Cataloging-in-Publication Data
A catalog record for this book has been requested

ISBN: 978-0-367-86021-9 (hbk)
ISBN: 978-1-003-01647-2 (ebk)

Typeset in Sabon
by Apex CoVantage, LLC

To Kris, for loving this ChicaNerd for over 20 years,
and to all ChicaNerds out there, especially Elena:
I see you.

Contents

Acknowledgments ix

Introduction: *ChicaNerds in Chicana Young Adult Literature: Brown and Nerdy* 1

1 Not Your Nerd or "At Risk" Chicana Student: On ChicaNerds and Stereotypes 19

2 "Those White Girls Don't Like It": Community and ChicaNerd Feminist Resistance in Jo Ann Yolanda Hernández's *White Bread Competition* 38

3 "The College Girl From the *Barrio*": Calculus and ChicaNerdiness in *What Can(t) Wait* 55

4 Theater and Chicana Poetic Development in Guadalupe García McCall's *Under the Mesquite* 70

5 Band Shirts and Rebellion: Resisting the "Buena Hija" Trope Through Nerdiness in *I Am Not Your Perfect Mexican Daughter* 88

6 "Tis the Life of a Misunderstood Teenage Poet": ChicaNerd Poetics in *Gabi, A Girl in Pieces* 105

7 To Be or Not to Be: Shakespeare, College, and Chicana Feminist Consciousness in *Ghosts of El Grullo* 121

Conclusion: Reflections From a (Grown-up) ChicaNerd: Or, Why I Wrote This Book   139

Works Cited   147
Index   158

Acknowledgments

This book would never have seen the light of day without the guidance, support, and encouragement from the many friends, colleagues, and family members who have uplifted and sustained me. To people I may have inadvertently left out, please forgive this oversight.

For their enthusiasm of my project and unparalleled professionalism, I thank the staff and editors at Routledge's Children's Literature and Culture Series, especially Michelle Salyga. Many thanks to the anonymous reviewers, whose suggestions for revisions greatly improved the book.

Without the brilliant writers whose words inspire me, there would be no ChicaNerds to write about: Ashley Hope Pérez, Jo Ann Yolanda Hernández, Erika Sánchez, Patricia Santana, Isabel Quintero, and Guadalupe García McCall.

I could not have survived those trying days of high school and after were it not for the many books I read along my journey that taught me that I could and should dare to dream beyond the walls of my bedroom. I especially thank the brilliant writers who have gifted me with their kindness over the years, including Melinda Palacio, Lucrecia Guerrero, Carla Trujillo, Dahlma Llanos-Figueroa, and Denise Chávez.

At Fresno State, I consider myself incredibly fortunate to have met colleagues that I consider my chosen family. I owe many thanks especially to my colleagues in the Department of Chicano and Latin American Studies who have taught me the meaning of friendship and solidarity: Maria-Aparecida Lopes, Annabella España-Nájera, Ramon Sanchez, Luis Fernando Macías, and Mai Vang. I thank colleagues outside of my department and university as well for their friendship, conversation, kindness, and for their support of my work: Andrew Jones, Amber R. Crowell, Jennifer Randles, Adela Santana, De Anna Reese, Ravi Somayajulu, Jenna Tague, Laura Alamillo, Larissa M. Mercado-López, Rosa I. Toro, R. Joseph Rodríguez, Patricia D. López, Ana Soltero-López, Diane Blair, Samina Najmi, Katie Dyer, Gina Sandí-Díaz, David Campos, Shane Moreman, Kathleen Godfrey, Aimee Rickman, John Beynon, Melanie Hernández, Jaime Rodríguez-Matos, Maritere López, William Arcé, Lori Clune, William Skuban, Kathryn Forbes, Takkara Brunson, Yolanda

x *Acknowledgments*

Doub, Davorn Sisavath, Jenny Banh, Romeo Guzmán, Leece Lee-Oliver, Elvia Rodríguez, Carissa García, Carribean Fragoza, and Brenda Venezia. Mil gracias to my students for keeping me grounded.

Thank you to the College of Social Sciences and Dean Michelle DenBeste at Fresno State for funding my conference travel, which planted the seed for this project. Bernadette Muscat, dean of undergraduate studies, has patiently fielded my anxious questions over the years. Thank you as well to Xuanning Fu, vice provost of faculty affairs, for the incredible kindness he has always shown me. Mil gracias to my amazingly supportive provost, Saúl Jiménez-Sandoval, for his mentoring and encouragement.

A special thank you to my labor union, California Faculty Association, especially the Fresno State chapter, for tirelessly advocating for faculty during trying times. My campus's executive board deserves a medal for their work.

Over the years, I've been privileged to be part of a circle of amazing scholars of Chicanx/Latinx literature and Chicanx studies, whom I also count as some of my dearest friends. Much love and respect to Trevor Boffone, Marci R. McMahon, Eliza Rodríguez y Gibson, Lourdes Alberto Celis, Ella Díaz, Gabriella Gutiérrez y Muhs, Marisela Chávez, Patricia Pérez, Magdalena Barrera, Marion Rohrleitner, Rita Alcalá, Marta López-Garza, Carolyn González, Amrita Das, Naida Saavedra, Sandra Ruíz, Helane Adams Androne, Claire Massey, Georgina Guzmán, and Sandra D. Garza. Britt Ríos-Ellis, Debi Cours, María Gurrola, Rebecca Koltz, Katie Gantz, and the rest of my fabulous HERS sisters, class of 2018: thank you!

I first presented an earlier version of what would eventually turn into this book, "Soy Brown and Nerdy," at the John Jay College Latinx Literature Conference in 2017. The organizers, Belinda Linn Rincón and Richard Pérez, have shaped this biennial conference into a Latinx literary force to be reckoned with, and for that, I remain in awe of their vision.

The journal *The Lion and the Unicorn* published my article in the September 2017 issue, volume 41, number 3, which would later become the springboard for this book.

I could not breathe, think, or create without my family, especially my beloved husband of 15 years and partner of 23, Kristopher W. Kunkel, who has been by my side since I was a shy, incredibly insecure college student who liked to read and who dreamed of one day being a professor. Thank you, mi amor, for your patience, loyalty, generosity, and love.

To the rest of my family: gracias. My other half, my twin sister, Elena, has walked this ChicaNerd path with me since the womb. You survived and thrived those lonely years with me, mi cuatita, to be the fiercely smart, compassionate, loyal, and strong person you are today. My mother, Serafina, has taught me the meaning of hard work, persistence, and the necessity of speaking out, and nothing I have done is without her. Te amo, Mama. Thank you to my older brothers, Chavita and Marcos, for sticking up for their little sisters. My precious girls, Carmelita, Cleo, and Cindy, teach me every day the meaning of unconditional love through their tail wags, purrs, energy, drool, and endless cheer.

Many family members, furry and human, have departed this earth, but I feel their presence every day. My abuelos, Mamá Chonita y Papá Tomás, fed me with stories, nurturance, and fierce pride in our Mexican roots, and I hope that I have honored their memory. Los extraño. My beloved in-laws, Robin and Roland Kunkel, have left me with the most precious gift I could ask for, their son. Life simply is not the same without them. I also write in loving memory of my faithfully departed doggies, many of whom slept by my side as I wrote, studied, and labored. How I miss you, my Minnie, Lucy, Otto, Sam, and Hazel.

Lastly, I wish to thank and acknowledge ChicaNerds, near and far, for their brilliance, tenacity, resistance, and bravery. I hope that in this book you find the power to shout, scream, and claim your rightful space of nerdy fabulousness. I hold you all in my heart. ¡Adelante!

Introduction
ChicaNerds in Chicana Young Adult Literature: Brown and Nerdy

Introduction: Why ChicaNerds?

The year was 1992. I had just turned 14 and was about to enter high school—a moment in life that I would look back upon with fondness when I'd meet my classmates years later at our reunions, according to my older brothers and the movies I watched. At 14 years of age, I was a painfully shy young woman, quiet, some may even say timid, and scared shitless. High school turned out to be the opposite of what everyone around me had promised it would be like, not the haven it was for my handsome and popular older brothers, not by a long shot. Instead, my identical twin sister, Elena, and I found ourselves like lost fish trying to swim upstream, doing everything we could to simply survive a day in our invisibility; 1992 was that year we entered the iron gates of high school, and it proved to be the year we would face some of the most devastating obstacles for young women to endure: the sudden abandonment by our father, Salvador, who never returned and the breast cancer diagnosis of our mother, Serafina—events that occurred seemingly out of the blue, life's cruel joke that gave no notice, no advance warning. Amid these life-altering events, high school beckoned, a terrifying place for quiet and unassuming Chicana bookworms who struggled to make friends. My solace was reading, but no matter how I tried to escape within the pages of the *Sweet Valley High* book franchise, the privileged lives of identical twins Elizabeth and Jessica Wakefield were light years away from the world I knew. Like the Chicana scholar Tiffany Ana López said of her adolescence, the same would be true for me: "When I was growing up Chicana, I never read anything in school by anyone who had a *z* in their last name. No González, no Jiménez, no Chávez, no López. And I grew to accept this and eventually to stop looking, since no one showed me that indeed such writers existed" (*Growing Up Chicana/o* 17). There were few books that could capture what it meant to be Chicana—to live with the daily struggle of trying to make ends meet; to speak Spanish with my mother, English with my siblings; to love reading as much as I loved the Mexican music and food that surrounded me.

2   *Introduction*

Elena and I would no doubt have been considered nerds by our classmates, a cruel taunt that I would struggle with throughout high school. Nerd: that awkward, bumbling kid with the mismatched clothes; pocket protectors; braces; acne; horn-rimmed glasses; few friends; straight As. These are the images I saw when I heard the word "nerd," a fate nobody I knew wished upon themselves.

Decades later, as I began my study of Chicana young adult (YA) literature, I suddenly found protagonists who were refreshingly familiar. In books by Ashley Hope Pérez, Guadalupe García McCall, Jo Ann Yolanda Hernández, Erika Sánchez, Patricia Santana, and Isabel Quintero, I was reminded of my teenaged self, a young Chicana who immersed herself in books and who desperately wanted to go to college to leave high school, that cruel place, behind. Years later when I met these relatable and now celebrated protagonists, I remember uttering to myself, "These are nerds. Chicana nerds. ChicaNerds!" Gone were the narrow stereotypes that I had inadvertently believed to be true, that to be a nerd was to be a rejected pariah. Instead, these were curious, smart, ambitious, bookish Chicanas who *liked* to study, who wanted to learn more, beyond their high school surroundings, and who relished in that studiousness. This unabashed pleasure in learning, I argue, exists alongside their burgeoning Chicana social consciousness, their insistence on uniting these disparate (if they were to believe those stereotypes about them) parts of themselves. As I argue, these young women can be Chicanas and nerds, what I call ChicaNerds: interesting, sometimes quirky, smart, astute young women who exist outside the white mainstream and on the fringes of the Chicanx communities they love *and* critique. Moreover, these novels display the importance of claiming a ChicaNerd identity as a refreshing statement on brown girl self-love, seldom visible in popular culture. By representing smart, studious, and politically conscious Chicanas in their novels, the writers normalize these qualities in Chicana teenagers, and in doing so, insist to their readers that ChicaNerds exist, if we only dare to see them. Normalizing Chicana intellectual curiosity and love of learning, I argue, is a resistant strategy that attempts to undo the common script of adolescent Chicanas as "at risk" and their families as uncaring about education. As this book demonstrates, the fictional portrayals of a diverse range of Chicana adolescents as smart, funny, and eager learners *are* acts of Chicana feminism, as they challenge the limiting, narrow representations of young Chicanas.

This book examines college-bound Chicanas in novels by five Chicana YA writers and one Anglo writer: Jo Ann Yolanda Hernández's *White Bread Competition*, Ashley Hope Pérez's *What Can(t) Wait*, Guadalupe García McCall's *Under the Mesquite*, Erika Sánchez's *I Am Not Your Perfect Mexican Daughter*,[1] Patricia Santana's *Ghosts of El Grullo*, and Isabel Quintero's *Gabi, A Girl in Pieces*. As an established genre, Chicana YA texts abound, but what these literary texts share is an examination of Chicana adolescence that is tinged with nerdiness and where love of learning amid family, school, and community pressure are central concerns the protagonists must navigate. As I argue, these protagonists are young women who insist on their right to pursue intellectual knowledge and curiosity, all while expressing distinct working-class Chicana feminist beliefs—traits I define as "nerdiness." Combining the term "Chicana" with "nerd," I have coined the term "ChicaNerd" to argue how these young women voice astute observations of their identities as non-white teenagers specifically through a lens of nerdiness—a reclamation of brown girl self-love for being a nerd that demands a more complex, honest representation of Chicana adolescence that we rarely see in mainstream culture. In their representation of studious and smart Chicanas who love their families and who aspire to attend college, the writers insist that we reclaim these aspects of Chicana identity to include traits of nerdiness that have traditionally not been associated with this population. We are all too familiar with the common stereotype, visible in popular, mainstream culture that aligns Chicana identity with "urban" problems of teenage pregnancy, poverty, and the looming threat of high school dropout rates. While these remain concerns among scholars and activists, to be sure, the ChicaNerd texts demand acknowledgment of multiple ways of being Chicana, refusing to ascribe to stereotypes that deny Chicana intellectual curiosity and talent. In my examination of ChicaNerd protagonists in the proceeding chapters, I discuss variations of nerd identities that distinguish each protagonist in her process of claiming a ChicaNerd identity. Luz Ríos, the protagonist in *White Bread Competition*, is an avid speller who wins her high school's bee, only to face opposition by white community members in her attempts to compete at the citywide district bee. Marisa Moreno, the protagonist in *What Can(t) Wait*, is a ChicaNerd with a talent for calculus and whom I classify as a Chicana math nerd. Lupita, *Under the Mesquite*'s protagonist, is a thespian who enjoys writing poetry, and the novel itself employs a verse narrative structure. Likewise, Isabel Quintero's protagonist, Gabi, is also a budding poet who discovers enthusiasm for performing her poetry in the spoken word tradition. In a similar vein, Julia (*Mexican Daughter*) and Yolanda (*Ghosts of El Grullo*) are literature nerds, although in a humorous twist, Yolanda's literary nerdiness and infatuation with Shakespeare later conflicts with her emerging Chicana consciousness that she develops as a new MEChA (Movimiento Estudiantil Chicano de Aztlán) club member in college. Julia's rejection of her family's strict gender roles is expressed through rebellion, and her love of literature and writing serves as an emotional balm to cope with the tragedy of her older sister's sudden death.

While the majority of the writers examined in this study are Chicanas, I have chosen to include a novel by an Anglo YA writer, Ashley Hope Pérez, who has written predominantly about Chicanx communities in her critically acclaimed novels. Pérez's positionality as a white woman married to a Chicano man is important to note, but I offer a brief explanation of my decision to include her novel in a study on Chicana young adult literature. First, Pérez's novels, from her most recent text of historical fiction, *Out of Darkness*, to her understudied novel *What Can(t) Wait*, are distinctively situated in Chicanx communities, and the protagonists themselves are of Mexican descent. Spanish phrases and words are commonly found in her novels, marking connections between her texts and those written by the Chicana novelists included in this book. However, I do not wish to discount the significance of what it means for a white woman to write texts about Chicanx characters and my decision to include her novel as Chicana. While for some it may be problematic to include her in this book, I have chosen to do so because despite her position as a white woman, the text's important elements, from the Chicana protagonist to its sympathetic examination of the Chicanx family, connect the work to the other YA novels included. A white woman's positionality undoubtedly raises the question of the "white savior" trope I discuss in my chapter on *What Can(t) Wait*, but her book's critical examination of this savior ideology is refreshing and subversive. This in itself also unites the novel with the Chicana-authored YA texts. I am interested in the ways Pérez compassionately and critically writes about a ChicaNerd, Marisa, shedding light on the circumstances of her life, her Chicanx family, and her community without shaming, castigating, or otherwise attempting to suggest that what Marisa needs is salvation by a white character or that assimilation via rejection of her Chicanx family is the path she should take. By no means am I suggesting that Pérez's own personal proximity to Chicanidad via her marriage to a Chicano male is sufficient to make her Chicana, but her familiarity with this community allows her to write about characters like Marisa in a way that few Anglo writers have. With nuance and great insight, Pérez traces Marisa's process of claiming a distinct Chicana adolescent path that honors her family and community. Marisa is undoubtedly a ChicaNerd.

In fact, in my chapters on *Mexican Daughter*, *Gabi*, and *What Can(t) Wait*, I also briefly examine the three novels' representations of their white teachers who mentor them in the college application process. Although the teachers are earnest in their attempts to help their ChicaNerd pupils, the protagonists struggle to negotiate their own desires to attend college while recognizing their teachers' privileged perspectives that do not take into account the young women's familial, cultural, and economic backgrounds. The teachers demonstrate what education scholars Michelle Fine and Lois Fine describe as educators' efforts "under the best of circumstances and often under the worst . . . to create classrooms, schools, and communities in which youth engage in critical inquiry, produce rich and provocative conversation, generate significant social projects, and emerge as young scholars with civic and moral sensibilities" (5). *Under the Mesquite* also factors in a teacher/student dynamic, but the teacher is Chicano, and though he shares Lupita's ethnicity, his advice to her encourages assimilation via language erasure as a means to excel at dramatic poetry. While my analysis does not necessarily privilege the student/teacher dynamic in the novels, I engage in a brief discussion of the relationship as one aspect of the development of ChicaNerd identity. All the characters in this study are on the cusp of college life, with the exception of Yolanda Sahagún from *Ghosts of El Grullo*, whose four years of college at the University of California, San Diego, are chronicled in this sequel to Patricia Santana's award-winning YA novel *Motorcycle Ride on the Sea of Tranquility*. A further note on Santana's novel, *Ghosts*, is warranted. Scholars of YA literature may question my decision to include this text in my study, given that the novel ends when the protagonist is approximately 22 years of age and about to enter graduate school to study literature. While YA literature would not often consider Yolanda a young adult, this novel's inclusion rests on the fact that the text deftly traces Yolanda's ChicaNerd identity during her final year of high school and her college years. The majority of the text examines Yolanda's growth during her formative years, including the end of adolescence. Further, the death of her mother, which occurs during this peak transition from young adult to adult, is a common element of YA literature, as the protagonist must learn to navigate her future life as an adult and as a motherless young woman. By closing this study with an examination of *Ghosts*, I also aim to show a trajectory of ChicaNerd identity—that is, Yolanda's graduation from college and eventual graduate school attendance; plot events that occur at the novel's conclusion symbolize where the younger ChicaNerds will follow.

Representations of young girls and their schooling is a common trope found in both children's and young adult literature, but my examination of ChicaNerds should not be conflated with another type of identity, the schoolgirl. While the term "schoolgirl" has often been used as a descriptor for an earnest, smart, even "goody two shoes" type (indeed, when I was in high school, to be called a "schoolgirl" was akin to being called a "nerd"), it is important to note that "schoolgirls have long been associated with misery," according to Elizabeth Marshall (93); they are quiet, seemingly disembodied, young women who are under the control of the mean schoolmaster. Within this traditional narrative, the schoolgirl is obedient, passive, and white. Because of this tendency to align the schoolgirl with white girlhood, the term "is also exclusionary, and often operates in tandem with the law and with educational policies to bar, segregate, and/or criminalize black, brown, and queer youth" (Marshall 6). Within this ideology, to be a "schoolgirl" and a girl of color is apparently impossible. But I insist on the term "ChicaNerd" to account for how the Chicana writers examined in this manuscript align nerdiness with academic intelligence, Chicana feminist resistance, Chicanx community and familial love, and joy. Rather than bask in misery like their schoolgirl counterparts, ChicaNerds learn to develop their brown-girl identities around the qualities of feminism, community support, and agency. As first-generation, working-class Chicana teenagers, the young women protagonists maneuver academic settings that have been hostile for women of color. Although most of the novels I examine largely use the high school setting as a subplot for the Chicana characters' cultivation of a ChicaNerd identity, the protagonists' academic pursuits often mirror the challenges faced by first-generation college students of color: struggles with imposter syndrome, including combating the all-too-familiar stereotype of the "at risk" Latina student. Defying these stereotypes, I argue that the ChicaNerds insist on their inherent intelligence, resisting the tokenization of young women of color. In my analysis of these ChicaNerds, I examine what I see as a reclamation and powerful acceptance of one's nerdy Chicana self. While popular culture and mainstream media have shaped the well-known figure of the nerd as synonymous with white maleness, Chicana YA literature subverts the nerd stereotype through its negation of this identity as always white and male. As I argue, these ChicaNerds unite their burgeoning sociopolitical consciousness as young nonwhite girls with their "nerdy" traits of bookishness, math and literary intelligence, poetic talents, and love of learning. Combining the sociopolitical consciousness of Chicanisma with one aligned to the well-known image of the "nerd," ChicaNerds learn to navigate the many complicated layers of coming to an empowered declaration of themselves as smart Chicanas. I point to the writers' politicized projects of normalizing Chicana intelligence and love of learning via the nerd identity. The novels call for more critical and diverse representations of Chicana identity, including those marginalized identities like nerds that have seldom been aligned with young women of color. As I discuss in more detail in Chapter 1, to be a nerd, although it has been a stigmatized identity, has also been equated with intellect, a quality that educational deficit narratives have proclaimed does not exist among Chicanx/Latinx communities. I insist on uncovering the ways that these novelists, through their compassionate representations of ChicaNerds, undo damaging, harmful stereotypes of Chicanas and their communities as deficient or uncaring about education or learning—something I examine in more depth in Chapter 1. By portraying Chicanas as intelligent subjects who are nurtured and supported by their families and communities in their nerd paths, the political implications of the novels cannot be underestimated. Unlike deficit narratives that advocate for assimilation at the expense of their Chicanx communities, the novels celebrate the Chicanx communities not as hindrances to academic achievement or intellect but as the source of profound support, love, and acceptance for the protagonists to embark on their ChicaNerd paths. As empowered ChicaNerds, these adolescents also profess a love of one's nerdy, brown-girl self, modeling confidence, intelligence, and pride to their families and the communities that surround them.

Classifying the characters as nerds is not to suggest that there is something unique or unusual about Chicanas who enjoy reading, theater, writing poetry, or math. This logic narrowly frames ChicaNerds as outliers, as young girls who are not "supposed" to have these types of interests. Instead, I argue that this nerd identity offers teenaged Chicanas an empowered subjectivity in stark contrast to the all-too-familiar stereotypes of the fumbling, rejected (white male) nerd in popular culture. While these characters do not necessarily refer to themselves as nerds, they do, in fact, claim their right to intellectual curiosity and enthusiasm for "nerdy" school subjects, qualities I read as nerdiness.[2]

The ChicaNerds in the YA texts struggle with warring expectations of "appropriate" teenage girlhood in their working-class Chicanx families amid their own desires to excel in their studies and go on to college. By successfully battling the gender, racial, and class dynamics of their families and their communities, these protagonists learn to accept and proudly claim their Chicana nerdiness. Although a number of studies have examined the nerd as a symbol of white, socially awkward, tech-savvy maleness, this study expands existing scholarship to focus on a group that has been overlooked by scholars as well as media outlets: young Chicana women who enjoy calculus, theater, reading, and poetry. As Amy Cummins and Myra Infante-Sheridan claim, "Education as a priority for Mexican American families is a major theme in many works of Mexican American YAL" (23). These texts share an emphasis on voice, demonstrated in their first-person narrative structures, which allows readers to see the significant process of a distinct ChicaNerdy feminist voice in formation. Like many young adult texts, these novels pose questions on identity and the self, given that "adolescence is often presented as the time set aside for such existential questioning" (Larkin 160). Examinations of the self and subjectivity are common in young adult literature, when protagonists are considering their identities and the spaces they occupy (McCallum 3). Not surprisingly, many of these texts thus employ the first-person narrative voice. This structure is highly common in YA literature, as Rachael McLennan claims: "If, as the many first-person narratives of adolescence seem to imply, a search for identity involves a search for voice, then the act of narrating one's self through story is vital to constructions of adolescence" (27). Although speaking of Chicana "adult" novels that feature younger protagonists, Annie O. Eysturoy's analysis of Chicana literature applies much to the YA novels examined in this manuscript: "In the case of the child and adolescent protagonist, the emphasis is on social and environmental influences on her rite of passage" (4). The YA protagonists, in their quest to authenticate their ChicaNerd identities, insist on defining themselves on their own terms, rather than as socially or culturally ascribed. The ChicaNerds featured in the novels are also vastly different, and these varying intellectual interests give a seldom seen diversity and complexity to young nerds of color.

8 *Introduction*

Among other questions, I ask the following: What does it mean that these Chicana YA texts employ narratives around Chicanas who are not only talented at certain subjects but also enjoy them? How do these texts defy, challenge, and critique mainstream myths of Chicana teenagers as defiant young women who do not enjoy or excel in school?

Including these complex ChicaNerd characters in books intended for younger audiences is significant, given that Chicana YA writers "have turned to children's and young adult writing to invoke critical consciousness at a young age" (Herrera 100). Given the tendency of mainstream culture to portray Chicanas and Latinas as hypersexualized and "hot," the prevalence of ChicaNerds in Chicana YA writing is all the more significant. Further, "Issues specific to identity, assimilation, and education remain critical concerns in the Latina community, especially for second and third generation adolescent females. Addressing this information is fundamental to understanding the motives of authors who write about themes central to an underrepresented culture" (Baxley and Boston 65). Chicana literary scholars, since at least the early 1990s, have written extensively on Chicana literature's confrontation with prominent stereotypes of Chicana and Mexican women. As the pioneering Chicana feminist scholar Norma Alarcón reminds us, "The name Chicana, in the present, is the name of resistance that enables cultural and political points of departure and thinking through the multiple migrations and dislocations of women of 'Mexican' descent" ("Chicana Feminism" 185). Reading the YA texts through this Chicana feminist critical lens highlights the ways in which contemporary Chicana YA writers follow in the tradition of earlier Chicana writers who have contested and resisted narrow understandings of Chicana identity. Further, according to another prominent theorist, Yvonne Yarbro-Bejarano, scholars within the field of Chicana literary studies must "[work] with the terms 'Chicana' and 'Chicano' as constantly producing identities (rather than as fixed and immutable categories) and as engaging productive tensions that are vital to continued projects of theoretical expansion" ("Sexuality" 229).

Reading ChicaNerds as Chicanas in the midst of developing their sociopolitical consciousness lays claim to Yarbro-Bejarano's call for literary scholars to examine the fluidity of Chicana identity, and in the case of the YA texts discussed here, the need to recognize young Chicana nerds as part of this process of "constantly producing identities." Indeed, Chicana literature has a long-standing tradition of portraying smart, inquisitive, and curious female protagonists. Novels like Lorraine López's *The Gifted Gabaldón Sisters* (2008), Bárbara Renaud González's *Golondrina, Why Did You Leave Me?* (2009), and Denise Chávez's *Loving Pedro Infante* (2001) portray adult Chicanas with nerdy interests, while Latina YA texts not featured in this study, including Viola Canales's *The Tequila Worm* (2005), Meg Medina's *Yaqui Delgado Wants to Kick Your Ass* (2013), and Elizabeth Acevedo's *The Poet X* (2018), also represent intelligent teenagers we could deem nerds. The novels examined in this study also share concerns with non-Latinx African American YA writers—most notably, Angie Thomas and Renée Watson. While undoubtedly intended for younger audiences, the YA novels nevertheless address much of the same themes examined in Chicana literary criticism from the early 1990s to the present. The texts examined in this study subversively embrace nerdiness as a source of empowerment. Rejecting the notion that nerdiness "belongs" to white males, I argue that the Chicana YA novels examined here call for a critical reclaiming of nerdiness and intelligence—traits deemed undesirable, inappropriate, or even nonexistent in young Chicanas.

In my examination of YA texts by Chicana writers that centralize the experiences of adolescent Chicanas, I recognize the limitations of my point of inquiry. Indeed, Chicano YA writers, including Benjamin Alire Sáenz and Rigoberto González, present characters in their works that could also be considered nerds—seen in *Aristotle and Dante Discover the Secrets of the Universe* and *The Mariposa Club*, respectively. In their unapologetic representations of queer Chicano masculinities and boyhood, these texts also explore themes related to the academic pursuit of knowledge and nerdiness. Like their Chicana YA counterparts, male-centered novels by Sáenz and González, among others, examine the familial, cultural, and societal pressures of "fitting in" and being an outsider or outcast as a brown, queer, male nerd.

While it is not my intent to suggest that Chicana YA texts are more concerned with nerd identity or any other simplistic reductions, this book's central point of inquiry—Chicana teens I see as nerdy and empowered as a result of this nerd identity—insists that an examination of young Chicana womanhood matters, particularly when a combination of racist *and* patriarchal structures of power that operate on macro levels and familial levels has denied ChicaNerds the privilege of academic exploration and intellectual curiosity. "Adolescence is often the time period in one's life when searching for individual identity, struggling with society's norms, and grappling with moral issues can create constant personal conflicts," and this is especially true for young women of color who must also confront age-old stereotypes that refuse to recognize them as intelligent, worthy, and capable of educational excellence (Baxley and Boston 18). The ChicaNerds examined here must not only contend with the all-too-familiar societal and media stereotypes of pregnant, "at risk" Chicana teenagers but also patriarchal-encoded expectations to be the obedient "buena hija" that exist alongside the common media script. The ChicaNerds' daily battles surrounding familial, cultural, and societal constraints around young women of color demonstrate a common theme in YA literature: the negotiation of "oppressive power dynamics at play" (Suhr-Sytsma 3). As young women of color, the ChicaNerds at all times struggle with what this means within the context of their families, schools, and communities. Although referring to Asian American YA literature, Ymitri Mathison's observation resonates with what Chicana YA writers represent in their works, particularly "how they . . . create their own uniquely blended and interstitial selfhood and place within the larger mainstream and their own ethnic societies" (10–11). ChicaNerds must come to terms with the many layers of coming into being, as women of color, as daughters of Mexican immigrant parents, and as nerds. The ideal good daughter, by traditional patriarchal standards, does not question her unequal status within this family structure, even while the family does encourage educational attainment, and these additional gender expectations are notably absent in many Chicano YA texts.

Significantly, in all of the novels I examine, the maternal relationship in particular is a guiding force in the ChicaNerds' many navigations among their community, school, and familial social circles.[3] In their edited volume *Mothers in Children's and Young Adult Literature*, scholars Lisa Rowe Fraustino and Karen Coats correctly note the still relatively underexplored theme of mothers in texts for young audiences, suggesting that this has much to do with the "vexed relationship between feminism and motherhood studies" (9). The ChicaNerds in five of the six texts are all daughters of Mexican immigrant mothers, and these differing perspectives—Mexican immigrant mother versus first-generation Chicana daughter—offer complexities to this relationship. While the texts broach many other important themes beyond the maternal relationship, the novels are invested in representing mothers in a way that that sympathetically addresses the many tensions that exist between them and their daughters. In her research on Chicana YA literature, scholar Laura López argues that Chicana protagonists mostly have to navigate treacherous social spaces without maternal and familial support (45) but that is not the case in the texts examined in this book. While at times overbearing or even unsympathetic, the maternal figures do support their daughters' intellectual aspirations, and this mother-child relationship operates in more thematically significant ways than in the Chicano-centered texts.[4] Although referring to picture books for children authored by writers of color, Dorina K. Lazo Gilmore's assessment of maternal representation is an apt way to consider the ways in which Chicana YA writers address the mothers in their novels, for these mothers "reject the mainstream 'good mother' model and prove more multidimensional, serving as a different mothering example for the future" (97). In her work on Chicana mother-daughter pedagogies, Alma Itzé Flores's research sheds light on how her critical analysis "disrupt[s] the narrative that Chicana immigrant mothers do not care about their children's education by showing how these mothers envisioned higher education for their daughters, despite never being part of that world themselves" (195). Likewise, the novels examined in this book also critically reclaim the maternal bond as a significant source of the ChicaNerds' academic achievement. Gender, in addition to ethnicity, social class, and even school peer pressure to lose one's virginity, constrain Chicana nerds in unique ways that may be seldom visible in YA texts that center on Chicano young male experiences. ChicaNerds, in contrast, struggle to balance what potential burdens their families place on them, even as they recognize familial sources of support, especially from their mothers.

Chicanas in YA Scholarship

Although the primary aim of this book is to show the significance of the ChicaNerd identity to combat the simplistic myths that have construed Chicana teenagers as always on the verge of teen motherhood, dropping out of school, or chola gang life, this study also takes to task the invisibility of Chicana-authored YA texts in young adult literary scholarship, including scholarship on Chicana literature that has seldom examined texts for younger audiences. *The Cambridge Companion to Latina/o American Literature*, for example, is a major volume that examines the Latinx literary canon, yet there is a major oversight, as not a single chapter addresses Chicanx or Latinx young adult literature. This oversight supports Marilisa Jiménez García's assertion that "scholars in Latinx studies rarely consider the position of literature for youth and writers for young audiences in the study of historically oppressed peoples. That is, in ethnic and postcolonial studies, literature for youth, remains, for the most part, marginalized" (115). Many YA writers in this study, including Guadalupe García McCall and Ashley Hope Pérez, have earned distinguished honors and awards, and their success demonstrates the growth of Chicana YA literature as an established (and highly marketable) genre. Yet this success has not translated into more visibility in the scholarship. In fact, my coedited volumes, *Voices of Resistance: Interdisciplinary Approaches to Chican@ Children's Literature* (2017) and *Nerds, Goths, Geeks, and Freaks: Outsiders in Chicanx and Latinx Young Adult Literature* (2020), are two of the first anthologies of essays on Chicanx/Latinx children's and YA literature. My colleagues and I embarked on those collections precisely because we were disturbed by the reality that Chicanx/Latinx young adult and children's literature remains vastly understudied in both Chicanx/Latinx literary scholarship and YA literary scholarship.

While the study of YA and children's literature is hardly a new field, evidenced by the number of scholarly journals and literary associations dedicated to the study of these genres, benchmark anthologies have rarely included discussions of Chicana-authored YA texts. As Frederick Luis Aldama points out, "The two-thousand-plus-page behemoth, *The Norton Anthology of Children's Literature* (2005), does not include one US Latino author" (10). The same can be said of studies such as *Contemporary Dystopian Fiction for Young Adults: Brave New Teenagers*; *Reading Like a Girl: Narrative Intimacy in Contemporary American Young*

Adult Literature; *The Edinburgh Companion to Children's Literature*; *Power, Voice, and Subjectivity in Literature for Young Readers*; and *Children's Literature: New Approaches*, to name just a few. Although not necessarily focusing solely on YA texts, other studies, such as *The Girl: Constructions of the Girl in Contemporary Fiction by Women* and *Growing Up Female: Adolescent Girlhood in American Fiction*, do not include discussions of Chicana or Latina-authored novels. Karen Coats's very recent publication laments that representation of diverse children's and YA literature "has a long way to go to claim equity on the shelves in the children's and teen section" (37), yet even her lengthy book avoids sustained discussion of Chicanx/Latinx YA writers despite recognizing the scholarly absence of this critical work. Roberta Seelinger Trites's new study *Twenty-First Century Feminisms in Children's and Adolescent Literature* similarly does not include a broader discussion of Chicana or Latina texts beyond *Gabi, A Girl in Pieces* and Pam Muñoz Ryan's *Becoming Naomi León* (2018). Jiménez García's claim regarding the erasure of Chicanx and Latinx children's and YA literature from the "canon" of American children's literature is apt: "when it comes to fundamental questions within the overall field of children's literature such as 'Who is "the child"?' 'What is childhood?' 'What is children's literature?' scholars have mainly drawn on a heritage of Anglo literature to create theory" (114–15). Mandy Suhr-Sytsma's description of Indigenous YA literature is particularly insightful as a mode of understanding systemic erasure and the response to it via works of fiction: "In short, YA books are centrally concerned with young people finding their place vis-à-vis 'the system.' That both resonates and strikes a discordant note when Indigenous subjects are involved, because they are operating in multiple systems—their Indigenous societies and the colonial systems imposed on those societies" (xviii). The prevailing whiteness of literary theory and scholarship, coupled with the tendency to deny YA and children's literature as viable points of inquiry, makes the work of Chicana YA scholarship all the more pressing and urgent.

Taking these facts "side-by-side," as Jiménez García references, scholars in the fields of literature and Chicanx studies have much work to do to address the large gap of critical theory on Chicanx/Latinx children's and YA literature. When scholarship avoids discussion of ethnicity/race, or worse, does not consider the works of writers who do not comfortably fit within the dominant mainstream, students and readers are left with an incomplete, even flawed, understanding of the realities of the present day—they "miss something," argue Yvonne Atkinson and Michelle Pagni Stewart (2). I reference these scholarly collections to address what I see as an alarming truth regarding the fields of both Chicanx literary scholarship and the YA scholarly fields at large: there is no shortage of texts by Chicana YA authors, but their important works are seldom included as part of the Chicanx literary canon, much less the long-established canon of American children's and YA literature. In addressing the theoretical absence of Chicanx/Latinx children's and YA literature, I recognize the path-breaking scholarship of Sonia Alejandra Rodríguez, Marilisa Jiménez García, Larissa Mercado-López, Isabel Millán, Tiffany Ana López, R. Joseph Rodríguez, Phillip Serrato, Amy Cummins, and others.[5] This study urges publishers, general readers, scholars, and students to see Chicanx teenagers, young women in particular, as readers and as characters. Chicana YA literature, in its representation of this often overlooked demographic, contests the invisibility and erasure of Chicana teens, especially maligned ChicaNerds, whose stories deserve critical, scholarly attention.

Chapter Overview

This book is divided into seven chapters. In Chapter 1, "Not Your Nerd or 'At Risk' Chicana Student: On ChicaNerds and Stereotypes," I provide a critical context for understanding the significance of ChicaNerds in Chicana YA literature. Using a theoretical framework influenced by scholarship in girlhood studies, psychology, education studies, and sociology, I examine how these disciplines have theorized stereotypes around Chicanx/Latinx educational attainment, nerds and intelligence, and young womanhood. Popular mainstream culture defines the "nerd" around a stigmatized identity, visible in films and even technology repair companies like the Geek Squad, and these representations are considered. Most importantly, however, this identity, even as it stigmatizes, nevertheless is complicit in the social script of the nerd as not only socially awkward but also as white and male. Most often used as a punch line or comic relief, the nerd is an ostracized figure, an outsider whose gifted intelligence marks him as uncool and socially inept. As a consequence, the overall lack of popular representations of nerds of color points to a harmful stereotype of Chicanas on the opposing end of the spectrum: the Chicana student labeled "at risk" by teachers and counselors and who is in danger of being pushed out of schools and thus abandoning her studies without choices. My analysis of six Chicana novels positions the characters as resistant to both stereotypes.

In Chapter 2, "'Those White Girls Don't Like It': Community and ChicaNerd Feminist Resistance in Jo Ann Yolanda Hernández's *White Bread Competition*," I discuss Hernández's work, which has surprisingly received little critical attention thus far, despite its publication in 1997, several years before we would see works published by the other writers included in my study. Perhaps more so than the other novels, *White Bread Competition* gives a sobering account of 14-year-old Luz's confrontation with racist classmates and white community members who threaten to jeopardize her participation in a spelling competition in the San Antonio, Texas, school district. I discuss Luz's eventual achievement of ChicaNerd agency, which begins as a reluctant process of voicing frustrations with her Chicanx community's high expectations of her; in doing such, I argue that the novel traces Luz's empowered ChicaNerd path through community and family, especially her mother and grandmother. To participate in this bee, Luz must learn how to embrace her Chicanx community as her staunch supporters and fierce advocates against the white supremacy that is rampant in her city.

In Chapter 3, "'The College Girl From the *Barrio*': Calculus and ChicaNerdiness in *What Can(t) Wait*," I examine Ashley Hope Pérez's debut novel, which centers on the life of 17-year-old Marisa Moreno, who lives with her Mexican immigrant parents, Patricia and Omar, her older sister, older brother, and young niece in Houston, Texas. Due in large part to her enthusiasm and talent for calculus, I classify Marisa as a math nerd, arguing that the novel presents readers with critical insight into Marisa's calculus ChicaNerd identity. As I argue, this text rejects, among other issues, problematic stereotypes of working-class Chicanx families perceived as "obstacles" that prevent Marisa from obtaining a college education, the "white savior" myth, rape culture, and racist beliefs that Chicanx families do not care about education. Though not authored by a Chicana writer, as I discussed earlier in the introduction, I classify the text as Chicana because of its validating representation of Marisa and the Moreno family.

Chapter 4, "Theater and Chicana Poetic Development in Guadalupe García McCall's *Under the Mesquite*," discusses the representation of thespian and poetic ChicaNerd identity through an examination of the protagonist Lupita's growing interests in theater acting and poetry. In the novel's chronology of Lupita's four years of high school in Eagle Pass, Texas, tragically marked by her mother's death from cancer, Lupita struggles to maintain her artistic and writing interests afloat while balancing the mourning and caretaking of her younger siblings. However, it is by honing her poetic talents—in particular through her use of poetry to honor and remember her mother—that Lupita grows into her ChicaNerd identity. In Lupita's rejection of some of her classmates' taunts that her poetic interests make her, in their eyes, "white," the novel challenges stereotypical messaging that denies Chicanas the right to embrace poetry, dramatic arts, and self-exploration.

In Chapter 5, "Band Shirts and Rebellion: Resisting the 'Buena Hija' Trope Through Nerdiness in *I Am Not Your Perfect Mexican Daughter*," I examine the protagonist Julia Reyes's ChicaNerd identity as a literature and poetry nerd, much like Gabi and Lupita. Significantly, of all the ChicaNerds I explore in this book, I suggest that Julia is the most rebellious. The novel provides particular attention to an extremely tense relationship between Julia and her mother and emphasizes the ChicaNerd's struggle to construct an authentic sense of self amid familial pressure to be the "good daughter." As a teenaged Chicana living in Chicago and who dons band tee shirts, Doc Martens, and jeans on a regular basis, Julia frames her ChicaNerd identity around this rebellion to her family's gender expectations. While Julia struggles to live within the confines of what she sees as her parents' old-fashioned and oppressive ways, the novel, like the others examined in this study, does not comfortably accept the common belief that Mexican/Chicanx parents merely groom their daughters for eventual heterosexual marriage and motherhood.

In Chapter 6, "'Tis the Life of a Misunderstood Teenage Poet': ChicaNerd Poetics in *Gabi, A Girl in Pieces*," the novel *Gabi, A Girl in Pieces*, is examined for the poetry lens it presents. Gabi Hernández is in her senior year of high school in the fictional town of Santa Maria de los Rosales, California. Like Lupita, Gabi cultivates a ChicaNerd poetic and writer identity, but whereas Lupita combines her love of theater and poetry, Gabi discovers her passion for the spoken word poetic tradition. In addition to Gabi's senior year, the novel presents a period marked by traumatic events, such as her best friend's pregnancy as a result of rape; another close friend's rejection and abandonment by his family when he reveals he is gay; her mother's pregnancy; and finally, her father's death from a drug overdose. In the process, the novel rejects myths of Mexican female identity around stereotypes of overt sexuality; skin color as an indicator of "authentic" Mexican identity/colorism; and family struggles, such as her mother's pregnancy, her father's drug overdose, and her younger brother's behavioral problems.

I conclude the book with Chapter 7, "To Be or Not to Be: Shakespeare, College, and Chicana Feminist Consciousness in *Ghosts of El Grullo*." As I stated earlier, Patricia Santana's novel is the only text that features a Chicana protagonist's journey through her four years of college. In contrast to the other texts, which examine Chicana teenagers in their final years of high school and on the verge of college life, the novel ends as Yolanda Sahagún gains admission to UCLA's literature graduate program. While at first Yolanda expresses a love of literature through her appreciation and admiration for Shakespearean poetry and theater while attending UC San Diego, her introduction to the Chicanx political club, MEChA, broadens her ChicaNerdiness to include radical politics and social consciousness. Her transition from Shakespeare nerd to MEChA nerd largely takes place as a result of her mother's untimely death, which propels Yolanda's quest to learn more about her mother's origins and to trace a maternal nerd legacy. My decision to conclude with Santana's novel is informed by what I argue as a progression of ChicaNerd identity that culminates with the college graduate Yolanda's astute proclamations of Chicana politics that weave in nerdiness with critiques of social, racial, class, and gender inequalities.

In a stroke of significant coincidences, the writing of this book took place during a time when ChicaNerds and other nerds of color began gaining much-needed publicity. For example, on a Netflix comedy special that aired in late January 2017, the Chicana/Tejana comedian Cristela Alonzo made several lighthearted, self-deprecating references to her nerdiness—a theme she has also addressed in interviews and on her personal blog. Similarly, the now defunct Comedy Central series *The Nightly Show* featured host Larry Wilmore who, while not Chicana or a woman, consistently commented on his love of science while also describing himself humorously as a blerd (black nerd), an undoubted attempt to normalize his own black, nerdy intellectual attributes and interests. As a Chicana literary scholar, these are refreshing examples and moves that signal a radical rethinking of nerdiness that both destigmatizes and illuminates the empowering possibilities of nerd self-love. These highly visible nerds attest to the power of reclaiming an identity that has traditionally been aligned with marginalized, demeaned, and outsider status. Nerds of color *do* exist, and as the Chicana YA texts argue, the intelligence, smarts, and "nerdy" interests of Chicanas should not be—and must not be!—read as unusual, odd, or worse, as nonexistent.

In his important book, *Teaching Culturally Sustaining and Inclusive Young Adult Literature*, R. Joseph Rodríguez maintains that YA literature provides a rich foundation to uncover "society's distortions, fears, images, questions, indifferences, misunderstandings, privileges, and stereotypes" (10–11). The reality that ChicaNerds must work through or push against forms the crux of their daily struggles, albeit agonizing and even punishing in social scenarios and academic spaces. The authors Pérez, Quintero, Hernández, García McCall, Sánchez, and Santana center on the worlds of ChicaNerds who must carve their own paths to college, adulthood, and beyond as witnessed in their novels.

Chicana YA literature is an established tradition, and with the publication of texts I discuss in the following chapters, Chicana writers craft nerdy Chicana characters that powerfully reclaim the traditionally negative associations of nerdiness and even self-love as adolescent Chicanas come of age. Although popular culture is ripe with images of the white male nerd, this figure is often reduced to comic relief and a stigma to be avoided at all costs. However, the acceptance of such mainstream representations as fact, leads to the inference that no one should *desire* to be a nerd, a member of an ostracized and alienated group, particularly a young woman. Nevertheless, Chicana YA literature expands existing nerd discourses and representations by featuring intelligent and ambitious Chicana nerds who dare to embrace nerdy traits of academic excellence with self-affirmation and self-love. The nerdy voices that readers of YA literature experience provide critical and necessary contributions to US literatures, Chicanx YA literature, and YA literature as a whole. The literary contributions of Pérez, Quintero, García McCall, Hernández, Sánchez, and Santana articulate a nerdy way of achieving agency to children and teenagers who otherwise remain in the shadows or unknown to a wider readership.

Beyond the importance of redeeming nerd identity, the novels analyzed in this book challenge age-old stereotypes of Chicanx underachievement and, in so doing, remind vulnerable populations of the importance of embracing Chicanx cultural heritage as motivation, not as a hindrance, to higher education and for self-actualization. Lupita, Marisa, Gabi, Julia, Luz, and Yolanda must navigate the gender expectations within their families as ChicaNerds who slowly experience the encouragement and pride of their families. By maintaining their love of learning amid daily battles and recognizing the importance of cultivating their nerdy voices, the adolescent ChicaNerds come of age and experience an empowering and affirming reclamation of identity and love. Although "coolness" and popularity are deemed to be characteristics to which all teenagers should aspire, these novels call for an affirmation of intelligence, and thus, critique the myth of academic underachievement among Chicanas. Unlike the typical plot line of nerd girls in need of makeovers that appear in media and advertising, the ChicaNerds refuse to alter themselves in order to shed evidence of nerdy traits that also value self-affirmation and self-love. Instead, these five young women cultivate their growing sociopolitical consciousness as Chicanas to powerfully proclaim and accept their identities as ChicaNerds.

Finally, I offer a brief note on why I selected these particular texts and my very specific intentionality around the concept of ChicaNerds being "brown" and nerdy—what I see as a Chicana feminist theorizing that is intersectional at its core. To be brown and nerdy functions in contrast to the "Weird Al" Yankovic parody to which I allude, where whiteness and nerdiness appear to go hand in hand. Within the "Weird Al" frame of reference, being white makes one distinctly less "cool" and, by definition, more socially awkward or odd—qualities I discuss in Chapter 1 and that have been consistently framed around nerdiness. Less as a descriptor of color, I consider brownness as one's critical self-consciousness as a distinct Chicana subject, a political identity that uniquely connects all the ChicaNerd protagonists, although to be sure, these paths to ChicaNerd consciousness occur in vastly different ways. For example, as a light-skinned Chicana protagonist, Quintero's Gabi Hernández possesses a modicum of privilege that her Chicanx and white communities bestow upon racially ambiguous peoples. Yet, as an adolescent Chicana who learns to use poetry and the spoken word tradition to voice astute observations around fat-shaming, slut-shaming, and identity policing, Gabi's unique ChicaNerd brownness is undeniable. The novel, like the others examined in this book, encourages open and honest conversations around Chicanx identity and the need to include ChicaNerds as part of, not separate from, their Chicanx communities that they love and claim. I am very specific in my intent to examine Chicana young adult literature's depiction of the ChicaNerd, but I admit that in doing such, I overlook the many Chicanx/Latinx YA texts that warrant future study for their representations of adolescent intelligence, intellect, artistic, creative, and talented identities. Literature scholars know the frustration that accompanies the study of contemporary works, for it is impossible to study every new text that is published. In particular, there is still much work to be done on representations of Afro-Latinidad in YA texts, especially in Elizabeth Acevedo's novels, *The Poet X* and *With the Fire Set on High*. Daniel José Older's *Shadowshaper* series also comes to mind. In my study of Chicana young adult protagonists in the six novels, I consider how nerdiness is one way that these young women assert their brown Chicana identities, and in doing such, the texts call for more expansive, creative, and critical expressions of Chicanisma.

Notes

1. Hereafter, *Mexican Daughter* and *Ghosts*.
2. For the purposes of my argument, I do not engage in a discussion of the label "geek," which, for some, may be read as synonymous with "nerd," although scholars such as Alexander G. Weheliye distinguish between the two. While I classify studiousness, bookishness, and love of learning as "nerdy," Weheliye defines geekiness as extensive knowledge of a particular subject, such as comic books, for example—a quality that does not necessarily denote a geek's interest in intellectual subjects. Full citation in Works Cited.
3. While I do not engage in a discussion of the mother's educational influence on her daughter, please see the important work by Dolores Delgado Bernal, C. Alejandra Elenes, Francisca Godínez, and Sofía Villenas, *Chicana/Latina Education in Everyday Life*.
4. See my 2014 book, *Contemporary Chicana Literature: (Re)Writing the Maternal Script* for an in-depth analysis of the maternal relationship in Chicana (adult) writings.
5. Full citations listed in Works Cited.

1 Not Your Nerd or "At Risk" Chicana Student
On ChicaNerds and Stereotypes

In their 2016 music video for the song "Soy Yo," the Colombian duo Bomba Estéreo, features an unknown but instantly lovable young Latina girl as the protagonist.[1] In her long braids, overalls, thick-rimmed glasses, and Crocs shoes, one thing is certain: this young Latina is unabashedly a nerd. With the self-assured strut of a young girl comfortable in her own skin, she takes on New York City streets, snickers from "cooler" white girls, and confused glances from teenaged black and Latino boys, who are left speechless by her dance moves and her refusal to be mocked or rendered invisible. The protagonist combines confidence, swagger, and self-love while navigating potentially unsafe and unfriendly urban spaces. Within a few days of the video's debut, a number of online articles were published in homage to this young Latina named Sarai González, who had struck a chord with Latina nerds everywhere.[2] At the video's conclusion, the girl playfully yet confidently declares, "Soy yo" ("I'm me"), her own brown girl "Declaration of Independence," if you will, or a powerful acceptance to be who she is, haters be damned. To put it plainly, this is one badass chiquita who relishes her nerdiness.

I reference this adorable chiquita nerd to assert the power of nerd visibility that uplifts without reducing the young Latina to a joke or a punch line. Sarai's popularity, as evidenced by the many publications following the video's debut, is a testament not only to her brilliant performance, but, I would add, to what she represented for grown-up Latina/Chicana nerds (including myself). There was something endearingly *familiar* about her, a kindred spirit who visually represented what we craved to see: someone who looked like us and dressed like us and who was not mocked but instead was celebrated, defiantly and lovingly. But although the video subversively commented on the power of nerd self-love, this chapter addresses the pervasiveness of harmful myths around nerds and Chicana teenagers that contextualize the surroundings that the ChicaNerd must navigate. This chapter employs an analysis of ChicaNerd identity through educational and sociological scholarship that has examined educational inequality and sociological studies of nerds as well as the growing field of girlhood studies that has overwhelmingly ignored young girls of color. To understand the complexity of what it means to be a ChicaNerd, this chapter borrows from educational scholarship, which exposes how it is inequality—not an inherent aversion to education—that explains the persistent myth that Chicanx students and their families do not value education. When combined with sociological and girlhood studies that position nerds as white, male, and socially awkward, and the "dangerous" Chicana on the opposing end of the spectrum, we see the ways in which ChicaNerds must carve their own spaces within nerddom and the classroom. ChicaNerds, along with their communities, work to undo and resist ideologies that construct them as "deviant" rather than as curious learners and thinkers.

While ChicaNerds like myself know that we exist, what does it mean that the term "nerd" still denotes a white male identity, while on the other hand, "Chicana," as it is constructed in mainstream stereotype, is associated with the problematic "at risk" label, a teenager who dislikes school and whose future portends a life of only potential criminal activity? Why cannot "nerd" and "Chicana" unite, and why must being a nerd mean you are not Chicana? What does it mean to be a Chicana teenager who, because of her interests in reading, writing, or math, seldom sees herself reflected in popular culture except as a stereotype? When reflecting on my own high school years, I distinctly remember hiding my interest in reading from classmates, never bringing my books to school, for fear of being labeled a bookworm or nerd. I read books only at home, a secret I could keep within the safety of the four walls of my bedroom. On the other hand, my sister and I were rarely approached by our teachers or encouraged to attend college; instead, our teachers focused their energies on our white, middle class schoolmates. Our classmates did not consider us "real" Chicanas, while our teachers neglected to see us as worthy of their attention because we were Chicana. Caught between these two myths about us, my sister and I kept to ourselves, rarely divulging our educational dreams to anyone but each other. I often think about how now, many years later, reading Chicana YA texts like the ones examined in this book, could have served as a lifeline for my sister and me.

In fact, when I casually asked Chicana/Latina colleagues via Facebook what being a "nerd" meant to them, I was struck, but not surprised, at their comments. Like me, they recalled being teased by both white and Latinx peers in school for "trying to be white" because they earned high grades and that they were supported by teachers to excel in school but simultaneously encouraged by these very teachers to distance themselves from "bad" Latinx children. As one colleague recalled, "I was frequently put in with the white kids because of my reading level which isolated me further from other children of color, again making the 'nerd' label feel very negative and a sort of betrayal to my ethnicity." Within this academically segregated environment, being smart meant being "white," and high achievement was perceived as an attempt to deny her ethnicity.

In a similar vein, another Chicana colleague said, "I was definitely called 'white' by many of my peers, and most of my friends were white because of the classes I was in (there were few students of color in my [high school] honors classes." My colleague's feelings of ethnic isolation in honors classes is not surprising, given that "in general, Latinas/os are a minority in honors and advanced placement courses and predominate in non-college preparatory classes" (Ochoa xiii). Although my colleagues credit this academic placement as beneficial for their eventual attainment of higher education, their comments nevertheless reveal the emotional toll of these deeply problematic and widespread social assumptions that classify Chicana intellect, or nerdiness, as odd at best, and at worst as attempts to assimilate, deny, or even reject Mexican cultural heritage. As R. Joseph Rodríguez reminds us, "In the process of becoming educated, the characters created by YA literature authors experience angst, challenges, and turmoil in navigating schooling worlds, home and family lives, and becoming educated citizens in their civic communities" (68). The ChicaNerds in Chicana YA literature, however, maintain not only pride in their ethnic heritage, but in addition, they define their intelligence and nerdy attributes as *part* of their ethnic identities, not as separate facets of their heritage that they must erase and hide to be "authentic" Chicanas.

White and Nerdy?[3] On Whiteness and Maleness in Nerdland

To be called a nerd, many of us have learned firsthand, is a social death sentence. From now classic films that feature nerds, such as *Revenge of the Nerds* or a John Hughes favorite like *Sixteen Candles*, to the contemporary HBO series *Silicon Valley*, nerd protagonists struggle with social awkwardness, bullying from "jocks," and rejection from attractive women. The nerd is ubiquitous in popular culture, television, and film, and although male nerds of color have earned almost cultlike popularity, as evidenced by the African American character Steve Urkel from the early 1990s sitcom *Family Matters* and the Chicano character Pedro from the 2004 film *Napoleon Dynamite*, the alignment of nerdiness with whiteness and maleness in mainstream ideology is firmly intact.

Scholarship on nerd identity has similarly cast it as pervasive with whiteness and an assumed trait of maleness. As Lori Kendall explains in her 2011 study "Computers, Race, and the Nerd Stereotype," even the nerd's appearance in popular culture can be reduced to "two essential items: the short-sleeved white dress shirt worn with a tie. Thick rimmed glasses and pocket protectors full of pens are optional" ("White and Nerdy" 507). Technology support companies, such as the Geek Squad, have capitalized on this stereotype, suggesting that computer savviness is a trait shared by all (male) nerds. "Regardless of who wears the uniform," adds Kendall, "these elements of dress, and the stereotype to which they allude, derive from and continue to convey a male identity" ("White and Nerdy" 509).[4] Within this narrow mainstream paradigm, nerdiness is shaped not only as distinctly white and male but as a particular kind of white maleness that allows little room for a varying range of intellectual interests beyond technology, let alone racial or gender diversity. In contemporary television shows, such as *The Big Bang Theory* and *Silicon Valley*, which center on the lives of mostly male professionals in STEM fields (science, technology, engineering, and mathematics), "underrepresented minorities are non-existent, and storylines reinforce negative stereotypes about gender roles and STEM professionals overall" (Reid, np). David Anderegg elaborates on the stereotype of the bumbling white male, explaining that nerds can be defined by "what they lack: Nerds and geeks are, by definition, not jocks" (27). Lacking athletic prowess makes one primed for the lab, not the field, which problematically suggests that intelligence and athleticism cannot coexist, which is strange, to say the least, given that some of my best students have been athletes on academic *and* athletic scholarships.[5] Nerds apparently do not date, nor do they possess any athletic ability, given that their free time outside school is spent building hard drives with other girlfriend-less nerds.

Indeed, as scholar Mary Bucholtz claims, "Nerds are members of a stigmatized social category, who are stereotypically cast as intellectual overachievers and social underachievers" ("The Whiteness of Nerds" 85). What defines nerdiness, according to myth, is not only strength in subjects like calculus or science but an inability to relate socially with anyone outside a nerd network; lack of fashion sense and a penchant for decidedly "uncool" clothing goes without saying. In ethnographic studies of American high schools, for example, researchers have commented on the realities of daily teasing or lack of social lives for most nerds (Ortner; Kinney). As David Anderegg explains, children "know [nerd] is a bad thing to be, and they know they don't want to be one, even before they know what it is. They know from other kids' intonation that it is a term of scorn, and therefore something to be avoided" (8). This solidifies the ubiquitous connection between "nerd" and outsider, making it impossible for this identity to mean anything but a school bully's ideal victim.

Although the term "nerd" has evolved over time in popular culture that now designates it a cool identity, as Jonathan P. Eburne and Benjamin Schreier note, the underlying notion of nerd as synonymous with lonely outsiderness is not so easy to dismantle within environments like the schoolyard:

> Hipsters in their twenties might find it empowering to sport giant glasses and dress in carefully curated unfashionable clothing, pursuing their counterhegemonic passions in small intentional communities. But the same cannot be said of most middle-school children, for instance, who still view the "nerd" as a maladjusted outsider,

manifesting a "queerness" defined less in terms of sexual preference than in terms of phantasmatic notions of scholastic normality. Nerds may be everywhere, finding economic and social prestige later in life, but as children and adolescents they often remain painfully invisible, or, for that matter, hypervisible as archetypal outcasts, rejects, nobodies.

(3–4)

Traditional nerd attire, like glasses and odd clothing, are now "trendy." Indeed, one need only to conduct a casual online search for clothing items that feature the word "nerd" on them to witness this cultural shift from stigma to cool. The number of students I teach who wear large glasses and cardigans, according to my own informal research, increases every year. "Once the derogatory name for a socially maladjusted enthusiast of arcane or otherwise difficult knowledge," add Eburne and Schreier, "'nerd' is now increasingly embraced in an effort to recognize laboratories, reading circles, and dragons' lairs as productive sites of youthful interest and attention" (11). The increased visibility of the nerd in popular culture suggests that the nerd identity has evolved into a more socially acceptable form of being, as evidenced by the tendency to casually identify oneself as a nerd in everyday conversation (e.g., "I'm such a nerd!"). While the visibility of the nerd has perhaps had some positive impact on shifting the nerd to a less stigmatized and more desirable paradigm of self-expression, we cannot yet claim that this cultural move has erased the tendency to designate the nerd, no matter how cool he may now be in 21st-century ideology, as anything but white and male.

Accepting nerdiness as a "stigma" erases the possibility of claiming this identity as a source of empowerment, liberating subjectivity, acceptance, or radical self-love, as in the case of Bomba Estéreo's young Latina girl who yearns to be nobody else but her own nerdy, badass, brown girl self. Perhaps the most insidious aspect of equating nerdiness with white male identity is its implication, overt or not, that intelligence is also "natural" to this group, excluding the presence of intellectual achievement, curiosity, and love of learning in young Chicanas and children of color. In one study, for example, Mary Bucholtz cites instances of academically gifted black high school female and male students who were ostracized for trying to "be white" (qtd in "The Whiteness of Nerds" 95). To suggest that smartness is inherent to white students not only promotes the myth that academic "underachievement" runs rampant in young students of color, but it also reinforces the belief that children of color must reject their racial identities to achieve smartness, as if these two attributes could not possibly coexist. This troubling lens positions nerdiness and gender-cultural identity on opposite ends of a very limited binary.

Scholar Alexander Weheliye notes in his study "Post-Integration Blues: Black Geeks and Afro-Diasporic Humanism" the relatively few images of black nerds in literature and mainstream culture that partially account for these deeply problematic accusations of "trying to be white" (214). Addressing the tendency to separate "black" from the "geek" identity, Weheliye posits, "What are the conditions of possibility for the merging of 'black' and 'geek' given their seemingly adversarial nature?" (221). Asking this question alludes to mainstream culture's problematic tendency to place blackness and nerdiness as oppositions rather than as cohesive and intersecting points of identity. To be both black and a nerd, according to this logic, is apparently unrealistic, suggesting the necessity of stripping one identity for another, as if that is possible.

Yet in a refreshing and subversive essay titled "Being Weird and Black Doesn't Mean You're Interested in Being White," writer Heather Jones recalls with fondness her adolescent years as a "weird black girl" (np). In its very title, which challenges problematic accusations of "selling out" or "trying to be white," Jones unites blackness with nerdiness by confidently proclaiming "both weirdness and blackness as incredible gifts" (np). By proactively claiming a nerdy, "weird" black girl identity, Jones rejects the binary split of "black" and "nerd."[6] Citing "weirdness as a badge of honor," the writer critically reclaims her authentic nerdiness. Like Jones's admiration for these nerd traits, a website, *Black Girl Nerds*,[7] professes love for nerd girls of color, stating on their website, "I named this site Black Girl Nerds because the concept of Black women as geeky-dorky beings is somewhat of an anomaly . . . the mission is to . . . know that many Black Girl Nerds exist on this planet" (*Black Girl Nerds*). The website's visual images, mainly drawings of young black girls and women wearing natural hair and glasses, lay claim to the founder's insistence on making powerfully visible a diverse range of expressions of black womanhood and girlhood. In a similar vein, the texts I examine insist on the necessity of uniting "Chicana" and "nerd" to provide smart Chicana teens with a liberating subjectivity that blends sociopolitical consciousness and self-love with nerd qualities.

Another notable exception to the white nerd rule is the fictional character Chidi Anogonye, from the NBC sitcom *The Good Place*. In a recent interview with the actor who portrays Chidi, William Jackson Harper, a *New York Times* columnist describes the cultural impact of this nerdy character's screen presence. Columnist Kwame Opam's description of Chidi as a "huge nerd" is a testament to the significance of the character's qualities that normalize and affirm nerdy traits: "Chidi is the sort of character who, in past generations, might have been the butt of the joke more often than not. . . . For a viewer like me, who grew up being compared to characters like Steve Urkel, the ubernerd portrayed by Jaleel White on the '90's sitcom 'Family Matters,' he summons a welcome, if skewed, sense of recognition." As Opam notes, Jaleel White's representation of the rare black nerd on television, while undoubtedly subversive for its time, nevertheless reaffirmed the ideology of the nerd as a bumbling outcast, not at all intended for viewers to emulate, and viewers were supposed to understand that his appearance and interests were rare exceptions to the "typical" young black male script. Urkel was undoubtedly the comic foil, and in his incessant, doomed attempts to woo the kind but out-of-his-league Laura Winslow, the sitcom declared to American viewers that nerds and pretty girls do not mix. In contrast, Chidi's nerdiness is acknowledged and celebrated, and in his role as a romantic interest, the sitcom deftly works to undo the tendency to align nerdiness along the fringes of accepted social scripts, providing writers like Opam, and others for that matter, a seldom seen legitimacy as black nerd subjects.

In one of the few examples of ChicaNerds featured in popular culture, however, the television show *Ugly Betty*'s central protagonist, Betty Súarez, relied on her intelligence, rather than her looks, to gain career advancement, which puts a spin on the nerd of color label. In their analysis of the show's gender and racial dynamics, *Humor and Latina/o Camp in* Ugly Betty*: Funny Looking*, Tanya González and Eliza Rodríguez y Gibson argue that the show challenged all-too-common stereotypes of the "hot" Latina by its construction of Betty as a complex Latina who "is also a feminist; she is an aspiring professional, but she constantly functions in a maternal capacity; she has multiple love interests, but she is labeled ugly" (103). Further, she is "intelligent, resourceful, hard working, and kind" (González and Rodríguez y Gibson 114), not unlike the ChicaNerds I examine in this book. Certainly, qualities that González and Rodríguez y Gibson use to describe Betty are not unusual among contemporary Chicanas, but it must be noted that smart Chicana characters who rely on wits over appearances are rarely, if ever, visible in popular culture, which makes *Ugly Betty* all the more significant. Betty's success depends not on rejecting her Mexican cultural heritage, but on outsmarting characters and overcoming obstacles that stand in her way, an important challenge to the "trying-to-be-white" argument. Betty's so-called ugliness functions in opposition to popular culture's tendency to create overtly sexualized characters who are closely associated with curvaceous bodies rather than sharp brains (think actress Sofía Vergara). While González and Rodríguez y Gibson do not identify Betty as a nerd, she, undeniably, exhibits nerdy qualities.

Nerdy, smart, and creative characters are ever present in Chicanx and Latinx young adult literature, although scholars have yet to investigate this subject matter in detail. In YA texts, Chicanx and Latinx characters struggle to claim nerdiness amid peer pressure, working-class familial expectations, and stereotypes of Chicanx/Latinx underachievement that deny the existence of intellectual attributes among this population.[8] But whereas a fair amount of scholarly attention has been paid to male nerds of color in literature,[9] research on women nerds of color is virtually nonexistent. In one of the few studies to examine female nerds, Mary Bucholtz states that "for girls, nerd identity also offers an alternative to the pressures of hegemonic femininity—an ideological construct that is at best compatible with, and at worst hostile to, female intellectual ability" ("Why Be Normal?" 213). When female nerds are presented in popular culture, according to scholar Marnina Gonick, the story line tends to follow the formulaic plot of a nerd-girl's "transformation" in order to find "the love of an eligible man" ("From Nerd to Popular" 48). Within this plot line, the nerd-girl's unpopularity and her supposed disinterest in boys are problems in need of solving. But perhaps another question to ask is how this nerd-girl identity intersects with ethnic/racial identity and working-class family backgrounds. For as we shall see, the nerd-girl protagonists not only have to grapple with school and peer pressures to lose their virginity and follow the latest fashion trends, but they must also confront racist and sexist myths that young Chicanas are not smart or must be "respectful" daughters and obey their families.

"At Risk"? Chicana/Latina Educational Stereotypes

There is a simple class activity I have conducted for the last several years that I know will always get my students talking. At the beginning of the semester, I set my computer up in the classroom and simply type in the word "Chicana" into Google Images. In addition to the number of images that appear on the screen, mostly depicting young women in oversized flannel shirts, hoop earrings, and baggy pants, I point the students to the brightly colored squares at the top of the images. In these squares, we see terms like "gangster," "homegirl," "chola," even "sad girl," and the like—terms people use when they search for "Chicana." "Why don't we see words like 'smart,' 'student,' 'college-bound,' or even 'nerd'?" I ask my students. My students, the majority of whom are Chicanx, have answered the question in a number of ways. Some will admit that they had not thought to ask that question. Others will express anger that they are represented in simplistic ways, while still a small number of students have blatantly said, "But that's how it is. Latinos don't care about school." When I show students research that proves the opposite, we discuss the ways in which they have internalized harmful beliefs that "Latinos don't care about school," exploring the problematic implications of those beliefs. As my students learn, a simple Google exercise exposes uncomfortable truths about power, identity, and stereotype that directly affect how they see themselves as students and as Chicanxs.

But what does this Google exercise have to do with Chicana YA literature? For if we interrogate the intentions or consequences behind the Google images, a bleaker reality is unveiled. The Google images suggest that dominant groups are quite comfortable with these visual examples of Chicanas as cholas and gangsters rather than as readers or nerds. Taken a step further, the hyperpresence of Chicana teenagers as gangsters and high school dropouts also reflects that other Chicana identities are erased from literature: "For a young reader not to see himself or herself reflected in the pages of [young adult] literature implies the value or level of worth associated with the individual is minimal" (Baxley and Boston 4). That my students have only been exposed to this narrative of Chicana adolescence makes the YA literature examined in this study all the more pressing. Not until my students grasp the concepts of power and who is erased versus who is upheld as *the* image of what it means to be Chicana, do they begin to address the dangers of subscribing to such problematic and deeply pervasive stereotypes. As my students learn, they have been taught to believe the troubling myth that "real" Chicanas are cholas, and more importantly, Chicanas are not smart, do not excel in school, and should not express interest in studying and learning.

Indeed, as some of my own colleagues' experiences suggest, academically segregated environments largely account for the misguided perception that Chicanas struggle to do well in school. A close friend of mine, a fellow Chicana academic, says that at her majority white high school, "the 'smart' kids were all white." Within my friend's segregated school setting, it was race, not actual intelligence, that determined who was considered smart or worthy of being mentored by teachers for college preparation. This connects to the Google exercise, which shows that Chicanas cannot be smart and can only be cholas, regardless of what we know to be true. I insist to my students that we should take Google searches and images with a grain of salt. But I remind them that although we know these images are simplistic reductions of Chicana identity, we should not underestimate the power these stereotypes hold over our collective imaginations. Stereotypes shape how we understand (or misunderstand, rather) groups of people.

In the novels I examine, in fact, the ChicaNerd protagonists at times voice insecurities about their right to perform well in the classroom and to attend college. Part of this has to do with how "smartness" has been defined in the first place. As Juan F. Carrillo and Esmeralda Rodriguez explain, "Smartness is culturally produced within various discourses and spaces. To be considered smart within school settings, one has to perform identities that meet whiteness and middle class cultural capital standards" (1238). It is no surprise, then, that in my discussion of *Under the Mesquite*, for example, I address how Lupita is chastised by her classmates, who are actually her friends, for what they interpret as a performance of whiteness. My colleagues' recollections of being called white for being in advanced placement classes further affirms that high academic achievement is narrowly construed as an aspiration to be white. Within a school system that continually "pushes out" students (Carrillo and Rodriguez 1238), it is all the more significant when Latinx students do remain in the classroom, much less excel in it and attend college. In their 2016 article, Carrillo and Rodriguez define a concept they call "smartness trespassing" to account for the ways in which a young Latina student negotiates smartness within a system that was not designed with her in mind. This concept can readily apply to the ChicaNerd protagonists examined in this book, who are all astutely aware that their very desire to study, learn, and eventually attend college renders them suspect, falsely "trying to be white," or reaching for the stars—in other words, having unrealistic aspirations: "trespassing in this case consists of disrupting the white-Asian *smart space* . . . and negotiating the regional definitions of brown bodies, their perceived abilities, and 'justified' place" (1238, original italics). In their discussion of a "smart" high school Latina student named Maria, they expand the concept of smartness trespassing to account for the ways that she must navigate her high academic achievement amid damaging stereotypes, a topic I further discuss later in this chapter:

> It is a complex struggle, for within the context of the new south, she has to deal with many stereotypes, including the notion that Mexicans are the community's manual laborers, and not necessarily gifted in the classroom. She also has to deal with being dehistoricized and with an uneasy relationship with possibly feeling that she can only be of value to society if she excels on the terms of the dominant class. Maria explains what students often say of her: 'She doesn't even act Mexican. She is actually kind of smart.'"
>
> (1240–41)

That Maria's classmates are unable to believe that one can be both Mexican and smart, Carrillo and Rodriguez's study highlights that students like Maria essentially "trespass" or cross over into uncharted territory; that is, they enter spaces that construct them as exceptions to the rule—that is, "Mexican students simply are not smart." As this book argues, however, ChicaNerd protagonists not only excel in the classroom in the manner in which smartness is narrowly defined via the achievement of high grades, but they do so without discarding their Chicana identities, much less the familial and communal role in shaping this identity. In claiming their right to be ChicaNerds, they also learn to acknowledge their families' ways of learning, tracing nerd identities from their communities. Many ChicaNerds, in fact, directly attribute their high academic achievement to their familial love and encouragement, disrupting the false premises that higher education is solely an individualistic pursuit. Their burgeoning Chicana adolescent feminism occurs alongside their acknowledgment of their familial support and their fundamental right to study in the classroom, charting new paths along the way.

Educational scholarship on Latinx youth has long examined how this population trails their white counterparts in relation to academic testing and high school attainment rates (Vega, Moore, and Miranda 37; Neseth, Savage, and Navarro 59). As Heidi Lasley Barajas and Jennifer L. Pierce have examined, Latina students are cognizant of existing stereotypes that depict them as lacking or "deficient" in intellect; they are "acutely aware of . . . perceptions that their teachers and other authority figures held of them as lazy, uninterested in education, or culturally deficient" (863). Within this "deficiency" model, Chicanx culture, not structural racism and inequality, is supposedly culpable for low educational achievement. Research that documents Chicanx and Latinx educational attainment in relation to their white counterparts has contested this deficit ideology, which problematically suggests that these ethnic groups are inherently unable to provide the necessary tools for academic excellence (Valenzuela). Lisa Delpit's important scholarship that examines the relationships between white teachers and children of color has uncovered how these deficit concepts remain firmly intact (xx). Although "there is no 'achievement gap' at birth, argues Delpit (5), the harmful belief that "something is wrong with the children [of color] who are in the classroom, if not in their genes, then in their culture" (6) leads to the educational system's failure to see children of color as anything but "low-achieving."

These scholars have proven that the real culprit lies with systemic inequality that blames parents and punitively treats schools that serve children of color. In her landmark study, *Subtractive Schooling: U.S.-Mexican Youth and the Politics of Caring*, Angela Valenzuela states that Mexican American students have historically been construed as "fundamentally lacking in drive and enthusiasm" for education (4). Gilberto Q. Conchas affirms Valenzuela's argument, stating, "Schools often replicate social and economic inequality present in the larger society and culture" (75). These deep-seated perceptions that Chicanx youth simply do not care about school, or are not smart enough to care, are at the root of what I discussed earlier in this chapter, as evidenced by my colleagues' experiences in the K–12 academic classroom. My mostly Chicanx schoolmates, in their accusations of intelligence and book smarts as counter to Chicanx cultural heritage, had no doubt internalized the harmful stereotypes that only white kids can and should do well in school.

Beyond contributing to internalized racism among Chicanx youth that earning good grades makes one "less" Chicanx and thus "white," education sociologists such as Gilda Ochoa claim that pervasive stereotypes may lead to what she calls "academic profiling," which is "rooted in historic and systemic processes, and similar to police profiling, academic profiling teaches students their place in society" (*Academic* 2). If racial profiling deems certain spaces off-limits, such as neighborhoods where people of color "should not" inhabit, then academic profiling exposes how the school environment is one such place where children of color do not belong. Much as racial profiling renders people of color "criminals" or "suspicious" if they trespass where they supposedly do not belong, Ochoa's analysis of academic profiling reveals the ways in which certain attributes around academic performance are construed to designate who gets to be labeled smart or who belongs at the top of the class. The so-called model minority myth is one such example, according to Ochoa, which defines "Asian Americans as the example for successfully adapting to the United States. [They are] depicted as hard working, passive, compliant, and malleable in opposition to Latinas/os and African Americans" (*Academic* 164). According to Ochoa, this problematic myth aligns Asian American students with "nerdiness," a trait seldom used to describe Chicanx students (*Academic* 164). The myth of the model minority has been critiqued by a wide number of scholars for its problematic assumptions that do not take into account structural racism and the realities of discrimination faced by Asian American students (Museus and Kiang 6). Another problem with the myth, however, is how it not only erases the painful experiences of Asian American students who struggle with it but also contributes to the "disparate expectations and treatment based on racialized assumptions" and stereotypes of academic achievement (Ochoa 165). While Asian Americans may be expected to live up to the unattainable "model minority" mythos, Chicanx students, particularly young Chicanas, must grapple with its opposite, that they are not smart enough to be in school.

As the research I have cited thus far reveals, the terms "Chicana" and "nerd" have been seen as incompatible and incongruent. If we believe that being Chicana renders a teenage girl a troublemaker no matter her academic interests and excellence, then the logic claims that there is something intrinsically "troubling" about Chicana girls. But as Nilda Flores-González explains, "Schools—in formal and informal ways—hinder the development of academic identities" for some students of color, including the Latinx children she studied (12). According to Flores-González, schools play a crucial role in determining whether children of color construct their identities around the "street" or school. She elaborates:

> More than an identity bounded to school, this school-kid identity represents an image of how these youths view themselves and how they want to be viewed by others—as good kids. . . . Because students want to maintain this image, identities that have the potential to conflict, disrupt, or negate their claims to being school kids are quickly discarded. As a result, students are successful in school to the extent that they are able to adopt and sustain a school-kid identity. Students who do not become school kids and who behave contrary to school norms are usually labeled "bad kids" . . . images of the bad kid invariably evoke images of the street and street culture—gangs, rowdy boys, teenage mothers. . . . It is not that these students are intrinsically street-oriented, or want to have—and maintain—a street-kid identity, but rather that circumstances often beyond their control force them to take on an all-encompassing street-kid identity. Once they have adopted this identity, it is very difficult and very unlikely that they will or can become school kids.
>
> (11–12)

Similar to "smartness trespassing," Flores-González's important observations also point to the ways in which certain ethnic groups, particularly Latinxs and African Americans, have also been historically connected to more urban or "street" backgrounds that do not encourage educational attainment. Rendered *barrios*, 'hoods, or worse, ghettoes, urban spaces of color are "complex and contradictory social space[s]," yet popular culture has simplistically reduced these neighborhoods as dangerous and their communities as counter to high academic potential (Villa 8). "Street" and "school" do not mix, according to Flores-González, and even when Chicana students perform well academically, their gender, ethnicity, and socioeconomic status place them at the risk of being labeled as troublemakers, flawed, or as the inevitable dropout. As Tiffany Ana López states, "Narratives produced by the dominant culture portray the individual as responsible and, if only properly motivated, fully capable of remedying problems. Lack of access to economic resources (employment, education, health care) is seldom portrayed as tethered to the workings of the larger social fabric" ("Reading Trauma" 207). Deficit standards, as mirrors of the dominant culture from which they emerge, define Chicanx and Latinx communities as incompatible with intelligence and academic success, troubling beliefs that Chicanx students risk internalizing.

Chicanas and Girlhood Studies

The stereotypes of Chicana academic underachievement that the ChicaNerd confronts must also be contextualized within the field of girlhood studies that examines sociocultural influences that relate to the process of maturation and growing up female. If, as Catherine Driscoll maintains, "Girlhood and daughterhood are consistently articulated in relation to a future role—who or what the girl will be or do as a woman" (108), this is certainly true in the texts examined in this book. To some extent, all the ChicaNerd protagonists, although to varying degrees, spend much time thinking about what their lives will encompass and who they will become after they leave high school and their parents' homes: college student, mathematician, writer, scholar, or poet. The hyperpresence of teenage girls in media and popular culture would lead us to believe that dominant culture is increasingly concerned with these young girls. However, as Catherine Driscoll explains, seldom have girls been the subject of dominant feminist inquiry and criticism (9). Significantly, we see the overlapping influences of girlhood studies and education studies, according to Marnina Gonick, when we consider how the meritocracy myth can be gendered: "When girls encounter neoliberal discourse espousing a conviction that "anyone who works hard can get ahead" and "women have made great gains toward equality," they are led to understand their own experience of successes and failures as a product of their individual effort," to say nothing of interlocking forces of sexism, racism, and classism ("Between" 6). This myth of meritocracy, discussed earlier in the chapter, promotes a false notion of individualism that essentially lets white supremacy and patriarchy off the hook.

Perhaps even more insidious to this pseudo-feminist discourse, argue Shauna Pomerantz and Rebecca Raby, is the false assertion espoused by popular rhetoric that "girls are taking over the world" (*Smart Girls* 3). Pomerantz and Raby point to the overwhelming popular representation of high-achieving girls that suggests that not only are girls unstoppable, but moreover, that sexism is a thing of the past, leaving out the intersections of gender with race and class. But which girls are "taking over"? Undoubtedly, state Pomerantz and Raby, these girls are "white, middle- or upper-middle-class, Western, and from a progressive household, where higher education is not just valued but ingrained in the family's culture" (5). The ChicaNerds I examine are intimately aware of their exclusion from this "girl power" rhetoric, and their realities as working-class Chicana daughters of Mexican immigrants conflict with the girl-empowerment rhetoric that fails to take into account young women like them who navigate multiple facets of structural inequality. As I stated in the introduction to this book, the overwhelming lack of literary scholarship on Chicana YA literature within Chicanx literary studies points to a similarly troubling trend—that is, the relatively scant amount of critical attention that literary scholars have paid to Chicana YA texts.

Elline Lipkin's text *Girls' Studies* addresses the importance of studying girls, raising similar concerns voiced by Catherine Driscoll:

> Girls' studies is an academic field that specifically considers the experience of gendering girls, starting at the earliest moments of their lives and continuing into their transformation to young women. Historically, studies that explore "childhood" broadly, or the experience of growing up generally, have often been biased to represent the experiences of boys. Separating out the realities within girls' lives uncovers new issues, topics, and concerns that are unique to being female and brings attention to experiences that might otherwise be subsumed into what are considered "standard" experiences of childhood, which presume the experience of boys to be the norm.
>
> (4)

As Anita Harris elaborates, this interest in girls' studies "was borne out of the commonplace disregard for issues of gender within youth studies and age within women's studies" (xviii). To be sure, as Rachael McLennan points out, "Male adolescent experience is often rendered universal" (22). A combination of gender and age warrants young women's erasure from fields that would seem particularly interested in the lives of young women and adolescents. While gender may be upheld as a major reason that accounts for this invisibility of young women's issues, Harris's reference to age points to the reality that young women are further erased from scholarly inquiry because of their youth. This inattention to youth is not lost on the ChicaNerds in the texts examined in this book, as many of the protagonists' chief complaints in relation to the familial and social inequality they experience has much to do with their young age and their feelings of confinement or not being taken seriously. When we consider age alongside gender, social class, *and* ethnicity, the ChicaNerds' daily navigations reveal the many struggles of what it means to be a Chicana teenager.

But while an established discipline, girlhood studies has not thoroughly examined Chicana girls and young women of color, and many benchmark texts overwhelmingly do not take into account the unique experiences faced by this demographic. In their chapter, "Women, Girls, and the Unfinished Work of Connection: A Critical Review of American Girls' Studies," Janie Victoria Ward and Beth Cooper Benjamin correctly identify some of the gaps in the early stages of this discipline's growth—namely, the limitations of basing "narratives of girls' psychosocial and academic development on predominantly White, middle-class samples" that "[overgeneralize] the experience of girlhood in a multicultural America" (20). Christine Griffin goes further in her critique, arguing that girls' studies remains "Anglocentric": "This Anglocentric perspective remains pervasive in contemporary academic and popular representations of girlhood, though this is seldom acknowledged" (31). Within this narrative, which narrowly frames what it means to grow up female in the United States, important aspects of identity, such as race and socioeconomic status, are left out, as if white middle-class girlhood is the norm to which all girls should aspire, not to mention that it positions this demographic as the point of reference from which we should compare "other" girls. In Sheila J. Walker's thorough study of African American girlhood, the researcher's critical examination of developmental research on gender exposes that, much as Latina girls have been construed as a "problem," African American young women have also been negatively gendered and racialized from a deficit lens that positions them as the antithesis to the white female ideal: "when developmental psychology 'has chosen to see' black adolescents females, it often 'sees' those who are unmarried and pregnant, those who have dropped out of school, and those who belong to girl gangs or are affiliated with male gang members" (9). As Walker correctly points out, girls of color, particularly African American and Latina girls, are rarely examined beyond a deviant/deficient lens, erasing the experiences of adolescent girls who enjoy "normal" activities like going to school, making friends, dating, or participating in athletics. Studies like Walker's examine the limitations of girlhood studies when girls of color are excluded and intersectional identities are not at the core of the study.

While Ward and Benjamin address the limitations of this early work in girlhood studies, they also believe that such differences along racial and class lines belie the ways in which "all American girls are influenced by, and must negotiate, persistent gender bias in institutions (e.g., schools, health care systems, organized religion) and the ubiquity of American popular culture" (21). But it is rather shortsighted to presume that "all American girls" are impacted in the same way by these institutions they name, particularly when we consider sociohistorical realities that have denied that Mexican-descent people are "American" in the first place.[10] At a time when Mexican and Latinx communities are under attack from the right wing sectors of this country, including by the nation's commander-in-chief, how accurate is it to proclaim that all young women residing in this country navigate these institutions in the same way?

Of further significance, as I have discussed in the introduction and to which I will return throughout the book, we must also contend with the fact that Chicana young womanhood, as it is understood within dominant media culture, has long been associated with negative images that rarely take into account a diverse range of Chicana representations of identity. My classroom Google activity is one such way that exposes how Chicanas are understood under the monolithic marker of the tough girl, homegirl, or chola. While these identities do exist and deserve the scholarly attention they have received, it is problematic, to say nothing of it being shortsighted, that this identity remains the most visible and most recognizable among Chicanx and non-Chicanx people alike. As sociologists Vera López and Meda Chesney-Lind explain, stereotypes such as the Google images are far more insidious than we may think:

> While the good, innocent, virginal girl continues to be an idealized image of womanhood associated with white females, it remains largely unattainable for young women of color, who are often characterized as hypersexual, manipulative, violent and sexually dangerous. The available gender scripts for girls of color, particularly Latinas . . . emphasize their innate "badness."
>
> (528)

The Google classroom exercise supports this supposed "badness" that Chicanas cannot escape, for if we are to believe not only the images but the words associated with them, we would think all Chicanas hang out on lowriders and all possess gang names like Sad Girl. But as one of my Chicana colleagues describes of her own high school experience, these labels are often imposed onto Chicana students even when they perform well in the classroom:

> In middle school [my sister and I] were in trouble a lot. My mom says that we were always fighting with the white girls because none of our

white teachers believed in our potential. That followed us to high school and we had to work hard to overcome the perceptions of us as troublemakers even though we always got good grades.

For my colleague, her academic achievement meant little for the likes of her white teachers and classmates who labeled her as the "troublemaker" when she assertively defended herself from the racism she experienced. Lipkin affirms my colleague's sentiment, stating that "when girls choose loudness as a strategy for attention in school, they defy an expectation of the 'good girl student' and risk punishment and disconnection from teachers" (95). As a "troublemaker," the smart identity is removed, and even the grades, as evidence of her intellect, are not acknowledged or praised. Within this imaginary, Chicana means "bad," and bad means not smart.

As Rosalinda Fregoso maintains, Chicana cholas, as the quintessential "bad" girls, have historically been "characterized as a deviant in studies about adolescent girl gangs" (317). In their important text, *Beyond Bad Girls: Gender, Violence and Hype,* Meda Chesney-Lind and Katherine Irwin argue that these views of Chicanas as always bad cholas can be traced to centuries-old constructions of women possessing a "duplicitous nature—appearing superficially 'innocent' and 'nice' while actually being manipulative, devious, and occasionally evil" (12). They caution, however, that young girls of color face real-life consequences as a result of the "mean girl" myth, such as harsher policing of their behavior within school settings and the criminal justice system (Chesney-Lind and Irwin 135). "More frustrating, although perhaps also liberating," adds Lipkin, "is the idea that it is harder for girls of color to see themselves fitting into society's standard of the 'good girl' " (95). But how, precisely, is this "liberating," as Lipkin asserts? While undoubtedly we must take to task the sexism inherent to the "good girl" ideology, we must also address that sexism alone is not the only culprit in this ideology. Other facets of identity, especially race, undergird the "good girl" ideology. Young women of color must contend with the reality that no matter their actions, their gender and ethnicity make them more likely to be accused of being bad or deviant. The ChicaNerds in the YA texts explored in this study are astutely aware that their intelligence contradicts gendered *and* raced ideologies of smartness, success, and visibility. They are acutely cognizant of the precariousness of their situations: while their intelligence marks them as potentially "good," any perceived or overt deviance from this myth will render them "bad," and this is especially the case with Quintero and Sánchez's protagonists, who face being pushed out of school. Perhaps the most common of the "bad" Chicana stereotype is that of the "at risk" young woman, the inevitable high school dropout that plagues the Chicanx community. Few popular culture references exist for the smart Chicana teenager, although there are a few exceptions.[11]

In the proceeding chapters, the ChicaNerds' navigations of racist and sexist stereotypes of Chicanas as bad, failing at school, and disinterested in academics will be explored. As the young women engage in the complex process of constructing and affirming their identities as ChicaNerds, they must wrestle with pressures from within their families but most especially from their school and peer environments. ChicaNerds demonstrate incredible resiliency in the face of educational and social inequality within a culture that is far more comfortable in casting off Chicanas as academically deficient cholas rather than as smart, motivated, and inquisitive students of color. As smart Chicanas, these young women are marginalized within multiple systems that refuse to see them as college bound, and this is complicated by the mainstream rhetoric around "girl power" that presumes that young women face no challenges to educational opportunities (Pomerantz and Raby, "Oh, She's *So* Smart" 550). Undoubtedly, popular culture is also more likely to present "nerds" as synonymous with white maleness, leaving little room for variations in gender and race, let alone intellectual interests. Confronting the stereotype of the socially inept white male, ChicaNerds must learn to construct a nerd identity that reflects their ambition alongside their burgeoning Chicana feminist awareness. Rather than subscribe to racist ideologies that define their families and ethnic groups as incompatible with academic achievement, ChicaNerds proudly identify as Chicanas, as products of their families and communities. Further, their growing Chicana feminist consciousness helps them to dismantle the most problematic stereotypes of Chicana adolescents as the inevitable high school dropout. As ChicaNerds, Chicana young women embrace their identities, claiming that they are truly themselves, or as Sarai González would say, "Soy yo."

Notes

1. To view the music video, please go to www.youtube.com/watch?v=bxWxXncl53U.
2. See, for example, an article titled "Why Bomba Estéreo's New Music Video for 'Soy Yo' Sings to My Brown Girl Heart" on the *Huffington Post*.
3. I am referring to the parodist "Weird Al" Yankovic's song "White and Nerdy."
4. In particular, this portrays a cis male, heterosexual gender identity that does not account for gender or sexual fluidity. In Rigoberto González's YA novel *The Mariposa Club*, the queer Chicanx characters embody nerdy traits while also rebelling against the heteronormative and cisgender nerd stereotype. While I do not discuss a queering of the nerd identity, there is definitely room for scholarly growth on the subject.
5. A notable exception to the "Nerds are not jocks" rule is the former NFL player John Urschel, who retired from the Baltimore Ravens in July 2017 to pursue his PhD in mathematics from Massachusetts Institute of Technology (*Washington Post*).
6. In a similar vein, the web series *The Misadventures of Awkward Black Girl*, created by writer Issa Rae, chronicles the protagonist J's weirdness, which

undoubtedly causes socially awkward situations, but her blackness is never viewed as incompatible with this weirdness. The series aired on YouTube from 2011 to 2013. Rae also launched a brand-new HBO series, *Insecure*, which premiered in fall 2016.

7. See also the Twitter handle @LatinxGeeks.
8. An early play by Gary Soto, *Nerdlandia*, treats nerdiness in much the same stereotypical way we see in popular culture. However, "adult" literature by Latinx writers offers examples of intellectually curious, intelligent, weird, or nerdy characters. See, for example, Junot Díaz's *The Brief Wondrous Life of Oscar Wao* and Denise Chávez's *Loving Pedro Infante*, among many other texts.
9. See work by Monica Hanna and Ron Eglash. Full citations listed in Works Cited.
10. See Francisco Balderrama and Raymond Rodríguez's important book *Decade of Betrayal: Mexican Repatriation in the 1930s*, which examines the period of mass deportation of people of Mexican descent, including US citizens. See also Guadalupe García McCall's YA novel *All the Stars Denied*, a fictional account of this period of US history.
11. One of the few examples of films that feature smart and academically gifted Chicana teenagers would be low-budget films such as Aurora Guerrero's *Mosquita y Mari* and *Real Women Have Curves*, based on Josefina López's well-known play of the same name.

2 "Those White Girls Don't Like It"
Community and ChicaNerd Feminist Resistance in Jo Ann Yolanda Hernández's *White Bread Competition*

I take from my title a line uttered by a character named Olga, who warns her friend Luz Ríos of the possibility of racist backlash should she win the spelling bee at her local school district in San Antonio, Texas. Throughout the novel, Luz's friends caution her against performing too well, suggesting her smartness and talent at letters make her "unapproachable" to boys, but most importantly, that success at the spelling bee will make her the target of racist and sexist vitriol within a community that still grapples with school integration and Chicanx upward mobility. In a shortsighted attempt to protect her friend against the wrath of white community members, Olga goes so far as to lie to their school principal, accusing Luz of stealing the spelling bee words prior to the competition she wins, where she beats a wealthy, white classmate from an influential family in San Antonio. However, this false accusation leads to Chicanx community outrage that eventually succeeds at gaining Olga's admission of the truth and Luz's ability to compete in the district bee.

While all the ChicaNerd texts examined in this book address the multilayered path of empowered ChicaNerd identity development and self-love as nerdy, brown girl subjects, Jo Ann Yolanda Hernández's 1997 work *White Bread Competition*, more so than the other novels, gives a sobering account of 14-year-old Luz's confrontation with racist classmates and white community members who threaten to jeopardize her participation in the district spelling competition. Although the ChicaNerd texts examined in this book address family gender roles and parental strife as negotiating factors in the Chicana protagonists' efforts to claim an identity for themselves, Hernández's novel suggests, more so than the rest of the novels, that it is institutionalized racism found within schools and communities that truly threaten the ChicaNerds' journey. *White Bread Competition* exposes the white resentment of Chicana academic excellence.

In this chapter, I engage in a discussion of Hernández's work, which has surprisingly received scant scholarly attention thus far, despite being one of the earliest Chicana YA novels to receive critical acclaim, such as being honored as a finalist for the prestigious Tomás Rivera Mexican

American Children's Book Award. Hernández's text was also published several years before the novels by García McCall, Pérez, Sánchez, Quintero, and Santana, making the overall absence of scholarship on her work all the more significant. In this chapter, I discuss Luz's eventual achievement of ChicaNerd agency, which begins as a reluctant process of voicing frustrations with her Chicanx community's high expectations of her; in doing such, I argue that the novel traces Luz's empowered ChicaNerd path through community and family, especially with the support of her mother and grandmother. Luz initially expresses irritation over her community's enthusiastic support of her academic success, at first not understanding that the Chicanx community's pinning their hopes on her is a consequence of their long-standing struggle to overcome racist educational practices and policies. Once she is able to compete again, Luz begins to recognize the strength in her community's staunch support, utilizing community and familial (maternal) love to embark on her unique ChicaNerd path. Though the novel privileges Luz's voice, as well as that of her younger sister, Justina, it should also be noted that the text utilizes multiple narrative points of view, including the perspectives of her mother and grandmother. Through the voices of Luz's mother, Rosaura, and grandmother, Aura, we learn that both women were artists and painters who, because of a combination of gendered/marital obligations and lack of socioeconomic power, were unable to pursue their talents. Luz only realizes her calling—that is, her passion to compete in a spelling competition despite the numerous risks that it entails—by (re)discovering this ChicaNerd maternal legacy and by accepting the support of her extended community network. Thus, I point to the novel's insistence on uncovering this maternal backstory to trace Luz's development of ChicaNerd identity and agency.

The novels examined in this book affirm the significance of community and family support in the young protagonists' ChicaNerd lives, but in doing so, the texts also stress the importance of brown girl nerdy agency and subjectivity. According to Roberta Seelinger Trites,

> in [feminist children's] novels, the protagonist is more aware of her ability to assert her own personality and to enact her own decisions, at the end of the novel than she has been at the beginning. Unlike her literary antecedents in such novels as *Little Women* or *Anne of Green Gables*, the feminist protagonist need not squelch her individuality in order to fit into society. Instead, her agency, her individuality, her choice, and her nonconformity are affirmed and even celebrated.
> (*Waking* 6)

While I agree with Trites's argument regarding the significance of young female agency and nonconformity, it is important to note that Hernández's work acknowledges and honors the distinct working-class Chicanx community of San Antonio as a crucial part of Luz's path of claiming her rightful place as spelling bee champion and empowered ChicaNerd. Of course, we must also point out that ChicaNerd characters like Luz have little in common with the protagonists of 19th- and early-20th-century texts penned by white women, with the exception of possessing traits like intelligence and scholastic talents. Early in the novel, for example, Luz's younger sister, Justina, correctly addresses the significance of Luz's spelling bee victory as the entryway to eventual university admission: "She had a straight-A report card and each correct answer got her closer to the scholarship she wanted for college" (10). Justina's awareness of the spelling bee's importance, not merely for the prestige it will bring, but for its potential to make college a reality for her older sister, points to the novel's insistence on recognizing the unique struggles faced by first-generation college students of color and their familial support. In particular, it is a strong, extended network of Chicanas, including Luz's younger sister, Justina; their mother, Rosaura; grandmother, Aura; and Rosaura's longtime friends, who serve as Luz's most ardent supporters and feminist nurturers and encourage Luz's confidence in her intelligence and talent. Although the novel affirms Luz's individual identity as a young Chicana who wants to excel at school, it does so while simultaneously emphasizing the importance of Chicana family and community members who have paved the path for her. By portraying the Chicanx community's role in nurturing Luz, the novel, like the other ChicaNerd texts, resists long-standing racist, deficit narratives that define Chicanx communities and families as barriers to scholastic achievement.

Before I begin my discussion, a note on the text is warranted. Like *The House on Mango Street*, Hernández's text reads as a collection of short stories or vignettes, even as a novel. The text's generic classification—that is, whether to call it a novel or short story collection—raises similar concerns as those I pose in Chapter 3, regarding how scholars interpret novels in verse, such as *Under the Mesquite*, as traditional novels or poetry in narrative form. While the book jacket describes the text as a series of "linked stories," I suggest that we examine it as a novel, and I say this for a number of reasons. First, unlike *Mango Street*, which, in its structural format has led multiple scholars to refer to it as a series of vignettes, a novel, or a hybrid work that refuses easy classification,[1] some of the narratives in *Mango Street* are not necessarily interconnected, unlike *White Bread Competition*, which all in some form or another implicate the core of the plot: 14-year-old Luz Ríos's victory in her San Antonio school spelling bee over a wealthy white student and her attempt to compete at the district-wide event after false accusations that she has cheated her way to success. Second, each chapter, whether narrated by Luz, Justina, or other characters, essentially depends upon this fact of the spelling bee, and each narrative voice has some stake in the competition. All the chapters additionally provide insight into what Luz's spelling victory signals for the Chicanx community at large and how her talent in letters symbolizes the ever-present Chicanx intelligence, despite the white supremacist educational system in San Antonio (and beyond) that has systematically denied equal access to education for Chicanx communities. For me, however, what is most unique in this work is Hernández's use of multiple narrative voices that does not necessarily privilege the adolescent protagonist, a typical characteristic of young adult fiction. Aura Morales, Rosaura Ríos, and her two daughters, Luz and Justina, narrate some of the chapters, providing readers with insight into their histories and experiences that are woven throughout the narrative, a novelistic feature we cannot overlook. The chapters, even as they may alternate between narrative points of view, depend upon the overarching plot element of Luz's attempt to compete in the district spelling bee, making each chapter unit dependent on each other. This important feature—that is, the chapters' inability to function as independent units, unlike *Mango Street*—leads to my assertion that *White Bread Competition* is a novel.

"It's Going to be Different for Me": Challenging the Racist Narrative

Early in the novel, Luz articulates her growing frustration with her community's various plans and expectations for her. At a party to celebrate her accomplishments, elder women assert their hopes that she will one day marry and become a mother, to which Luz thinks to herself, "It's going to be different for me" (41). Luz's burgeoning Chicana feminism is evident in this line, as she acknowledges that she will reject gendered obligations that threaten her studies. Throughout the novel, however, Luz learns, like the rest of her ChicaNerd protagonists, that it is family and community support that ultimately provides her with the necessary tools to reject not only gendered expectations but racist structures of power that marginalize smart Chicanas. Perhaps more overtly than the other novels I examine in this book, *White Bread Competition* delves deeply into San Antonio's brutally racist past (and present) educational system that accounts for Luz's struggle to assert her right to intelligence and nerdy school interests. While Hernández's text is not a work of historical fiction that examines San Antonio's strife-ridden past, particularly its problematic schooling system, the novel insists that we recognize Luz's more contemporary fight to excel in academics as deeply rooted within her community's ongoing fight to resist institutionalized educational racism and segregation. In doing such, the novel shares many concerns with another Chicana YA novel, *The Tequila Worm*, by Viola Canales (2005). While I do not examine Canales's text in this study, it is important to note that the novels by Canales and Hernández both emphasize the distinct role of Texas history to communicate the further challenges faced by their ChicaNerd protagonists. Both characters come of age in South Texas, and in their school settings, the two protagonists face scrutiny and criticism by their white classmates. As a response to the racism and classism of their school communities, both novels also stress the strength of community and kin networks to empower the Chicana protagonists.

In her chapter titled "Entre Tejana y Chicana: Tracing Proto-Chicana Identity and Consciousness in Tejana Young Adult Fiction and Poetry," scholar Larissa M. Mercado-López calls for the inclusion of Chicana youth literature, which emphasizes a particular Tejana historical experience, into the educational curriculum precisely because of Texas's role as "an important site of colonization" (4). As Mercado-López argues, "Considering that Texas is currently embroiled in a battle over allegedly inaccurate and racist textbooks that are expected to be adopted for use in Mexican American Studies classrooms, it is especially critical that young readers have access to books written by and for Chicanas—books that tell Texas history from the perspective of those in an ongoing resistance to colonialism" (5). As Hernández makes clear, the educational setting is one such site of colonization, and Luz's struggle to legitimize herself as a smart student who beats a white student "fair and square" shows that schooling remains a by-product of the legacy of white supremacist colonization. Hernández's acknowledgment of this important fact of San Antonio history is evident throughout the novel, when community members encourage Luz to win the district spelling bee so she can "show" white community members that she is gifted, unlike the historical tendency to conflate all Chicanx peoples as intellectually inferior.[2] In fact, Luz's frustration with the community pressure placed on her is at first due to her (false) belief that racism and institutional barriers are a thing of the past, until she unfortunately is victimized by those same structures in the present.

The attention that Chicana YA writers pay to portraying educational barriers and pursuits is a hallmark of this body of work, evident in the novels examined in my study. According to scholar Sonia Alejandra Rodríguez's article "School Fights: Resisting Oppression in the Classroom in Gloria Velásquez's Latina/o Young Adult Novel *Juanita Fights the School Board*," this is because "systemic oppression and discrimination make access to education difficult for [Latinas]" ("School Fights" 62). While to some degree being a ChicaNerd brings a modicum of privilege because of the positionality of the protagonists at the opposite end of the stereotype of the pregnant and struggling or gangster Chicana teenager, I caution against suggesting that being a nerd means that access to education is a given, even when the protagonists are singled out by their teachers or communities as symbols of community "progress." Too often, it is precisely because students of color may be singled out that they can access educational opportunities, leaving the majority of students along the margins. In Chapter 1, in fact, I cited a number of my

Chicana colleagues and friends who witnessed the double-edged sword that accompanied their intelligence. On the one hand, their academic success provided access to the privileged space of advanced placement and honors classes that prepared them for college admission. But on the other hand, this placement also meant that as teenagers, my Chicana colleagues faced scrutiny by their classmates, who unfairly accused them of "not being Chicana enough." No more is this evident than in Hernández's novel. Luz is indeed a smart ChicaNerd, but her intelligence, alongside the community support she receives, does not negate the structural barriers she faces and with which she must contend. Luz's talent means that she and her sister, Justina, face bullying by white classmates who antagonize the girls so that they will "learn their place." Hernández's novel contests similar concerns raised in Rodríguez's analysis—namely, the fact that Luz is immediately suspected of rigging the competition and must be vindicated by her community; her guilt is automatically presumed by the majority white community and school board members. The novel critically examines the white community's ability to wield power in a way that makes Luz guilty until proven innocent. The white community's presumption of guilt demonstrates the reality that, despite the privilege of smartness, Luz may still be subjugated to the margins and deemed a liar, cheater, or worse, criminal.

For example, at the school board meeting that members hold to determine if Luz is guilty or innocent of stealing the spelling words and whether she will be stripped of her title in favor of a white classmate, Hernández describes this meeting in deliberate, careful language to convey how Luz is criminalized by the white community before any evidence of her guilt is presented. A school board member tells Rosaura, Luz's mother, and the crowd, "The person who reported seeing your daughter with the list of words before the competition is a student. We don't want the vindictiveness of others to cause undue suffering for the child" (176). Ironically, of course, this board member shows little concern for Luz's "undue suffering," even though she is also a child, which reveals Hernández's not-so-subtle critique of the ways that white supremacy removes the "innocence" associated with childhood when those children are young people of color. Although Rosaura presses the school board member to admit whether the student who falsely accuses her daughter is white, the member responds with, "The student who stood up for honesty was a very responsible Hispanic" (177). Readers eventually learn that it was Luz's friend, Olga, who falsely accused her and who later admits the truth (188), but the board member's pointed use of the term "responsible" to describe Olga reveals his inability to see Luz as "responsible," only guilty. The descriptor further points to his need to justify his belief of the witness. She's not simply any "Hispanic"; to be worthy of believing her, she must be "responsible"—everything Luz is apparently not, according to the board member.

The white community's treatment of Luz as a criminal who has overstepped into a space where she does not belong, a district-wide spelling bee, illustrates the ways that educational racism is entrenched—a point that Hernández wants to convey to readers through her representation of multiple white characters who attempt to jeopardize her participation in the bee. Although Luz and her family are not privy to this information, Hernández narrates a telephone conversation between Harriet Whitting and her brother. As we learn, Harriet is the mother of Debbie, Luz's classmate whom she beats in their school's final spelling bee, which decided who would represent them at the district-wide event. Harriet attempts to block Luz from attending the competition, and it is largely her actions that fuel the rumors that Luz has stolen the spelling words. In the phone conversation, she describes Luz not only as a threat to her daughter's image, but as an inferior "Mexican girl" who must be reminded of her "place" within the community of San Antonio: "Brody, she lost to a Mexican girl.... Some girl named Luz Ríos. Such funny names" (107). Harriet's anger over her daughter's loss, of course, has more to do with to whom Debbie lost rather than the actual sting of defeat. As a "Mexican girl," Luz is "supposed" to lose, but in addition to that, the descriptor of "Mexican girl" conveys Harriet's fear of foreign otherness and the invading threat to white supremacy represented by Luz's win over the supposedly more "deserving" white girl. Despite being a Chicana, a US citizen, Luz is rendered "Mexican," thus, illegal; thus, a trespasser. When she repeats the lie to her brother, that Luz has stolen the words, her explanation of this as being highly plausible rests on her racist assertion that "she probably stole the words because she's used to having everything handed to her.... You know. Affirmative action" (108). The irony of Harriet's rhetoric, that Luz has been "handed" things to her as a result of affirmative action, is intended to be a focal point of critique that Hernández anticipates readers will see. But the larger point, unfortunately, is that Harriet's point of view, no matter how racist it may be, is a common point of contention. As recently as October 2019, a judge ruled in favor of Harvard University's policy of using race as a factor in admissions decisions, spurred by a complaint brought forward by a group, Students for Fair Admissions, who had accused Harvard of discriminating against Asian American students (Harris, "Harvard"). In even recent debates such as this, the fundamental question of whether race should ever be part of admissions decisions undermines the historical legacy of a white supremacist system of power that has made American higher education a deeply unequal institution. Harriet's flawed assertion that affirmative action is merely a tool that "hands" things out to undeserving students of color, however, suggests that she is not above handing things out to her daughter, such as an unearned trip to the district bee.

But the racist violence subjected onto Luz and her sister, Justina, is not confined to the realm of the adult school board setting. Both Luz and

Justina are subjected to racist taunts by their white classmates as well, and interestingly enough, much of this vitriol occurs in their school's cafeteria, pointing to the culinary implications of the novel's title, including chapter titles.[3] The "white bread" of the title refers to the girls' struggles to gain acceptance by their white classmates, but it also hints at the Mexican version of white bread, the baked breads known as bolillos. Of course, the term "bolillo" has also been used as a derogatory word in the Chicanx community, similar to the hurl "coconut," which implies that a person is "brown on the outside, white on the inside," or rather, like a floury bolillo, trying to be white.[4] For example, early in the novel, white classmates mock Justina in the school cafeteria when they discover that she is eating a tortilla slathered with peanut butter for lunch. The girls' cruel and racist bullying is clear, but beyond that, we see Justina's confusion over her sister Luz's reaction to the taunts:

> "You're eating peanut butter on a tortilla! How gross!" Debbie cried for everyone to hear. I looked into Kathy's blue eyes as she said, "You're in America now. Why don't you eat American food?"
> . . .
> Debbie took Kathy by the arm. "C'mon, Kathy. You know, you can take them out of the field, but you can't take the field out of them." The four girls, my two classmates, and all the students eating lunch laughed. Everyone except us at our table. I hung my head. My sister hissed at me from across the table. "Keep your head up high, Justina." I did as she told me. "I'm sorry to ruin your happy day," I said. "Eat your taco with pride." I stared at her, trying to see if some monster from outer space had taken over her body. My bossy sister was telling me to eat this tortilla with pride? Just yesterday she made me walk with her down the hallway to throw away the plastic wrapper with "Tortillas made in San Antonio" written across the front that *abuelita* had used to bag the tacos. Now she was telling me to eat my food with pride just because some white girls made fun of me.
> (13–14)

As a marker of "otherness" for the white girls, Justina's tortilla relegates her as an alien and a foreigner who cannot fit comfortably within the academic setting because the only place deemed "fit" for her is the agricultural field. For the white girls, as we see, the fields are more "appropriate" for Justina because of the backbreaking labor, and their racism is rooted in centuries-old white supremacist logic that historically defined peoples of color as intellectually inferior and therefore only capable of physical toil.

In this passage, we see Hernández's understanding that food is used as a tool to oppress Justina within the cafeteria setting. The cafeteria is not only a site of cruel bullying but a school and social setting where identity negotiation takes place. Within this setting, the racial hierarchy designates who is an outsider or an insider, and the white girls use food to determine one's belonging (or not) in the school's social circle. Justina's confusion over her sister's solidarity is justified, given that she is aware of Luz's own inner struggle with assimilation and belonging. While Luz openly defends her sister and urges her to not succumb to the girls' hatred, Justina correctly points out her sister's internalized sense of shame and her attempts to hide evidence of her Mexican food. Further, Justina recognizes Luz's futile efforts to "fit in" by hiding the tortillas, recognizing that within the racialized school and community setting, it matters little if Luz consumes white bread or tortillas. She will never be white, and her Chicana identity will always make her suspect and deem her intellectually inferior. In fact, when Justina's friends fight back against Kathy and Debbie, Kathy's menacing words to Justina and her friends, "My mother will make sure you are never permitted back into school" (32), demonstrate the power differential between the Chicana and white girls. While Kathy's youth does not grant her the authority to necessarily wield power against Justina and her friends, her status as the daughter of a wealthy white community member means she has access and proximity to power that Justina and Luz lack.

"You Show Them": Community and Resistance

In *White Bread Competition*, Hernández situates Luz's ChicaNerd identity within a community whose pride in her spelling talent at first is a source of exceeding frustration and angst—namely, because Luz is unaware of what her victory signals for her extended social network. Within her tight-knit Chicanx community, Luz's spelling bee victory is hailed as a type of underdog story in which "This girl here is going to prove to the world that all Mexican Americans are not like what they see in the movies," as one family member puts it (35). This family member's statement, though his sincerity is evident in his belief that his Chicanx community is more complex than what stereotypes may suggest, does little to acknowledge the reality that one individual alone cannot undo centuries of racist ideology. Further, Luz's experience with her white classmates' taunts and bullying emphasizes this point head-on. Rather than affirm that Chicanx students are "not like what they see in the movies," Luz's intelligence instead threatens the white supremacist narrative, subjecting her to allegations of cheating. Although her community undoubtedly expresses pride and love for their ChicaNerd kin, Hernández honestly portrays Luz's overwhelming sense of confusion, and in doing so, sympathetically narrates the complexities of being a Chicana adolescent who must navigate multiple competing narratives of Chicana intelligence. Even when their support is rooted in love and resistance, Luz nevertheless exhibits frustration with the obligation this entails. It is precisely this sense of obligation with which Luz is uncomfortable, as she understands the gendered layers of meaning embedded within the encouraging words she receives. For example, at a family party, another family member says of Luz, " 'She knows she has an obligation and a duty to our kind. We help each other out.' *Tía* Gloria dimmed the lights around her with her smile. Here we go again with that 'our kind' stuff. How am I supposed to know where I belong?" (36). Luz's gender combined with her youth, social class, and Chicana identity all contribute to her community's expectation that she must serve as a role model and example of Chicanx intellectual excellence. Beyond that, however, it is presumed that Luz welcomes this role. While her sarcasm is evident in her comment, "Here we go again with that 'our kind' stuff," her growing frustration is crystallized in her legitimate questioning of where she "belongs." Luz understandably recognizes that were she white, there would be no pressure to serve as a stand-in for her community. Although the novel pays homage to past generations of Chicanx activism, Hernández takes care in highlighting Luz's precarious role as recipient of generational knowledge that at first appears to have no legitimacy in her contemporary reality. As Luz tells herself, "So many words. Revolution. *La Raza*. Family obligation" (51). Luz's struggle to make sense of "so many words" is partly due to her fledgling notion of independence and autonomy; that is, her initial desire to win the spelling bee is solely for her own individual gain and the hopes that this victory will make college admission a guarantee. Her community, however, frames her victory as more of a community achievement than an independent one. Further, Luz begins to comprehend that ethnicity alone does not factor into her ChicaNerd path; gender as well plays a significant role in her community's expectations.

Luz's understanding of her identity as an adolescent Chicana is exemplified in her astute commentary (albeit to herself) in response to family friends' words of encouragement. At this same family party, yet another friend of her parents says to Luz:

> "You showed all those gringos at school that we Chicanas have brains. Brains and guts. . . . Don't let no one tell you you can't be smart just because you're a girl."
>
> That's dumb. They say I'm not smart because I'm Chicana.
>
> Mrs. Cuellar and Mrs. Ortiz traded looks loaded with accusations and experiences.
>
> "We need more women like you in the revolution. We have been oppressed for so long that we have to rise up and get stronger." Mrs. Cuellar poked her face so close that Luz felt her eyes cross. "Men think they can do it by themselves. But it's us women who do all the hard work. Women are stronger because we have to do more, put up with more."
>
> (42–43)

Mrs. Cuellar's words reference early Chicana feminist critiques of sexism within the Chicano Movement of the late 1960s and early 1970s.[5] Mrs. Cuellar's underlying anger with women's oppression within the Chicanx community is clear, but beyond that is what I see as her wish that her young Chicanita kin understand the ongoing feminist resistance to patriarchy. Of course, her insistence that "we have to rise up and get stronger" is resonant with not a small amount of aggression, evident in Hernández's humorous mention of Luz's eye crossing. As a Chicana teenager who simply wants to perform well at school and compete in spelling bees, Luz at first wants no part in the elder Chicanas' call for a revolution because she is unable to situate their revolutionary call to feminism and racial solidarity with the reality of her current experience. In Luz's correction to Mrs. Cuellar, "They say I'm not smart because I'm Chicana," she asserts that it is not gender, but ethnicity, that accounts for her struggle to claim her rightful place as spelling bee champion. Luz's initial reluctance to understand that gender *and* ethnicity intersect to shape her distinct ChicaNerd experience accounts for this early unwillingness to heed Mrs. Cuellar's words.

But even with these words of encouragement, Luz must navigate competing gendered messages around intelligence and academic achievement that arise among her community and family. While Mrs. Cuellar's feminist message acknowledges the reality of sexism within the Chicanx community, male community members prioritize Luz's racialized community obligations, exuding precisely the brand of sexism of which Mrs. Cuellar warns her: " 'This here girl is gonna whip all those *gringos*.' Mr. Cuellar thumped the air with his cup. 'You show 'em for us,' the other men chorused. . . . 'In two weeks, she's gonna win and show all those *masa* boys who's got what. She's gonna show them that us Chicanos got balls. *¿Qué no, niña?*' " (47). Mr. Cuellar's crass language juxtaposes his wife's feminism, even as both express pride in Luz's talent. Mr. Cuellar reflects a masculinist perspective that erases Luz's distinct gendered identity as a young woman. Nevertheless, I point to these competing messages to underline the complexities surrounding Luz's early struggle to articulate her ChicaNerd aspirations. As an intelligent Chicana teenager, Luz desires the apparently simple goal of winning a district-wide spelling bee without the added layer of community expectations of Chicana feminist resistance and ethnic solidarity. Essentially, her conflicting feelings reveal that she is uncomfortable with being framed as a Chicana success story because of how it potentially risks reproducing the ideology of Chicanx intelligence as an exception to the age-old rule of Chicanx intellectual inferiority. Hernández's novel thus critically calls for a normalization of Chicanx intellect and nerdiness, even as the text simultaneously acknowledges the significance of Chicanx activism and community engagement. Luz's ChicaNerd path begins with frustration and what she sees as unfair pressure placed on her by a community that still lives with the legacy of colonization and white supremacy, but by the novel's conclusion, her hesitation manifests into a distinct Chicana adolescent, feminist, and empowered nerdy identity.

Mother/Daughter Legacies

Throughout this book, I will discuss the significance of the mother-daughter relationship in the ChicaNerds' path to empowered identity. While I do not necessarily prioritize this element in the ChicaNerds' development, all the texts I explore pay homage to the maternal relationship's significance to Chicana adolescent academic achievement and smartness. In *White Bread Competition*, the maternal relationship is no less imperative to Luz's process of nerd development, although initially she is uncertain of her mother's own nerd history that is kept from her. As Roberta Seelinger Trites reminds us, "The most complex form of relationship in feminist literature, however, seems to be the mother/daughter relationship, for that is the primary relationship for many girls" (*Waking* 100). Despite this fact, Trites addresses what she sees as a common tendency in children's literature, stating, "Whether feminist or otherwise, more children's novels omit maternal subjectivities than include them" (*Waking* 102). However, in *White Bread Competition*, Hernández's narrative style allows readers insight into multigenerational accounts of Tejana/Chicana/Mexicana lives, replete with stories of unlawful deportation (Aura) and dreams of attending art school deferred (Rosaura), to the youngest generation, Luz and Justina, who struggle to vocalize their complex feelings on assimilation, community expectations, and racism. Luz is the predominant voice in the novel, but Hernández provides us glimpses into Rosaura and Aura's perspectives via dialogue and inner monologue. In doing such, Hernández insists on acknowledging this maternal legacy that shapes Luz's path to spelling champion. By providing readers access to Luz's maternal history of artistic creation and knowledge, Hernández documents the necessity of centering Chicana and Mexican women into a ChicaNerd lineage that honors their struggles that ultimately strengthen Luz's resolve to compete, study, and learn. Further, the novel's documentation of Aura and Rosaura's stories affirms subversive, Chicana modes of knowledge, what Chicana educational scholars define as the "activities and actions of everyday life" (Téllez 60). As Sofía Villenas maintains, "Latina mothers and daughters teach and learn through body and words" (147). She refers to these maternal sources of knowledge as "pedagogical spaces—indeed an intangible 'third space'—where dilemmas are negotiated and possibilities for creativity and self-love flow" (147). As the novel highlights, it is through this maternal nerd legacy that Luz can cultivate her unique brand of Chicana adolescent identity. To claim a Chicana feminist, nerd identity, Luz must uncover these stories as maternal, Tejana inspiration.

As an adolescent Chicana who solely wants to compete in spelling competitions so that she can make college a real possibility, Luz is initially unable and reluctant to situate her ambitions within a larger history of institutionalized racism that has denied Chicanx communities higher education access and attainment. But it is her grandmother, Aura, who demands that Luz recognize racist systems of power that threaten to suppress Luz's talent. In fact, Luz expresses frustration and inadequacy, believing that she cannot possibly represent her community when she has faced relatively few barriers in comparison to others: "'I mean I've never gone hungry. My parents have always given me everything I've wanted. . . . I mean, I've never even known a migrant worker. Who am I to be representing *La Raza?*' There. I've said it. So shoot me" (52). Luz's confusion is rooted in her naïve beliefs that being an "authentic" Chicana means experiencing poverty and hunger. These thoughts expose Hernández's resistance to identity policing that thwarts multiple ways of expressing Chicana identity.

But importantly, the novel sympathetically reveals Luz's transformation as a slow but empowered process of recognition of herself as a legitimate community member and Chicana. Her words, which are uttered to her grandmother, reflect her fears that her life of relative privilege thus far somehow makes her unworthy of her community's love and support. Aura, however, while sympathetic to her granddaughter's angst, reminds Luz that as a recipient of her community's histories and knowledge, she must learn the harsh truth about racism's continued legacy in the present: "Because you were born *raza*, the system will never let you forget it. . . . Racism. Genocide. Oppression. Whatever name you put on it, it's real. It's out there. And that's why it will be different for you than it will be for the white girls you compete with. No one is going to kill them for trying" (52–53). Aura's chilling words to her granddaughter resonate with the power of wisdom, but additionally, their truth is rooted in her traumatic, firsthand knowledge of the violence of white supremacy, which cares little about citizenship, or birthplace, for that matter. As a Chicana, but especially as an intelligent Chicana who threatens white power and authority, Luz will always be deemed lesser within a system that constructs all people of color as inferior, illegitimate, and always potentially at risk of death and violence for simply existing. Aura attempts to instill her granddaughter with social consciousness to challenge and resist structures of power that continue to deny her rightful place as student and learner.

Aura's traumatic history of unlawful deportation is revealed early in the novel, and in unveiling this crucial part of her past, Hernández underscores its significance to Luz's embattled competition in the present. Significantly, Aura reveals this harrowing experience in her own words, a key component that is seldom seen in young adult literature, the voice of an elder: "I was a young woman working a job I did not like, but it kept me home with the children in the day. I cooked *tortillas* at a restaurant until one night the *migra* came and rounded up all those that looked *mexicano*" (61). Aura's confession to her daughter, I suggest, functions as a warning to Rosaura that she must protect Luz from similar acts of racialized violence that threaten to jeopardize Luz's academic success. As a survivor of this brutal history of mass deportation, Aura understands firsthand that birthright citizenship does not matter if one "looked mexicano."[6] While her granddaughter may not suffer the extremes that she did, Aura draws connections between white community hostility at Luz's spelling success and her own deportation, recognizing the different strands of racism that ultimately share the underlying anxiety of a Chicanx/Mexican "threat," real or imagined. Rosaura attempts to assuage her mother's concern, telling her: "Oh, *Mamá*, it's not like when you were young. Some things are easier. We're fighting for more rights" (61). Although Rosaura acknowledges that racism continues to thrive, her belief that "some things are easier" suggests that she wants to shield her daughter from the brutalities of the past. Aura's insistence that the current generation remembers the past and its continued impact on the present, however, conflicts with Rosaura's tempered optimism. I do not mean to suggest that Rosaura denies the significance of her community's history of violent oppression, but in her encouragement that Luz fight for her right to compete, she reveals a fundamental belief that one should not remain tethered to the past.

This belief of hers, that the present and future are of greater concern than the struggles of the past, is evident in Aura's angry response to Rosaura: "'It is not in the history books that your daughters bring home from school, but it was us,' she points to herself, 'old Latinas, that picketed the pecan factories and made changes happen'" (61). Aura's refusal to silence her past trauma and activism reveals the novel's quest to document Chicana/Tejana contributions to Chicanx historymaking, evoking historian Emma Pérez's call to unearth these erased narratives. In Pérez's foundational book *The Decolonial Imaginary: Writing Chicanas Into History*, she states:

> I am more concerned with taking the "his" out of the "story," the story that often becomes the universalist narrative in which women's experience is negated. . . . How much have women been a part of the stories? Is it possible to recover much, given that the archives have been preserved for the "great men" who have made contributions in one way or another, whether presidents, generals, or imagined forefathers? The documents on or by women that have been preserved in libraries are often the papers of the wives, daughters, or family members of "great men."
>
> (xiv)

As Pérez argues, scholars must question "official" archival documentation that not only marginalizes, but outright erases, the presence of women throughout history. Aura's statement, "it was us," demands recognition and inclusion into a narrative of Mexican/Chicanx history and activism that seldom acknowledges women's leadership. Further, Aura insists on transmitting to her granddaughters her story of deportation and labor activism to challenge the systemic erasure of Mexican/Chicana women's roles within a larger American history of social change. Like more recent Chicana YA texts, such as Diana J. Noble's *Evangelina Takes Flight*, Ashley Hope Pérez's *Out of Darkness*, and Guadalupe Garcia McCall's recent two-part book series, the authors, including Hernández, center young women into Texas and broader Chicanx history to insist on young women's legitimate presence. While *White Bread Competition* does not utilize the genre of historical fiction in the same way as the texts by Noble, Pérez, and McCall, Hernández's careful insertion of Aura's history of unlawful deportation and activism underscores the significance of this facet of Luz's ChicaNerd identity development.

Luz's path to ChicaNerd feminism also entails learning about her mother's thwarted attempts to attend college and live on her own without her parents' consent or knowledge. This facet is revealed through dialogue between Rosaura and Aura, as well as inner monologue. In particular, readers learn that Rosaura's artistic talents and aspirations in college were derailed by racist and sexist professors, who condescendingly tell her "that there was no market for Mexican folk art. I should learn how to paint real art—if I could learn how to paint like a man, that is" (65). Significantly, the two primary maternal figures in Luz's life take on vastly different approaches to teach her the meaning of Chicana feminist knowledge production. On the one hand is the matriarch, Aura, who painfully yet vividly recounts her persecution and labor activism to insist to her granddaughter that little has changed in the present. In doing this, Aura fears for Luz's safety, going so far as to discourage her from competing in the district spelling bee (57). On the other hand, Rosaura, who has also firsthand experience with racism and sexism, instills in her daughter the tools of resistance as well as optimism.

Significantly, *White Bread Competition* delves into Rosaura's own ChicaNerd path of artistic resistance, and this path includes achieving her awaited dream of displaying her art publicly. Hernández uses the dialogue between two grown Chicana adults to draw similarities between multiple generations of ChicaNerds who aspire to create and compete. As Rosaura's trusted friend encourages her, when she is doubtful of displaying her art at a larger gallery, "You give people a glimpse of what and who we really are—not the stereotypes, but us as real people" (101). Hernández's examination of the adult world of Luz's mother—including several conversational exchanges throughout the novel between Rosaura and Aura, as well as between Rosaura and her friends—is a significant element we rarely see in YA fiction, where adolescence is the focal point by which we learn about gender, identity, race, and sexuality, among other issues. The added component of Luz's multigenerational, maternal past woven throughout the novel highlights Hernández's recognition of racialized and gendered histories that silence Chicanas/Tejanas. *White Bread Competition* insists on including Rosaura and Aura within Luz's ChicaNerd identity development.

Conclusion

Luz must learn to weave the legacy of her Chicana maternal stories with the community support she receives. As much as she is burdened by her community's demands, Luz eventually accepts her community's support when she recognizes their fierce demonstration of pride, solidarity, and love. At the novel's conclusion, we witness the community's presence at the school board meeting to determine the outcome of the false accusation launched at Luz. The significance of this meeting is not lost on Luz's supporters, despite the school board president's surprise at the large crowd when he states, "I wasn't expecting such a crowd. We have gathered here to address a simple matter" (176). For this white school board matter, Luz's fate is reduced to being a "simple matter," a failure to acknowledge Luz's suffering as a result of educational racism that presumes guilt simply because she is Chicana.

Although the truth eventually comes out, that Luz did not steal the spelling words, and she is at last able to represent her school in the district bee, the novel ends at the spelling competition, and readers can only guess if Luz wins. Hernández's decision to keep her readers in suspense is intended to emphasize Luz's path to this event, an endeavor riddled with false accusations, attacks from white community members and classmates, but above all, an experience that Luz shared with her family and community. In its realistic portrayal of the long-standing consequences of colonization in Texas, especially via the system of learning in San Antonio, *White Bread Competition* unapologetically reveals the depths of Chicanx community and maternal resistance that succeeds in supporting Luz Ríos's path to ChicaNerd spelling champion. By narrating the racist climate in which Luz must navigate, simply for the chance to represent her school at a spelling bee, Hernández refuses to paint a simplistic portrayal of a Chicana who overcomes racism. Indeed, the novel suggests that Luz is one of many ChicaNerds who continue to demand the right to learn and compete, but this persistence is a communal effort, and with the support of elder Chicanas in particular, Luz comes to understand the significance of Chicanx community solidarity.

Notes

1. See, for example, Paula Moya's important book chapter "Resisting the Interpretive Schema of the Novel Form" in William Orchard and Yolanda Padilla's volume *Bridges, Borders, Breaks* (2016), which gives a comprehensive overview of the scholarly debate surrounding genre and *Mango Street*.

2. See, for example, Ashley Hope Pérez's more recent novel *Out of Darkness*, which examines the racist, violent legacy of the Texas educational system that segregated Mexican-descent students into "Mexican" schools.
3. This chapter does not engage in a discussion of the novel's treatment of food and culinary undertones, although certainly this warrants future scholarship. For a more thorough account of the significance to food and consumption in children's literature, please see Kara K. Keeling and Scott T. Pollard's edited volume, *Critical Approaches to Food in Children's Literature*.
4. Celia C. Pérez's middle-grade novel *The First Rule of Punk* engages in a discussion of the derogatory slur "coconut," which refers to anyone who is assimilated, or "Brown on the outside, White on the inside." Although not a children's or YA text, Gwendolyn Zepeda's novel *Houston, We Have a Problema* makes references to characters' fears of being deemed bolillas, or white girls.
5. For more on Chicana feminist critiques of sexism and patriarchy within the Chicano Movement, also known as El Movimiento, see Alma García's benchmark anthology *Chicana Feminist Thought: The Basic Historical Writings* (1997) and the more recent collection *Chicana Movidas: New Narratives of Activism and Feminism in the Movement Era* (2018), edited by Espinoza, Cotera, and Blackwell.
6. For an excellent study on this period of mass deportation, also known as repatriation, which occurred during the Great Depression in the United States, please see Balderrama and Rodríguez's book *Decade of Betrayal: Mexican Repatriation in the 1930s*.

3 "The College Girl From the *Barrio*"
Calculus and ChicaNerdiness in *What Can(t) Wait*

Ashley Hope Pérez's debut novel centers on the life of 17-year-old Marisa Moreno, who lives with her Mexican immigrant parents, Patricia and Omar, her older sister, older brother, and young niece in Houston, Texas. The novel presents readers with critical insight into Marisa's ChicaNerd identity, rejecting, among other issues, problematic stereotypes of working-class Chicanx families as perceived "obstacles" that prevent Marisa from obtaining a college education; the "white savior" myth; rape culture; and racist beliefs that Chicanx families do not care about education. I provide a discussion of the novel's critical rejection of these myths through the text's portrayal of a Chicana teenager who excels in advance placement calculus, a rare glimpse into a Chicana math nerd that is seldom visible in popular cultural constructions of Chicana adolescents. In particular, I examine the ubiquitous "white savior" trope and rape culture, elements that feature prominently in the novel as complicated paths that Marisa must maneuver. As I discussed in the introduction to this book, I consider Pérez's novel a Chicana YA text because, despite Pérez's identity as a white woman, I point to the deft examination of a Chicana protagonist's nerd development that poignantly captures Marisa's reclamation of an empowered, subversive identity that honors her Chicanx community as part of this process.

The novel's representation of Marisa's academic talent in calculus marks the text's significance to the young adult literary canon for a number of reasons. First, in its unapologetic portrayal of a ChicaNerd who enjoys math, Pérez normalizes Marisa's talent, refusing to reinforce racist and sexist tropes that mark Marisa as somehow an exception to the rule that Chicanx adolescents, or all teenagers of color, for that matter, are incapable of excelling at a complicated subject. But perhaps most important, the novel is one of the few images of Chicana math nerds in print or on the screen. A notable exception is the Chicana filmmaker Aurora Guerrero's 2013 film *Mosquita y Mari*, a tender portrayal of young, queer Chicana love between the geometry whiz, Yolanda, and the girl she tutors and falls in love with, Mari. While the film and the novel tell two distinct stories of Chicana adolescence, they remain among the few portrayals of Chicana math nerds, which confirms that we have a long way to go in filling the gaps to tell nuanced, authentic tales of teen girls of color who possess, among other talents, math intelligence.

In Chapter 1, I discussed at length the multiple paths ChicaNerds must navigate—namely, stereotypes of nerds—and the "appropriateness" of Chicana scholastic aspirations amid damaging stereotypes of Chicanas as always troublesome cholas, bad girls who "belong" on the street rather than in the classroom. But in this chapter, I examine Marisa's efforts to chart her own path as a college-bound Chicana calculus nerd who is encouraged by her white teacher, Ms. Ford, to attend college. As we learn, Ms. Ford, though she is sincere, all-too-narrowly views college attainment as a simple matter of applying and gaining admission. Before I engage in a close reading of the novel and how it portrays Marisa's ChicaNerd development, it is important to first offer a discussion of the "white savior" trope, as it plays a fundamental role in how Marisa must reject Ms. Ford's attempt to rescue her. Marisa must learn to reclaim her family, cultural heritage, and emerging social consciousness as a Chicana to declare herself a ChicaNerd. By the end of the novel, it is Marisa's relationship with her family members, her mother in particular, that serves as the impetus to study engineering in college.

Although the "white savior" myth has largely been understood within the context of film, according to Matthew W. Hughey, examining the particularities of this cinematic trope allows us to gain insight into what these films tell us about how race, power, and inequality operate within a larger social structure. To be sure, this book focalizes Chicana YA fiction, not film, but the impact of these films is clearly not lost on the authors, several of whom portray the complex relationship between ChicaNerds and their white teachers. While I acknowledge that this teacher relationship is but one element of their lives that ChicaNerds must navigate to arrive at an empowered state of ChicaNerd self-love and confidence, these texts demonstrate a concern for smart, studious nerds of color everywhere, many of whom will likely be taught by teachers like Ms. Ford. The novels examined in this book thus point to the complex web of navigation, maneuvering, and negotiation on which ChicaNerds must embark to recognize their families, ethnicity, and mainly working-class communities of color as fundamental to their sense of love, worthiness, and intellect.

According to Hughey, white savior films refer to "the genre in which a white messianic character saves a lower- or working-class, usually urban or isolated, nonwhite character from a sad fate" (1). In his examination of 50 white savior films, Hughey's study investigates the ways in which these films reflect the realities of the myth of a "color-blind" society. While there is the tendency to simplistically reduce films such as *The Blind Side* to mere "entertainment," Hughey claims that we cannot underestimate how the white savior film "is an important cultural device and artifact because it helps repair the myth of white supremacy and paternalism in an unsettled and racially charged time" (15). Far from the films' supposed "good intentions," seen in showcasing romanticized plot lines that reveal the possibilities for egalitarian black/white friendships and social equality, visible in *The Help* as but one example only, the films construct black/white relations and an unequal power structure that "racializes and separates people into those who are redeemers (whites) and those who are redeemed or in need of redemption (nonwhites)" (Hughey 2). In the case of the novels examined in this book, this white savior trope finds its way in the classroom as well. As the novels demonstrate, the teacher/pupil is in itself reflective of an unequal power relationship, but the added reality of race further problematizes the ways in which some white teachers may internalize the white savior mentality to rescue "at risk" students of color who come from "damaged" or "broken" families and communities.

For example, in her study on white female teachers, scholar Amy Brown found that some public urban high schools reinforce the white savior ideology by describing the schools as "necessary" for the students' college preparation and ultimately, for the students' own good (124). Undoubtedly, schools play an integral role in socializing and educating children, but suggesting that the communities of color in which these students live are a detriment that can only be remedied by white teachers and the salvation provided by the schools, lays claim to Brown's argument. Across the country, according to Brown, school teachers are overwhelmingly white women (129) who do not reflect the reality of the communities they serve, as demonstrated in *What Can(t) Wait*, which takes place in a largely Mexican American neighborhood in Houston. But for Brown, the graver concern is not solely that the majority of teachers nationwide are white women; rather, teacher preparation programs continue to maintain a "deficit" perspective that reduces children of color and their communities to "problems" that can only be saved by white women and a color-blind education (129). While Ms. Ford does not overtly criticize Marisa's family or culture, the particularities of her language and word choice suggest that she believes that attending UT Austin will redeem Marisa from the woes of her working-class, Mexican family in Houston.

Marisa's relationship with Ms. Ford is more complicated when we consider that few girls of color are encouraged to pursue fields in STEM (science, technology, engineering, and mathematics). Not only must Marisa contend with her father's expectation that she passively obey his authority, as I explain in further detail, but she must further confront the overwhelming underrepresentation of Latinas and young women of color in a field that she is encouraged to pursue. The invisibility she will face as a young woman of color STEM professional is compounded by her father's insistence that she give up her mathematical aspirations. As Christia Spears Brown and Campbell Leaper note in their study, "Despite the narrowing of some gender gaps in STEM achievement, there are persistent gender differences in academic attitudes about STEM domains. Specifically, boys have both higher perceived competencies in math and science, as well as greater interest in math and science coursework and occupations" (861). When we consider how ethnicity intersects with gender, as in the case of Marisa who is both a young woman and Mexican/Chicana, research further documents that young girls of color face added obstacles in STEM achievement. Brown and Leaper report in their research that because of perceptions of sexism and discrimination felt by Latina teens in the classroom, "Latina girls' double-minority status—in which both their gender and ethnicity are academically devalued—may make them particularly vulnerable to negative group-based treatment" (867). As I discuss throughout my analysis of the novel, ethnicity alone does not account for Marisa's nuanced struggles in developing a ChicaNerd identity that empowers her to study and excel at calculus. Her identity as a young woman, in particular as the youngest child in a working-class Mexican immigrant family, informs the complexities of her struggle.

We must also consider Marisa's potential entrance into a specific branch of STEM, engineering, a field with few Latina professionals. In their article on engineering identity development, Sarah L. Rodriguez, et al., point out that only 2 percent of engineers in the United States are Latina (1). They add that,

> Many factors may contribute to Latina students' underrepresentation in engineering programs. For example, prior research has shown that Latina college students have difficulty envisioning themselves as engineers and feeling validated in the engineering community (Camacho and Lord, 2013; Carlone and Johnson, 2007). An inability to identify as an engineer and feel a part of the engineering community severely limits one's potential to persist in an engineering program and transition into industry (Camacho and Lord, 2013).
> (Rodriguez et al. 2)

Systemically, it is near impossible to be "at home" within institutions of power, such as the STEM industry, when one is a woman, a person of color, and from an otherwise marginalized community. Marisa, like all the ChicaNerd protagonists, must navigate the complexities of feeling like an imposter while at the same time insisting on their right to achieve higher education and training. As Marisa comes to learn, her talent in subjects like calculus not only subject her to ridicule from her father, but the very field in which she will eventually embark will also render her an outsider because of the invisibility of women of color in that profession. Throughout the novel, Marisa struggles with conflicting emotions regarding whether she should pursue engineering precisely because she is aware that her home life *and* status as a young Chicana potentially threaten her aspirations. Even before Marisa's entrance to college, she possesses a heightened awareness that she will be marginalized at an elite university, let alone within the engineering major and profession.

As the youngest daughter, Marisa's life is largely governed by her authoritative and emotionally distant father, Omar, who demands portions of her weekly paychecks to help support the family. Caught between her parents' expectations to help provide for the family and care for her young niece, and her own desires to excel at AP calculus so she can attend the University of Texas (UT), hours away from home, Marisa struggles with her nerdiness that is apparently at odds with her family and community. For example, Marisa admits to routinely leaving her report card in plain sight for her parents to notice, "hoping that one day my parents will say something" (24). Clearly, Marisa desires her parents' pride and wants to share a part of her life with them. Their silence, however, suggests her parents' inability to understand their daughter's high school experience, rather than their refusal to support educational pursuits. While her parents initially appear to be uninterested or even unsupportive of her intellectual pursuits, it is important to note that the novel in no way reinforces problematic stereotypes of working-class Chicanx families as "obstacles" that stand in the way of achieving (read: "white") academic success. Instead, Marisa learns to adopt her parents' example of hard work, particularly her mother's, to study engineering at an elite university.

Throughout the novel, Marisa struggles with feelings of being an outsider within her family and school community, while at the same time desiring her family's acceptance and pride in her intellectual achievements. This outsiderness does not denote her rejection of them, but she struggles to articulate her academic interests and aspirations to her family. This, of course, is complicated by the reality that her weekly paychecks from her grocery store job contribute to her family's economic survival. When her calculus teacher, Ms. Ford, encourages her to apply to UT Austin to major in engineering, a subject in which Marisa knows little, Marisa is burdened with the guilt that accompanies the knowledge that attending this elite university means leaving home: "If you put me in a world where all that matters is what I want, I'd go to UT and give engineering a shot. But that is definitely not my world. I can't just peace-out on my family" (13). In her working-class home, Marisa's wages help sustain the family's survival. While she wishes to attend college, she struggles with her complex feelings of abandonment, guilt, and perceived selfishness. Further, her first-generation status means that her family is unable to understand the extent of what attending college means, leading Marisa to feel that she is outside her family unit, even as they inherently understand that college may potentially mean upward mobility. This feeling of being an outsider is complicated by her intense feelings of shame that she is disappointing them.

The patriarchal structure of Marisa's family, however, coupled with her studiousness, often makes her the butt of jokes and the source of Omar's frustration. On the one hand, her older brother, Gustavo, teases her for refusing to "lighten up" and enjoy her senior year of high school (10), calling her a "*nerda*" (9) and "schoolgirl" (10), but more troubling are Omar's admonishments that she "[l]eave the mathematics to the men" (12). Omar's admonishment that she forego calculus training reveals the common stereotype that mathematics is not appropriate for women and that women are not good at it in the first place (Tomasetto, Alparone, and Cadinu 943). Marisa, however, learns to challenge her father's sexism by continuing to excel at a subject that she is aware she is not "supposed" to enjoy, much less a subject at which she should surpass her peers' achievement. Her bookishness and achievement in a challenging subject like calculus, rather than being a source of pride for the men in her family, instead makes her seem rigid at best, and at worst, a threat to her father's authority, given that Marisa admits that he is unable to read or write. As a ChicaNerd who aspires to attend college, Marisa struggles with guilt for venturing into a world in which she feels alone, and where she has been told she does not belong. In her UT admission essay, for example, she honestly and poignantly captures the complex web of emotions with which she grapples as a working-class, first-generation student of color:

> I watch the life that my parents lead, and I know that I want something different. They have worked hard their entire lives with no savings to show for it. . . .
>
> I want my hard work to get me somewhere. I want to worry about which engineering firm to work for, not how I'm going to pay the light bill.
>
> So why do I make my life so hard? Because I want to make something of myself. Because I want my mom to look at me in ten years and finally understand why a high school diploma wasn't enough for me.
>
> (29)

Marisa's honesty about her parents' hard work and sacrifices is not rooted in shame, nor is it an admission that she desires to be "more" than them. Instead, Marisa refuses to romanticize working-class life and the financial anxieties that accompany it. This awareness of how a college education offers the opportunity for more upward economic ability than her parents were able to achieve is reflective of her status as a first-generation college student. For example, in their research on first-generation college students, Rebecca Covarrubias and Stephanie A. Fryberg found that Latinx students were more likely to struggle with what they call "family achievement guilt," defined as feelings of guilt associated with "surpassing the achievements of family members" (426). In addition, the novel articulates Marisa's aspirations to achieve material comfort in a way that does not signal her desire to separate from her family and Mexican American community. Instead, as Elda María Román argues, much contemporary Chicanx cultural production represents how "upward mobility does not have to lead to cultural disavowal" (14). Admitting that she wants more financial stability does not reflect in any way a desire to abandon or discard her family and community. Rather, in her astute comment that her parents "have worked hard their entire lives with no savings to show for it," Marisa critiques the idealized myth of "The American Dream," which supposedly grants material wealth to those who have worked hard. But the ideal does not account for the reality of systemic racism that denies equal access to this wealth, as sociologists and Chicanx educational scholars such as Stephen J. McNamee, Robert K. Miller, and Angela Valenzuela have argued in their seminal works, *The Meritocracy Myth* and *Leaving Children Behind*. Though it is difficult for her to admit these facts, Marisa's raw honesty in the letter is crucial for its refusal to be silent; speaking of her family's economic struggles is necessary in the achievement of ChicaNerd agency. In particular, Marisa yearns for a college education to honor her mother, Patricia, who does not always understand Marisa's aspirations, but wants to support her in the best way she can.

On Not Being Rescued: ChicaNerds and White Teachers

In addition to navigating her family's expectations, Marisa must also battle her school and community's subtle but strong messages on the "appropriateness" of Chicana college aspirations. We see this especially in her interactions with her teacher and mentor, Ms. Ford, who works with Marisa throughout the college application process. Although Ms. Ford genuinely cares for her star pupil, the novel also comments on the limits of this care. On the one hand, Ms. Ford recognizes Marisa's unparalleled talent in calculus and her college potential; on the other hand, however, she is unable to comprehend structural forces in play that make moving away to college an emotionally *and* financially complicated endeavor on which to embark. When Cecilia, Marisa's sister, must return to work following her husband's workplace accident that leaves him temporarily disabled, Marisa is left responsible for the caretaking of her young niece, Anita. Marisa's commitment to fully care for her niece, as well as to teach her how to read and count, however, leaves little time for calculus preparation and tutoring. Ms. Ford cannot comprehend this arrangement, but in a touching letter, Marisa asks for her teacher's help to catch up on the lesson plans that she has sacrificed in caring for her niece.

This request for help, though, does not denote a desire to be rescued. Instead, Marisa insists on being honest and forthcoming about her family's circumstances, refusing to describe caring for her niece as a waste of time or as actions that do not measure up to studying for calculus: "At first I tried to do my calculus while I watched Anita because that was the only time I had.... I can't let her down. She didn't do anything to deserve all this trouble.... If you help me, I think I can catch up. I'm not just doing it for me. I want my niece to see that women just like her mom and grandma and aunt *can* do hard things" (106–7, original italics). In this raw honesty, Marisa insists on embodying intellectual pursuit and hard work to her niece, passing down Chicanerdiness to her young family member. What I also find particularly poignant and powerful is Marisa's desire to do both, to study for the calculus AP exam *and* care for Anita. Both tasks are equally valued, yet Marisa astutely understands that her teacher and society at large may refuse to see her caregiving as anything but an example of her "misplaced" priorities and her family's failure at raising college-bound children. By refusing to stop caring for her niece, Marisa rejects this narrative that she does not prioritize her schoolwork. Being a ChicaNerd means caring for her Chicanita kin and modeling reading and learning to her niece, even at the expense of her own grades.

For Ms. Ford, attending a "dream school" like UT is a simple matter of gaining admission, without an understanding of how Marisa's family depends on her for economic and emotional survival, not to mention Marisa's devotion to her niece that she feels will be jeopardized by leaving home. When Marisa struggles in her calculus class, mostly as a consequence of having to care for Anita and take on more hours at the grocery store where she works, Ms. Ford displays confusion over her top student's low test scores. In an emotional exchange between the two, Marisa critically rejects what she perceives as Ms. Ford's attempt to "save" or "rescue" her:

> She's thinking my life could be simple if I would just follow some stupid goal-planning worksheet and come to tutorials. She's thinking, *These Mexican girls, why won't they take their futures seriously?* She's thinking, *This Marisa, if she were more like me, she'd go far.* ...
> "I wish it were easier, but you've just got to make hard decisions. Education is your ticket."
> Like I don't know that! It's like she's reading right off one of those stupid motivational posters from middle school. I can feel the heat in my cheeks, and I want to tell her to back the fuck off. Those are the very words fighting to get off my tongue. Because she doesn't know my life. She doesn't know me. ...
> "I'm on your side, remember?" Ms. Ford says. ...
> "I don't care about UT! You want me to be this perfect success story, the college girl from the *barrio*."
> (63–64, original italics)

In Ms. Ford's simplistic advice that Marisa merely "be smart" with her schedule (63), she fails to understand Marisa's responsibility in caring for her niece. This advice is part and parcel of the "bootstrap" mythos ingrained in American culture, the message being that one merely needs to "work hard" to get ahead, without taking into account structural inequality and racism. While Ms. Ford is earnest in her beliefs that Marisa's intelligence makes her a perfect candidate for UT, Marisa struggles to accept her teacher's help, given that Omar distrusts this Anglo teacher's interest in his daughter's education, as he tells her: "It's only because some *gringos* want to feel good about themselves, want to feel like they're helping out some poor *mexicana*. Don't think that gets you out of working" (13, original italics). Although he views his daughter's college goals as attempts to evade familial responsibility, Omar does represent the novel's rejection of the "white savior" trope, and his skepticism is firmly rooted in knowledge of problematic stereotypes of struggling Latinx students who must leave their families and culture behind to achieve academic success, all under the guidance of Anglo teachers who come to their rescue. But at the same time, Omar's scathing comment also reminds readers of his earlier comment to Marisa that she "leave the mathematics to the men." In his reference to Marisa as a "poor Mexicana," he subtly conveys his suspicion at her math intelligence, affirming Brown and Leaper's research findings that show how, "as girls enter late adolescence, their interest in math and science may be negatively affected by negative comments about their math and science abilities. This has implications for the types of math and science courses girls may choose to take, and may lead girls to take the minimum required math and science courses to graduate and to opt out of advanced level courses" (868). Marisa's enrollment in AP calculus is temporarily threatened by her father, but her persistence in remaining in the course demonstrates her resilience and work ethic. But in documenting Marisa's resilience, I point to the fact that the novel does not suggest that resilience alone is what is required to excel and enroll in AP math courses. The bleaker reality is that few students like Marisa, because of a combination of racism, sexism, and systemic lack of educational opportunities, pursue AP mathematics and study it in college.

In her retort that the teacher merely wants her to be "the college girl from the *barrio*," Marisa refuses to be Ms. Ford's charity case, while also calling out the myth of equal access to education and the realities faced by first-generation, working-class Latinx students. Once again, giving voice to these struggles is a critical insistence on her right to an empowered nerd subjectivity, a harsh truth people like Ms. Ford may be unwilling to admit. Ms. Ford is undoubtedly sincere in her advice to Marisa that "education is [her] ticket," but these "motivational poster" words, as Marisa sarcastically refers to them, do not take into account the circumstances that make going away to college a difficult and painful decision to make for many first-generation students, whose financial contributions are necessary for the family's survival. Equating college attainment to a "ticket" also problematically suggests that Marisa's current life, embodied by her parents' physically laborious work, is an "undesirable" place in need of fleeing. Essentially, Ms. Ford is suggesting that education is her "ticket out" of the *barrio*. According to this logic, smart students like Marisa cannot possibly thrive in these settings.

But in a significant change of tune, Ms. Ford agrees to help Marisa, realizing that her student's family and home obligations require adjustments and accommodations, rather than charity. Ms. Ford's willingness to help her student shows the novel's belief that white teachers *can* help guide and mentor ChicaNerd students if their help is rooted in encouragement rather than a desire to "rescue." For Ms. Ford to adjust her interpretations of Marisa's home life, Marisa's decision to be honest and forthcoming is necessary. That is, Ms. Ford helps Marisa, and does not rescue her, only when Marisa openly asks for help in the letter in a way that does not reject her role within the family. Marisa's maturity and honesty are a precise example of the development of her ChicaNerd identity that refuses to hide the truth of her family's needs. Further, Marisa uses her teacher's assistance to her advantage, as she decides to apply for financial aid to make college a real possibility. Her savviness, resilience, and resourcefulness are evident in this process: "I spend three lunch periods in a row applying online for financial aid, glad for once that I've been stuck helping Ma with the taxes for ages" (111). Although Marisa's financial aid application process is a rather minor detail in the overall narrative, this additional plot element, I would argue, demonstrates the significance of her giftedness in using her familial responsibilities to her advantage—what I see as a distinct element of ChicaNerd identity. Rather than reinforce the racist myth that Chicanx families and culture are a "detriment" to Chicanx student success and college attainment, it is precisely this experience in helping her family that eventually serves her in the college application process.

On Being a ChicaNerd, Not a Teen Mother

Thus far, this chapter has examined Marisa's development of her ChicaNerd identity that is at times at odds with her family and teacher, especially her teacher's initial misguided attempts to come to her rescue. However, the novel takes great care in addressing Marisa's other social environment—her school and peers—which also play a role in how Marisa maneuvers her life as a ChicaNerd. As she learns quite painfully via her survival of an attempted rape, being the "schoolgirl" does little to protect young Chicana teens from the brutalities of rape culture. Marisa's growing sexual curiosity and desire to date freely additionally make her the target of her father's rage. If Marisa's nerd-like aspirations place her at odds with both her teacher's and parents' grand plans for her future, they also make her a target of physical and sexual violence. For example, when Marisa arrives home late from an evening double date with her new boyfriend, Alan, and best friend, Brenda, her father violently grabs her by her clothes and disdainfully tells her, "You have these big ideas that you're too good now" (98) and orders her to take on more shifts at work and help care for her niece. In his accusation that Marisa thinks of herself in superior terms, however, Omar also reveals his own deep-seated fears that intellectual achievement will cause his daughter to be ashamed of her family, culture, and working-class roots. While this in no way must be read as an excuse for his physical aggression, Marisa temporarily internalizes her father's accusation, shamefully believing that she deserves violence and disdain because of her perceived aloofness and arrogance.

Marisa's increased frustration with her father's austerity manifests in outright rebellion to his authority. While rebellion is often interpreted as the quintessential adolescent behavior, Marisa's rebellion should be read as highly charged outbursts that reflect her astute expression of her father's unjust harshness and sexism. In her refusal to be silenced by her father, Marisa breaks her family's cardinal rule of voicing aloud the realities of her father's abuse and drunken behavior: "His hand feels like a steel band on my arm, and I can smell the beer on his breath. 'What about you? What if you stopped drinking? That would free up some funds.' Now I've really done it, said the thing nobody's supposed to say" (123). Although her accusation renders her a "disrespectful daughter" by her father's standards, readers empathize with Marisa's growing sense of isolation and hurt. Rather than rebel for the simple sake of rebellion, Marisa's statement to her father reflects the novel's poignant representation of the many familial, cultural, and social codes that ChicaNerds must maneuver in the achievement of agency, subjectivity, and academic pursuits of knowledge.

Although I am not equating Omar's physical aggression with the violence Marisa experiences when she is the victim of attempted rape by a popular high school classmate, Pedro, it is important to acknowledge the ways in which Marisa's very human desires to date and explore sexuality are treated as evidence of her being "slutty" or "too good" for her family. Consider, for example, the seething words her attempted rapist utters, which are eerily similar to her father's: "You think you're different, but you're not. In the end, you're still a slut on the inside" (143). Pedro's hateful words imply that her intellect, her daring to be talented at math, makes her deserving of such brutality. In calling her a slut, Pedro echoes a common slur hurled at young women who engage in sexual activity, consensual or not. Moreover, Marisa at first withdraws from her friends and school community, fearing that "everybody at school is going to take one look at me and know. Slut! Cheat! Liar!" (149). In blaming herself for this attack, Marisa reveals the novel's critique of rape culture that suggests young girls deserve "what's coming" for rejecting narrow standards of femininity. This important critique made in a YA text follows in the tradition of Chicana feminist literature, which, according to scholar Norma Alarcón, has long vocalized its opposition to rigid understandings of female sexuality that "condemns [women] to enslavement. An enslavement which is subsequently manifested in self-hatred" ("Chicana's" 183). In Marisa's case, her attacker attempts rape to place her firmly where she "belongs." Rather than supposedly protect her from unwanted sexual attention, her nerdiness marks her as an easy target of violence because of misperceptions that a Chicana has no business being smart and studious.

If surviving an attempted rape exposes Marisa head-on to the common stereotype of Chicana girls as sexually available, visible in Pedro's misogynistic slur, alongside this occurs another troubling myth that Marisa struggles with: that of the teenage mother of color. As Vera López and Meda Chesney-Lind explain, "Latinas who fail to live up to this 'good girl' expectation are thought of as sexually promiscuous 'whores' who are often pregnant and unwed" (529). Throughout the novel, Marisa must contend with the realities of teen motherhood, given that her new relationship with Alan awakens a burgeoning sexual desire that she fears will manifest into unprotected sex and pregnancy. As the sister of a former teen mother, Marisa is intimately connected with the struggles of young motherhood, and when her boyfriend, Alan, confides in her that his younger sister is pregnant, she fears that this too could happen to her. Alan captures Marisa's angst over their families' confrontation with teenage pregnancy: "It's sick, how this happens all the time. Your sister, my sister. And all the other big bellies at school" (55). While she expresses sexual attraction and even desire for her new boyfriend, their sisters' young pregnancies serve as a warning: "Like maybe we both knew enough from our sisters' lives to be over the 'caught in the moment' thing" (72–73). While she and her boyfriend exercise restraint, she acknowledges how easy it is to succumb to sexual desire.

Marisa attempts to evade a "big-bellied" fate through her academic achievement, but even as she vows not to "end up" like her sister, she nevertheless expresses discomfort at being labeled the innocent, good girl. In contrast to Alan's sister, Jessica, who is pregnant, Alan's parents use Marisa as the example to which their pregnant teen daughter should aspire, as Alan tells Marisa: "When my mom and my sister are fighting, it always comes back to what a hardworking, respectful girl you are," to which Marisa responds in frustration, "Oh, God. . . *no me lo digas*" (101, original italics). Although the description of Marisa as hardworking is accurate, Marisa rejects being so narrowly understood as "respectful," given that she interprets this as coded language for passivity. What I find to be significant is that Marisa is *not* passive or silent, as evidenced by her argument with her father. As a hardworking and outspoken ChicaNerd,

Marisa insists on her right to determine her own path in life, even if this does not align with her parents' wishes that she remain in Houston, work at the grocery store, and marry Alan. She may not want to be a "big-bellied" teen mother, but she also refuses to reinforce her family's expectations of virginity and passivity.

Yet, Marisa remains steadfast in her college goals, combining her nerdy interests with a burgeoning Chicana consciousness to claim a ChicaNerd identity. Describing calculus work as "reclaiming a little something for myself" (114), Marisa unabashedly admits her enjoyment of a challenging subject. Claiming this enjoyment and talent foregrounds a growing sense of her nerdy Chicana self. Voicing this is a turning point, as it demonstrates her achievement of agency, which requires a vocal admission of daring to be herself among her family. In fact, when her mother and older brother concoct a plan to make up Marisa's lost wages so she can continue math tutoring, her older brother, Gustavo, humorously but affectionately tells her, "I mean, it's weird to care so much about school, but you've always been weird. And maybe that's not such a bad thing. . . . *Familia* takes care of *familia*. We're going to make it" (154–55). Earlier in the novel, Marisa keeps her tutoring sessions secret, but as she learns, hiding her talent in math succeeds only in alienating herself from her family members, who, in fact, do want to support her. In this loving exchange between older brother and younger sister, we witness the novel's refusal to reinforce racist myths that Chicanxs do not care about education. Although Gustavo may not understand or share his little sister's aspirations of college, he accepts her in her nerdy "weirdness" and vows to help her. And, in his subtle use of the plural "we," Gustavo takes on Marisa's burdens as his own, beautifully articulating the need for familia to support their nerdy kin. Gustavo's affection for his nerdy little sister encourages Marisa to discover her own agency and voice.

Marisa's older sister, Cecilia, also voices support for her ChicaNerd kin. While Cecilia does not fully understand Marisa's career choice, mistaking engineering for an electrician profession (146), she admits her admiration for her younger sister. In her encouragement that she not allow their father or Marisa's boyfriend to derail her college plans, Cecilia articulates what I read as a working-class Chicana feminism rooted in love: "You're going to be the one who really does something, you know? So don't let Papi or Alan or nobody slow you down. . . . You're going to college *y todo*, and that's that" (146, original italics). Telling Marisa, "The last thing I want you to do is end up like me" (146), Cecilia advises her to excel in college to achieve upward mobility. But whereas Cecilia voices shame in how her life has turned out, similar to their brother Gustavo's admission that he cannot fully understand Marisa's aspirations, the novel cautions against reading Marisa' family as obstacles to higher education attainment, nor are we supposed to frame Marisa as the "success" story. This point is evident in the growing scholarship in Girls Studies and Chicana girlhood, which has unveiled the unique position in which Chicana teens find themselves: their desire to "get ahead" amid their families' working-class backgrounds that are denigrated in the larger society as examples of those who "failed" in life. In her study with Chicana teens, sociologist Julie Bettie found that "Mexican-American girls wanted to point to the importance of mobility, yet did not want this to mean that their parents' lives were without value" (156). Likewise, as a ChicaNerd who is developing a working-class, Chicana feminist perspective, Marisa refuses to classify her siblings as failures, nor is she willing to uphold herself as a type of family success story, the "one who really does something."

At the novel's conclusion, Marisa is at last UT bound. Although she does not inform her mother that she is leaving for Austin until the night before her departure, Patricia, having correctly surmised her daughter's plans, does not scold her for her secrecy, but instead gives her an overnight bag. Through this gift, Patricia symbolically transmits to her daughter the means to carry her home items back and forth between the new world she is about to enter and the old one she has left. The gift also serves as a reminder to Marisa of Patricia's sacrifices and devotion to her college-bound daughter. In emotional words to Marisa, "I was never like you, so much confidence, so much brains. I was always *burra*, slow. . . . You were always special, curious, interested in everything. And smart. I never knew how to be the right mom for you" (224–25), Patricia initially expresses shame for not understanding her daughter's achievements. In her self-deprecating description of herself as a "burra," Patricia reveals what she sees as flaws, her supposed intellectual "slowness." Patricia's simple, loving encouragement of her daughter runs counter to the myths of Mexican families as deficient and not caring about education, what I discussed at length in Chapter 1. Instead, Patricia's actions demonstrate what Gilda Ochoa calls "transformational caring," or a "range of often unacknowledged and politicized caring and . . . the complex and situationally specific ways that some are redefining and resisting narrow conceptions of Mexican American women, mothering, and education" ("Transformational" 105). Particularly touching in Patricia's emotional words is the deep sense of pride, admiration, and love for her daughter. Patricia is aware that she cannot provide her daughter with the economic means to attend college, nor can she provide her with insider knowledge on navigating college student life. But what she does provide—love and acceptance—is not lost on Marisa, who reclaims her Mexican immigrant mother. In this passage, the novel exposes and adamantly rejects gender, racial, and class systems of power that define Mexican immigrant women like Patricia as deficient, inferior, and intended for manual labor, as if being a laborer renders one incapable of complex thought. Instead, it is precisely Patricia's model of dignity and work that she passes down to her daughter.

Without a doubt, assimilationist rhetoric pressures first-generation students of color like Marisa to reject working-class Mexican heritage as incompatible with academics, but in Marisa's heartfelt declaration to her mother that she is "the right kind of mom" (226), she lovingly reclaims her Mexican immigrant mother. While Chicana feminist scholar Aída Hurtado notes the prevalence of "idealized motherhood" (398) in Chicanx culture, it is important to note that Patricia is not constructed as a martyred mother but instead as Marisa's inspiration and source of loving empowerment. In fact, research has shown that young women of color excel in subjects like math and science when they have maternal and social support (Leaper, Farkas, and Brown 276). Patricia's love and pride in Marisa provides her daughter the means to achieve daughterly and nerdy agency.

Further, this loving connection between a ChicaNerd and working-class mother demonstrates the novel's ongoing insistence that readers recognize Chicanx families, especially mothers, as educational models that are typically not acknowledged in mainstream theories on education (Bernal et al.). Leaving for college does not denote her attempts to flee, deny, or reject her family and culture, as Patricia's gift symbolizes preparing for, rather than escaping from, a world she has yet to discover. In these simple but heartfelt words to each other, Mexican mother and ChicaNerd daughter reclaim each other. The many exchanges between Marisa and her family demonstrate Ashley Hope Pérez's insistence that readers recognize the emotional strength and resilience that Marisa inherits. As a soon-to-be first-generation college student, Marisa learns to use her family's hard-work ethic and loving support as sources of inspiration and radical love that she will need to attain a college degree. Rather than reject her family, home, and culture, Marisa embraces these elements of her life to declare herself a ChicaNerd.

4 Theater and Chicana Poetic Development in Guadalupe García McCall's *Under the Mesquite*

In an interview with R. Joseph Rodríguez, Guadalupe García McCall had this to say about the role that literature played in her adolescence, especially during a particularly gut-wrenching time: "[Books] showed me how to dream, to believe in myself, and to not care about glory as much as about personal growth. Books fed my mind at a time when my personal life was falling apart" (qtd in Rodríguez 165). For McCall, the beauty of words could transcend the darkness in her life. Guadalupe García McCall's award-winning novel *Under the Mesquite* chronicles the protagonist Lupita's four years of high school, a period that the novel beautifully captures in its verse structure that emphasizes the development of voice and consciousness.[1] Based loosely on García McCall's life, the novel examines, like the other ChicaNerd texts, the particularities of growing up as an intellectually curious, adolescent Chicana who struggles with the pressures of fitting in at school as a drama/theater ChicaNerd and issues punctuated by her mother's cancer diagnosis and her eventual death from the disease. García McCall's novel, much like Patricia Santana's text, discussed in the final chapter, charts the protagonist's ChicaNerd path in relation to her newly formed identity as a motherless young woman who is unable to fully articulate at first what it means to be Chicana, a student, daughter, artist, and learner without her mother. In this chapter, I examine Lupita's development of ChicaNerd theater/ poetic identity, arguing that it is her negotiation of maternal death and familial responsibilities, her love of drama, and the advice given to her by her Latino teacher that prove to be the major elements that drive her sense of ChicaNerd self. Lupita navigates an emotional path toward ChicaNerd self-love that entails accusations from classmates that she is "white" because of her interest in drama and poetry, but despite these hurdles, she adopts a unique ChicaNerd identity with the love and support of her immigrant parents, who encourage her to write and study. Significantly, although the other novels I examine in this book feature at times antagonistic relationships between the ChicaNerds and their mostly white teachers, it is important to note that Lupita's teacher, in fact, is not white but presumably Mexican American like her. However, despite their shared ethnic/cultural identity, her teacher, Mr. Cortés, at times encourages assimilation to his prized drama student. Mr. Cortés, while mainly an empathetic supporter of Lupita as she deals with her mother's death and the overwhelming responsibilities that ensue as the eldest child and daughter of her family, transmits an assimilationist message that aligns with what the ChicaNerds' white teachers proclaim to their students. As a ChicaNerd, Lupita learns to construct her own voice amid her teacher's desires that she assimilate.

The novel joins the large canon of YA writing that has used the verse genre, a common form of writing that we see in recent Latina YA publications, most notably Elizabeth Acevedo's 2018 novel *The Poet X*, for example. In Acevedo's verse novel, the teenage protagonist, Xiomara, learns to construct her identity in relation to the poetry she creates, and the verse form captures her sense of self that she must negotiate amid gendered expectations within her family and the racialized landscape that marginalizes her as an adolescent but especially as a teenaged Afro-Latina. Although this chapter does not privilege a discussion of the novel's employment of verse, it is useful to briefly document the ways in which this genre highlights Lupita's sense of self as a budding writer and ChicaNerd. YA literature scholar Joy Alexander states that the verse YA novel typically "is told in the form of non-rhyming free verse," which readily applies to *Under the Mesquite* (270). Read aloud, the text is nevertheless rhythmic while also possessing the effect of a story's plot line. For Alexander, however, the genre's similarity to poetry raises the "vexed question of distinguishing between a novel told in verse and a series of poems linked in a narrative sequence" (270). Mike Cadden's assertion that we examine "the novel, poetry, and drama in relation to each other instead of as separate and unrelated forms" (26) further complicates the ways scholars interpret verse texts as prose—that is, as novels—or poetic texts that take on the longer novelistic form. I am reluctant to describe García McCall's text as a sequence of poems in a narrative format, for it is important to note the manner in which the chapters function as *chapters* rather than poems; while indeed the chapters are presented in verse, their organization in the overall text follows the novelistic format. There is clearly a plot. But for both Alexander and Cadden, regardless of how we classify texts like *Under the Mesquite*, the writers' use of verse undoubtedly functions as a mode of privileging the protagonist's voice in connection with other themes the novels may undertake. Clearly, García McCall's verse structure does align Lupita's quest to discover her own voice with the generic form, although the novel does also feature conversations where other voices are present. Perhaps even more significant is what it means for a Chicana writer to use the verse structure to author a novel about a Chicana protagonist who yearns to write and act. In this subversive choice to employ a genre that privileges the protagonist voice, the novel introduces readers to a young, adolescent Chicana voice, one who is traditionally silenced by unequal power structures that marginalize the experiences and observations of teenaged Chicanas and other young women of color.

When we consider genre alongside the novel's thematic use of the emerging writer, *Under the Mesquite* further breaks ground within the realm of Chicana YA and "adult" literature. In doing so, the novel is also part of the large body of Chicana literature that has represented protagonists as writers, including those texts that challenge the conventions of literary form (Eysturoy; Quintana 55). In well-known texts, including Sandra Cisneros's *The House on Mango Street* and Denise Chávez's *The Last of the Menu Girls*, the protagonists are emerging writers whose first-person narrative voices frame stories around gender, violence, sexuality, and community. But what sets García McCall's book apart is its marketing for a distinct youth audience, connecting it to novels like *Gabi, A Girl in Pieces* or *I Am Not Your Perfect Mexican Daughter*, the subject of other chapters in this manuscript. By featuring the protagonist as a writer, *Under the Mesquite*, and for that matter, the novels by Quintero and Sánchez, not only normalize creative Chicanas who aspire to be writers but also point to a tradition of Chicana letters that portrays complex and creative Chicana protagonists who use the written word to vocalize burgeoning Chicana feminist thought and astute commentary on what it means to be young, working-class, female, and Chicana. Annie Eysturoy's study of the Chicana *bildungsroman*, published in 1996, examined what she identified as a common trend in Chicana fiction: "this process of becoming, whether it is that of the child and adolescent or the somewhat older woman" (3). In her discussion, however, Eysturoy omits a prolonged examination of literature for young adult audiences. In their more recent study, Amy Cummins and Myra Infante-Sheridan argue that the novel should be classified not only as a *bildungsroman* but as a distinct Chicana version of the well-known literary genre, explaining that the text represents a number of elements that warrant that classification: "narrating the coming of age of a Chicana protagonist over an extended period of time, portraying her developing an understanding of a dual identity as a Mexican American, and connecting the protagonist's development with valuing of family, community, and collectivity" (19). Lupita's distinct voice as a teenaged Chicana who contests racialized and gendered constraints of what it means to be Chicana is compounded by her realization that she occupies the complicated terrain of adolescence. Without a doubt, Lupita's identity as a ChicaNerd owes much to her family's influence, as I will discuss, and her "understanding of a dual identity as a Mexican American" is captured throughout her development into a ChicaNerd. In this chapter, I examine, in particular, Lupita's vocalization of a ChicaNerd writerly and thespian identity that is constantly under attack and under negotiation by the high school setting of her South Texas community.

Cultivating a ChicaNerd Identity: Familial Inspiration

Before I examine Lupita's development of a thespian and poetic ChicaNerd identity amid her school and peer racial politics, it is useful to begin with a discussion of the novel's representation of the Mexican immigrant family as the source of Lupita's inspiration and writing talent. As I argue throughout this book, all the ChicaNerds grapple with one of the most persistent harmful myths around Chicanx education: namely, that Chicanx and Mexican immigrant families do not care about their children's schooling. In contesting this myth, the ChicaNerds embrace their Chicanx, working-class families as creative inspiration, even if this path is ridden with pain and misunderstandings, most evident in *Mexican Daughter*, for example, or even when the protagonists feel pressured to "live up" to what their community expects from them, as in *White Bread Competition*.

Under the Mesquite tackles these destructive myths early in the text. Although the novel traces Lupita's four years of high school, she narrates memories of her early childhood to chart her writing path, particularly her father's praise of her talent when first teaching her how to write:

> Papi's hand guided mine as
> I clutched the pencil,
> holding it sideways against my fingertips.
> "The S is a *serpiente*, sitting up
> on its tail," he told me.
> Then we made the letter C,
> curled up like a tiny bug, a *cochinilla*.
>
> "You have a talent for letters,"
> Papi said, speaking softly in my ear.
> His hands were rough and scratchy
> against my skin, and the bits of sawdust
> clinging to his work clothes
> were tiny mosquitoes biting into my arms.
> But his voice was sweet and gentle.
> My pencil whispered the letters
> onto the paper like magic.
>
> (33)

In these visually stunning lines, García McCall reclaims immigrant parents as educators. It is important to note that while the novel does represent many classroom scenes to address Lupita's experience in high school, this moment in the novel revises the immigrant home space as her first classroom. Reclaiming the Mexican immigrant home space is one way writers such as García McCall challenge "systems of power [that] . . . threaten to invalidate certain kinds of knowledge," as scholar Cindy Cruz asserts

(662). It is her father who is the holder of knowledge, transmitting to her the power of using her home and culture as the foundations of literacy and learning. Her father's use of the Spanish language to teach her the letters of the alphabet is symbolic of the novel's reclaiming of a subversive Mexican literacy that engages with the home tongue as the root of speech and writing. In addition to upholding a Mexican familial literacy rooted in Spanish, their native tongue, the novel also symbolically places the working-class body, the father's hands, at the core of Lupita's learning. The novel reminds readers of multiple forms of knowledge, especially those not recognized as legitimate sites of learning. Rather than denigrate his "rough and scratchy" hands that toil in physical labor, García McCall elevates working-class bodies and families as artists in their own right. In recalling the "bits of sawdust" on her father's clothing, evidence of his labor, Lupita fuses her working-class roots with her education, capturing the significance of her family's role in her academic journey.

Lupita's mother similarly praises her daughter's writing talents, and though Lupita struggles to claim autonomy throughout the text, her mother's encouragement is gentle, subversive, and loving. Shortly after her mother's cancer diagnosis, Lupita invites local nuns to her home in a moment of fleeting desperation, even though it is evident that in reality she has no desire to join a convent. When the nuns speak to her mother about this possibility, Lupita's mother firmly tells them, "We've made other plans./Lupita's a gifted writer. She's going/to community college" (26). In acknowledging Lupita's writing talent, her mother's simple statement validates her daughter's nerd identity, and in doing such, her mother affirms her recognition of an integral part of Lupita's life. She *sees* Lupita for who she is, calling her a writer, and this statement's significance cannot be overlooked. While a brief and minor passage overall, the statement is significant in its simplicity, for its power rests also in her mother's affirmation of college as Lupita's eventual next step. The use of the plural "we've" reinforces Lupita's rootedness in her family, demonstrating that her eventual college attainment is not an individualized feat, but a collective, familial accomplishment. I reference this moment in the novel, coupled with the previous passage, to demonstrate how the novel normalizes the Mexican immigrant family's encouragement of education. It is her parents' affirmation of Lupita's writing that serves as the foundation for pursuing this talent, more so than outside forces, including her teacher. With her family's love and support, Lupita gains the tools to withstand hurtful accusations at school, learning valuable skills of resistance and confidence to forge her own path.

"Trying to be White"? Thespianism and Chicana Identity

Much as the ChicaNerds in *Gabi, Mexican Daughter*, and *Ghosts* construct their nerd identities around their writerly and creative interests, *Under the Mesquite* similarly traces Lupita's growth in poetic development. In addition to her poetic aspirations, Lupita develops a keen talent for dramatic performance, not so unlike Gabi's cultivation of the spoken word tradition. In their discussion of *Under the Mesquite*, Baxley and Boston describe the text's examination of "similar themes of gender, equality, and assimilation represented in the works of other Latina poetics like Ana Castillo, Sandra Cisneros, and Angela de Hoyos whose works have (re)defined the literary canon" (68). But as I have discussed throughout this book so far, while the ChicaNerd texts share similar concerns with well-known Chicana novels, the YA novels' central focus on distinct Chicana *adolescent* identities makes their works wholly unique. While the novels addressed in this book examine the gender, ethnic, and class constraints that define Chicana experiences in the United States, racial politics within school and adolescent peer settings are an added burden that teenaged ChicaNerds must confront head-on. In particular, Lupita's interest in dramatic arts forces her to reject her classmates' stereotypes that her interests "make her white." Much as in Hernández's *White Bread Competition*, which I discuss in Chapter 2, where peer relationships play an integral role in the ChicaNerd's navigation of racial and gender identity construction, Lupita must similarly contend with her classmates' troubling attitudes that attempt to police her expression of Chicana identity.

But in chronicling Lupita's talent and her inherent right to create art, García McCall's novel, like the other ChicaNerd texts, challenges these assertions and contests limited, narrow understandings of what makes a person Chicana. In her research on teaching drama to high school students, Carmen Medina argues, "Through drama the students actively engage in negotiating the text world with their own world" (198). This echoes the research conducted by Pablo C. Ramírez and Margarita Jiménez-Silva, whose work found that students "feel validated when performance poetry is conducted in the classroom" (89). The researchers' assertions regarding the potential empowerment students experience with drama certainly applies to Lupita's cultivation of this talent; however, Lupita must learn to negotiate these interests amid her peers' assertions that she is "trying to be white" because she is a thespian. In a painful scene, Lupita's friends accuse her of inauthenticity and being ashamed of her Mexican heritage:

> "You talk like you're one of *them*."
> She spits out the word in disgust
> and looks down at her lunch tray,
> like she can't stand the sight of me.
>
> "One of *them*?" I ask.
>
> "Let me translate for you,"
> Sarita sneers. "You talk like

you wanna be white."

. . .

"What," Sarita asks, "you think you're
Anglo now 'cause you're in Drama?
You think you're better than us?"

"No—"

"Then stop trying to act like
them," Mireya says accusingly.
"You're Mexican, just like the rest of us.
Look around you. Ninety-nine percent
of this school is Mexican.
Stop trying to be something you're not!"
                (80–81, original italics)

Her friends' accusations reveal how "culture becomes conflated with color, an assumption embodied in accusations of 'acting White.' Underlying the charge is the implication that the accused are not showing pride in being distinctive from the white mainstream, for if they were, they would be speaking the language or exhibiting the behavior patterns typical of the more 'authentic' ethnic community" (Román 17–18). As Román suggests, claims of "authenticity" are laden with problems, one of those being that such claims assert that there is only one way of being a member of that particular community, leaving little room for negotiation or creative expressions of identity. For Lupita's classmates, "Mexican" identity is one that can be measured up according to how one speaks. In her classmates' distorted accusation that her interest in drama makes her "Anglo," or at least her failed attempt at being so, we see how the girls are unable to accept Lupita as both an actor and a Chicana teenager, as if the two parts of herself could not possibly coexist. Within this logic, being an actor makes one white, but in addition to that, it is their focus on speech and Lupita's voice that stands out. While her friends align drama with whiteness, it is not her interest in drama alone that "makes" her white; their accusations that she "talks like *them*" highlight a delicate theme the novel tackles—namely, problematic and arbitrary markers of identity that police one's Chicanisma. As I discussed at length in Chapter 1, nerds of color face stigmas within and outside the school setting because of racist myths that conflate smartness and studiousness with whiteness. While scholars have studied what is known as "linguistic profiling," similar to racial profiling, in that "people use false assumptions about language to justify judgments that have more to do with race, national origin, regional affiliation, ethnicity and religion than with human language and communication" (qtd in Zentella 621), Lupita's experience shows that students of color may experience a different form of linguistic profiling from within their ethnic group. The reality, of course, is that even if Lupita "talks like *them*," she will never be *them*, that is, will never be white. Structural racism and sexism negate her ability to pass as white, even if she wished to do so.

Lupita's emotional response, however, demonstrates her critique of her classmates' linguistic policing and her astute ability to respond to these problematic accusations. In her statement that "Being Mexican/ means more than that./It means being there for each other" (83), Lupita insists on defining her identity on her own terms. Within Lupita's frame of reference, being Mexican means community, her family, as sources of support. Although her classmates' verbal attacks are painful, she refuses to internalize that she has "become white," telling herself, "*I couldn't be more Mexican/if you stamped a cactus on my forehead*" (83, original italics). In Lupita's English translation of the well-known and humorous Mexican expression to "tener el nopal en la frente," she defends her Mexicanidad, but rather than adopt the refrain to reinforce skin color as an indicator of Mexicanness, she instead rejects both linguistic and skin markers as determinants of one's authenticity. For Lupita, being Mexican "means more than that," as Cummins and Infante-Sheridan argue in their analysis of the novel: "Lupita's identity is connected to her interpretation of family and community and shown through caring for her siblings during their mother's illness" (29). In her astute response, Lupita rejects essentialist interpretations of ethnic identity, remaining true to her ideals, and rather than engage in a futile attempt to defend her Mexicanidad, Lupita chooses to continue with her study of theater and poetry. This experience painfully highlights that ChicaNerds must balance their discomfort with demands that they assimilate amid unfair accusations that they are "trying to be white." Further, Lupita later learns to find her own ChicaNerd voice that honors her family and her experiences. While she initially performs dramatic pieces selected by her teachers, she uses this performance to eventually craft her own voice in the poetry she writes that honors her mother, family, and community.

Chicano Teachers and Chicana Students

The classmates' accusations of Lupita's performance of whiteness occur shortly after a significant section of the novel when her teacher, Mr. Cortés, advises her to lose her accent so she can excel at drama. Its significance in the novel, I would argue, is not only for its relevance to one of the central themes of the novel, the pressure to assimilate or chart one's path, but as I have discussed in other chapters, it addresses the multiple ways in which school teachers may shape their students' futures, for better or for worse. *Under the Mesquite*'s representation of a schoolteacher is even more complex because unlike in the other texts, Mr. Cortés is not, in fact, white, but Latino. His advice comes seemingly out of nowhere, during one of their after-school meetings, when he presents her with a bag of Blow Pop candies:

> "If you're series about acting—
> and I think you are—then you need to
> lose your accent."
>
> Rolling the Blow Pops
> into position, I wonder if
> this is how Mr. Cortés
> got rid of his own accent...
>
> "Well? Say something,"
> Mr. Cortés demands.
>
> I swallow some spit and warble out,
> "I have an accent?"
>
> (67)

Lupita's initial confusion, evident in her question to her teacher, reveals the problematic ways that particular modes of speaking are framed. Essentially, everyone has their own unique sound, but Mr. Cortés suggests that Lupita must rid herself of sounding "too Mexican." Of course, he does not say this, but his meaning is inferred. According to Mr. Cortés, being "serious" about a future in acting means eliminating her style of speech that supposedly marks her as "Mexican" and, therefore, not acting material. Significantly, there is little further mention of Lupita's accent in the rest of the novel, with the exception of her classmates' comments about sounding white. This passage raises a number of critical questions—an obvious one being why Mr. Cortés, himself a person of color, would recommend that she alter her speech. Is it simply a matter of demanding that she assimilate and shed her Chicana/Mexican identity? Or is he astutely aware of the potential racist challenges Lupita will face in her future aspirations as an actor, where actors of color are rarely cast for leads? What I do find inherent in Mr. Cortés's advice that she lose her accent is his effort to make Lupita "linguistically pass"—that is, sound "less Mexican." In her discussion of what she terms "linguistic passing," literary scholar Melissa Dennihy describes this phenomenon as "situationally altering one's way of speaking, in addition to or instead of altering appearance, to pass as a member of or gain insider status within a particular racial group," which in turn "broadens traditional understandings of passing by shifting emphasis from the physical and visual to the linguistic and audible" (157). In Lupita's case, Mr. Cortés advises linguistic passing to gain access to the privileged, white-dominant world of theater. Linguistic passing occurs alongside linguistic profiling, as I discussed above. In his advice, Mr. Cortés not so subtly reveals his inability to see her as a successful actor without changing her speech. And while it is incredibly problematic that her teacher would see this in her future, theater scholar Brian Eugenio Herrera reminds us of the realities of "the mechanisms of exclusion embedded in conventions of American theatrical production, especially the habits of practice that guide how roles are cast" (23). Thus, rather than encourage Lupita to solely focus on honing her talent and challenge white supremacy, Mr. Cortés instead teaches her the intricacies of dramatic craft alongside these "voice lessons," as he refers to them (66).

While the novel spends little time on the issue of language loss and identity, the importance of this section to Lupita's ChicaNerd identity development cannot be underestimated. For all the ChicaNerds, juggling pressures to assimilate while remaining intimately connected to their Chicanx communities remains one of the constant struggles that all protagonists must negotiate. In considering her Latino teacher's advice to alter her voice, we are reminded of Gloria Anzaldúa's widely known theory that she names "linguistic terrorism," which she describes as using language as a weapon to oppress and shame Chicanx peoples. As Anzaldúa explains, this form of linguistic oppression occurs not only from whites but from other Chicanxs who try to "out-Chicano each other" (80): "If a person, Chicana or Latina, has a low estimation of my native tongue, she also has a low estimation of me. . . . We oppress each other trying to out-Chicano each other, vying to be the 'real' Chicanas, to speak like Chicanos. There is no one Chicano language just as there is no one Chicano experience" (80). Anzaldúa's words affirm Lupita's experience with her classmates, who shame her for her speech, but at the same time, I suggest, Mr. Cortés's attempts to erase her unique sound function also as a form of linguistic terrorism, given that he encourages her to rid herself of a mode of speaking that reflects her bicultural heritage and her family's history of immigration.

Further, while Lupita indeed discovers the power in performance and dramatic arts, what are we to make of the fact that the productions she performs are not representative of her community and culture? For example, she wins first place in a dramatic performance of "The Highwayman," a poem by Alfred Noyes and performs a scene from *The Trojan Women*, a Greek tragedy. Unlike the protagonist Gabi Hernández from *Gabi, A Girl in Pieces*, who claims Chicana poets as her muses for creative inspiration, Lupita is not introduced to dramatic literature and poetry that affirm and validate her bicultural lived experience. Undoubtedly, Mr. Cortés's choice in performance material reflects the limitations of the educational system's curriculum, which historically has not equally provided lessons around the histories, literatures, and arts of people of color in the United States. But while Cummins and Infante-Sheridan argue, "The lack of Mexican or Mexican American culture exposure at school contributes to Lupita's struggle with identity" (30), Lupita constructs her own ChicaNerd identity despite the dramatic pieces she performs and studies in school. As she tells her friend, "Changing how I talk/doesn't change who I am./I know where I came from" (95). Lupita performs the material as a ChicaNerd, using her experiences caring for her siblings and family to fuel her passion and artistry. Lupita does in fact find her own voice, her ChicaNerd voice, but it is not through the material she recites in school competitions. Instead, the poetry she creates while leaning against her family's mesquite tree *is* a burgeoning act of ChicaNerd feminism. This poetry becomes even more significant following her mother's death.

Negotiating ChicaNerdiness With Motherlessness: Loss and Poetic Development

Although the novel traces Lupita's development of a ChicaNerd identity through her growing talent in poetry and performance, this acceptance of who she is as a nerd must also be negotiated with her new life as a motherless daughter. Though not speaking of *Under the Mesquite*, Adrianna Santos's astute observation on Chicana teen protagonists is an apt description of Lupita's story: "There is a particular need to tell authentic stories of Chicanx/Latinx teenagers *as writers* due to the specific social conditions that silence their narratives" (Santos, 46, original italics). In Lupita's case, her mother's death potentially serves as one of these silencing forces, but with her father's aid, Lupita is able to transcend her mourning through poetry. Kelly Wissman notes that in YA texts that feature budding writers like Lupita, these characters "claim writing as an essential and efficacious practice for self-discovery and social understanding" (150). Lupita learns to use poetry as a means of mourning her mother while also delving into her own thoughts as a ChicaNerd who has recently lost her mother. The novel's treatment of death and loss is part of Lupita's development as a ChicaNerd. As Trites argues, "Death in adolescent literature is a threat, an experience adolescents understand as a finality" (118). For Lupita, the major struggle comes in adapting to this new reality of her mother's absence, a loss she is old enough to know is final and impossible to undo. When she visits her paternal grandmother's home soon after her mother's death, for example, her sense of hopelessness about her future is evident, as she divulges to a cousin:

> "I used to imagine myself
> moving to New York
> to be in a Broadway show,
> or becoming a photojournalist
> and backpacking through Europe,"
> I say, remembering it all.

"I had so many dreams
Mami and I used to talk about:
community college,
a career, traveling.
She wanted so much
to see me do those things.
But now that she's gone,
what's the point?"
                                                    (190)

Lupita's anguish and sense of hopelessness following her mother's death reveals the significance of maternal loss not only to an adolescent Chicana, but as Carolyn Dever argues, the death of the mother is a common literary trope that writers have used to underscore the relationship between a mother's death and the protagonist's development. Although speaking of 19th century British literature, Dever's assessment of this trope may be easily applied to Lupita's negotiation of her mother's death, which leaves her distraught over what this means for her creative aspirations and the future: "To write a life in the Victorian period, is to write the story of the loss of the mother. In fiction and biography, autobiography and poetry, the organizational logic of lived experience extends, not from the moment of birth, but from the instant of that primal loss" (1). Significantly, however, the death of Lupita's mother occurs approximately halfway through the novel, organizing the teenager's narrative up to and after her mother's death. That is, we glimpse very little of what Lupita's life will entail after her mother's death, given that the text ends as she begins college, which I discuss later in the chapter. This important narrative element, I believe, suggests that while her mother's death undoubtedly leaves Lupita feeling lost, doubtful, and unsure over what the future holds, the location of the novel's ending—the campus parking lot of her dorm—signals a new beginning, a hopeful one, even as Lupita must chart this path without her mother by her side.

Although Lupita's pain is evident in these lines, I point to the significance of vocalizing her aspirations—what I see as a distinct aspect of ChicaNerd identity; in addition, the reference to her mother demonstrates the integral role of her family in these aspirations. Yet her mother's death brings the reality of mortality to light, the painful admission that her mother will no longer live to see her daughter fulfill these plans. For Lupita, the process of ChicaNerd development entails the traumatic, painful process of learning to achieve her writing and career aspirations as a motherless daughter. Lupita's feelings of hopelessness and dejectedness point to the significance of her mother's influence on her writing identity; that is, the reality of her mother's death means she will no longer be present to validate, affirm, and support her young daughter to pursue her creative aspirations, leaving Lupita to wonder what this signals for her future as an artist. But though she is motherless, her father's strong presence also serves as a major influence in the achievement of these goals.

While she initially performs dramatic pieces selected by her teacher, she uses this experience and knowledge of performance to eventually craft her own creative voice in the poetry she writes that honors her mother, family, and community. With the mesquite tree as a creative muse, "Lupita learns the power of her voice and of her poetry" (Herrera, "Seeking Refuge" 202). For example, during a visit at her paternal grandmother's home, a sudden storm proves to be the antidote to the intense sadness she has felt following her mother's death. Heeding the storm's warning on the futility of challenging the inevitability of death and grief, she begins writing new poems:

> I sit on the grass,
> reach for my journal,
> and start to tear out pages.
> I rip out all the sad, tortured
> poems I've written
> since Mami's funeral
> and pile them on the ground
> in front of me. . .
>
> After everything that's happened,
> and everything that hasn't,
> it hurts, but it also feels good
> finally to let Mami go.
>
> Later I find a tall mesquite
> to sit under;
> and with my pen in hand,
> I open my journal
> to a blank page and begin
> writing a whole new batch of poems,
> poems filled with memories
> and hope, because that's
> what Mami would've wanted.
> (194–96)

The blank page of Lupita's journal is symbolic of this new "blank page" of her life, essentially a new chapter in which she has no choice but to embark. Though her mother's death occurs early in her life, Lupita learns to channel her grief and pain through poetry that remembers and honors her mother and family—what I classify as ChicaNerd feminism. Of equal importance is where this new poetry writing occurs: at her grandmother's home in Coahuila, Mexico, just across the border from her hometown of Eagle Pass, Texas. The location of this creative inspiration is not only significant for its status as her family's birthplace, but this location itself represents Lupita's bicultural, border identity that fuels her creativity. It is this home space—the land of her family's origins—that serves as the foundation for Lupita's ChicaNerd identity, impacting her more so than the dramatic arts taught by her teacher. Writing this "new batch of poems" in this significant setting reveals the impossibility of separating Lupita's creativity from her Mexican and border heritage.

But García McCall takes great care in not idealizing the mother-daughter relationship, evident in Lupita's contestation of gendered behavior that she is expected to perform. On the eve of her 15th birthday, for example, her aunts and her mother insist that she wear a quinceañera dress, which she humorously describes even as she expresses a staunch critique over what this represents:

> When my *tías* are done dressing me up
> like a big Mexican Barbie doll,
> I look at myself in the mirror.
> Mami stands behind me
> as I pull at the starched
> flowered fabric and argue
> with Mami's reflection.
>
> "Why do I have to wear this stuff?
> This is your style, not mine!
> I like jeans and tennis shoes.
> Why can't I just dress
> like a normal teenager?
> *En los Estados Unidos*, girls
> don't dress up like *muñecas*."
>
> "*Señoritas* don't talk back
> to their mothers," Mami warns.
> When my aunts aren't looking,
> she gives me a tiny pinch,
> like a bee sting on the inside
> of my upper arm. "*Señoritas* know
> when to be quiet and let their
> elders make the decisions."
> (74–75, original italics)

Like the other ChicaNerds discussed in this book, Lupita negotiates her own definitions of what it means to be a Chicana teenager, alongside her parents' expectations of being "una señorita." What I find most significant in this passage, which is evident in all the Chicana YA books I examine, is the complex nature of the mother-daughter relationship surrounding educational aspirations and gendered standards of behavior. Lupita's mother adamantly supports and encourages her daughter's writing talent, serving as a source of inspiration and strength, yet even while she displays pride, her scolding words, "*Señoritas* know when to be quiet and let their elders make the decisions," reinforce the parental hierarchy of the Mexican family structure that all the ChicaNerds challenge to some extent in their efforts to gain autonomy. While for her mother being a señorita means deferring to one's elders to make important decisions, for Lupita "*señorita* means/*melancolía*: settling into sadness./It is the end of wild laughter. . . ./*Señorita* is a *niña,*/the girl I used to be,/who has lost her voice" (76–77, original italics). Rather than signal more freedom and liberties, a rite of passage, Lupita instead interprets growing up as its own type of death, the loss of the freedoms associated with childhood. I cite these lines to underscore the complexities of Lupita's ChicaNerd development, struggles she shares with the other ChicaNerd protagonists. In addition to resisting widespread myths of Chicanx educational (under)achievement, teachers' attempts to "rescue" them, accusations of whiteness, and financial burdens of paying for college, ChicaNerds must also negotiate their families' expectations of appropriate female behavior, even as these families support their daughters' educational goals. ChicaNerds like Lupita maneuver multiple forces that stand in their way of attaining college admission and intellectual, creative autonomy.

Lupita's own quest to attend college is temporarily threatened shortly after her mother's death, given that her father relies heavily on her help caring for her siblings while he works to support the family. In an emotional passage that takes place the summer after high school graduation, Lupita and her father argue over her application to a university several hours from home. While mostly a sympathetic figure, Lupita's father nevertheless exposes his own gendered double standards of behavior surrounding his daughter's venturing far from home:

"What happened to staying home
and going to community college?"
Papi asks. "There's a reason girls
shouldn't go away to college.
Predators lurk on those campuses!"
Papi blusters, waving
a college catalog in his fist
like banned literature at a book burning.
"Oh yes," I tease him, "and let's not forget
the Lechuza and the boogeyman!
Papi—I'm not a child anymore!"

"Listen," he says, his green eyes
as intense as polished agate stones.
"I made promises to your mother.
I told her I'd take good care of you,
put you all before myself or anyone else.
Lupita, *m'ija*, there's no place
safer than home."

"But I want to go places
where I can see new things
and meet new people," I argue.
"I want a chance to explore
the rest of *los Estados Unidos*.
I can't help it, Papi! I'm like you!"
               (199–200, original italics)

Her father's machismo has been mostly absent up to this point, when he is confronted with the reality of his daughter's exit from their home. Lupita's description of banned books aligns her father's view of the dangers associated with the outside world for young women and the historical rationale of barring books that supposedly expose new, "dangerous" ideas to youth. He further justifies his stance in his assertion that "there's no place safer than home," upholding a binary that defines the domestic space as safe and the world outdoors as a formidable place for women to handle. But while her father's benevolent patriarchy frustrates Lupita, it is important to note that in no way does she defend her decision to leave her family home because she believes that remaining at home will stunt her educational journey. Instead, leaving home is a necessary act of ChicaNerd feminist development that honors her parents' immigration as the source of her aspirations, not as a hindrance to them. Referring to herself as being "like" her father, Lupita not only rejects his machismo, but in doing so, she proudly and honestly attributes her departure to his own experience of migration. Lupita's passionate declaration demonstrates her emerging feminist savviness, an ability to critique sexism while not rejecting her immigrant family.

Significantly, her father's initial reluctance sways when he chooses to drive her to Alpine, Texas, several hours from home, so she can attend college. When he drops her off at the parking lot of her new dorm, Lupita reflects on her future as a writer, symbolizing the newfound voice she will develop in this chapter of her life: "Someday my words will/take flight and claim the sky" (207). In these words, which read almost as a mantra to herself, we read "Lupita's promise to continue crafting a Tejana voice that speaks of her homeland and its significant role in her creativity and identity" (Herrera, "Seeking Refuge" 205). The importance of the Texas landscape in the novel cannot be overlooked, as it is this region that factors greatly in her quest to construct an authentic ChicaNerd identity for herself.[2] As Larissa M. Mercado-López argues, scholars must be deliberate in examining texts like *Under the Mesquite*, which center the Tejano landscape, thereby "compelling its inclusion within the Chican@ literary landscape as another source for tracing trajectories of collective identity formation and giving voice to voices marginalized within dominant narratives of colonial and imperial histories" (5). In this attention to Tejana-specific texts, Mercado-López argues "for the inclusion of *young* Tejana feminist consciousness in our conceptualization of Chicana feminist consciousness" (5), but taking this further, I insist on uniting these facets of Lupita's life—Tejana, Chicana, writer—into the marker of ChicaNerd to reclaim this identity as an empowered one. Although it is her father who drops her off at this new location where she will spend the next four years of her adult life, Lupita does not leave her home, family, or memories behind. Lupita arrives to Alpine with "Mami's old, blue suitcase" (207), a touching connection to the overnight bag Patricia Moreno gifts her ChicaNerd daughter, Marisa, as I discussed in the previous chapter. Arriving to college in her father's truck and her mother's suitcase in hand, Lupita symbolically carries her family with her, not rupturing the family tie but sealing it with her firm promise to write, study, and remember.

Guadalupe García McCall dedicates *Under the Mesquite* to her late mother, Tomasa Ruiz de García, and while it is perfectly common for writers to dedicate their fictional works to family members, this reference to her mother sets much of the tone of the novel. Lupita's role as eldest daughter in her Mexican immigrant family is a central aspect of her ChicaNerd identity development, a path that is ridden with the pain of her mother's death; she struggles to defend her Mexican identity, gendered responsibilities within the family, and her desire to honor her own aspirations to attend college far from home. Like *Ghosts of El Grullo*, which I discuss in the final chapter of this book, maternal loss factors greatly in the ChicaNerds' efforts to create art, study, and chart their own paths. For Lupita, it is precisely her mother's death that teaches her the power of writing as an emotional yet healing balm. Rejecting accusations of whiteness and negotiating her teacher's encouragement of linguistic loss, writing poetry that honors her Mexican immigrant family serves as her profound, empowering declaration of ChicaNerd self-love. Lupita's choice to write of her family, community, and bicultural lived experiences in this new landscape symbolizes her own ChicaNerd migration, a movement toward her own authentic identity, not away from it. ChicaNerd protagonists powerfully find a way to carve a space of intellectual and creative aspirations wrought out of experiences of loss, trauma, and angst, in addition to the profound possibilities of familial love and nurturance.

Notes

1. While the verse form is a key element of the novel, I will not delve at length on the significance of genre. Please see my 2019 publication "Seeking Refuge *Under the Mesquite*" for a more complete analysis of the relationship between form and content. Full citation listed in Works Cited.
2. See my article "Seeking Refuge *Under the Mesquite*" for a more thorough discussion of the novel's representation of nature, landscape, and identity.

5 Band Shirts and Rebellion

Resisting the "Buena Hija" Trope Through Nerdiness in *I Am Not Your Perfect Mexican Daughter*

In an interview with *NBC News* shortly after the publication of her debut novel, Erika Sánchez revealed that her manuscript was turned down multiple times by literary agents, some of whom "didn't like the voice. My character is not for everybody, she's a snarky brown girl, just as I was" (Ladish). Sánchez's observation that her protagonist's "snarky" voice did not appeal to these agents not only exposes the racism and sexism that is inherent in the publishing world, but it also points to the ways in which "having an attitude" makes one an unsympathetic character, particularly if one is a young woman *and* a person of color. In fact, when I taught the novel for the first time in 2017, many of my students, the majority Chicana, struggled with Julia's personality, even as they empathized with her frustrations and experiences as the daughter of Mexican immigrant parents. Julia is a challenging character, no doubt, as I agreed with my students. But if we dig deeper into this "snarky" persona, we discover Julia's painful attempts to forge a ChicaNerd path for herself, one that is unencumbered with the skeletons of her family's closet. However, as Julia discovers, uncovering these silences and secrets is crucial to her development as a Chicana and aspiring poet.

As I argue in this chapter, Julia's ChicaNerd identity first manifests itself as rebellion, even outright rejection of her parents at times, particularly her mother, with whom she argues throughout the novel. Julia comes to a space of healing and hope only through her confrontation with her family's secrets, the truths of which enable Julia to painfully, yet powerfully, reclaim her family's story, articulating her own path as a ChicaNerd as a result. This path is punctuated with and through loss—that is, through her older sister Olga's sudden and violent death and through Julia's investigation into her sister's secrets, which ultimately leads to the traumatic knowledge of their mother's brutal rape that she experienced when she crossed the US border. Julia's depression and subsequent suicide attempt shed light on Sánchez's attempts to not only critically engage in a discussion around stigmas surrounding mental illness but also to openly discuss the unique struggles faced by intellectual, smart ChicaNerds who feel like outsiders even within their own families.

Julia's search for an empowered ChicaNerd identity necessitates a painful path of rebellion, trauma, and finally, reconciliation. Julia's staunch rebellion to her parents' attempts to mold her into "the perfect Mexican daughter" is most visible in her poetry reading and writing, and she is initially unable to reconcile her college/intellectual aspirations with her family life. In my analysis of Julia's ChicaNerd identity development, I also pay close attention to the role of her white teacher and friendships, relationships that she must navigate as she affirms her right to study, write poetry, and eventually leave Chicago for college. Like my discussion of *Under the Mesquite*, where peer relationships at times cause Lupita incredible frustration, Julia's relationships with her Chicanx friends are also occasionally burdened by her sense of isolation as a ChicaNerd who desires to flee her hometown of Chicago to escape the pain, silences, and secrecy that overwhelm her family. Her white teacher, while earnest in his attempts to help Julia with the college application process, resembles Marisa's teacher in *What Can(t) Wait*, reinforcing my argument laid out in the introduction to this book, that ChicaNerds walk a tricky path where teachers, family relationships, and stereotypes about smart Chicanas threaten to undermine their quest for authentic self-love and empowerment through intelligence and nerdiness.

Rejecting the "Buena Hija" Trope: Silence, Secrecy, and the ChicaNerd

Julia's path to ChicaNerd development, much like the other ChicaNerds we have seen thus far, requires a negotiation of the identity she inhabits as the daughter of her mother, Amparo. For Julia, however, much of this negotiation necessitates unpacking the harmful myths surrounding Mexican/Chicanx families like hers that fail to recognize her culture and family experiences as rich sources of creative inspiration. In short, Julia must learn to see her family not as obstacles that prevent her from achieving a college education, but as intrinsically part of her ChicaNerd identity. While to some extent the other ChicaNerds struggle with gendered obligations constructed around their roles as daughters, *Mexican Daughter* features more antagonistic qualities in the mother-daughter relationship than what we have witnessed so far. As this chapter argues, Julia's ChicaNerd identity is shaped around rebellion, particularly visible in the maternal relationship, which manifests in hurt, accusations, resentment, and only later results in a profound love and reclamation between Julia and Amparo in their shared history of trauma. But initially, Amparo's attempts to protect her daughter are maintained in rigid and overbearing attitudes on sexuality and virginity, similar to what we see in *Gabi, A Girl in Pieces*. What Julia must uncover, however, is the source of her mother's fearful beliefs on sexuality. Amparo's traumatic rape experience, initially unknown to Julia, is at the core of her rigid beliefs on sex and the body, a marked departure from *Gabi*, where Mrs. Hernández's attempts to police Gabi's sexuality are more connected to her fear that her daughter will become white and therefore less Mexican.

In my previous work on literary representations of Chicana mother-daughter relationships, I have theorized this maternal relationship as a source of empowerment even when the relationship is fraught with tension and hurt:

> The daughters in these texts do not reject their mothers, but they do reject and contest cultural, patriarchal, and heteronormative gender roles that would have them follow in their mothers' footsteps. Although at first the daughters attempt to distance themselves from what they view as their mothers' complicity in gender role socialization, the same daughters grow to rewrite motherhood and daughterhood as a unifying, empowered experience that need not stifle or constrain Chicanas in achieving subjectivity.
> (*Contemporary Chicana Literature* 10–11)

Julia's rejection of her parents' expectations that she be the "perfect Mexican daughter" is more vividly pronounced in her relationship with her mother—a relationship that is more often than not laden with feelings of resentment and open hostility. In her study on mother-daughter relationships in YA literature, Hilary S. Crew explains that this relationship is typically more strained and conflicted in texts like *Mexican Daughter* because of the "daughter's growing up in a different racial or ethnic, and often social, milieu from the kind of world that had shaped her mother's cultural values and beliefs" (192). While Crew accounts for this fraught relationship as a result of cultural conflict, what we see in *Mexican Daughter* is Julia's perception that her mother is "old-fashioned" and "Mexican," without knowledge that the true source of her mother's overly cautious and fearful attitudes on sexuality stem not from cultural norms per se but from her racialized and gendered experience of trauma. In the case of mothers and daughters of color, as Elizabeth Brown-Guillory notes, this bond may experience "a love/hate relationship often because the mother tries painstakingly to convey knowledge about how to survive in a racist, sexist, and classist world while the daughter rejects her mother's experiences as invalid in changing social times" (2). Julia struggles with how to negotiate her mother's knowledge and attitudes about sexuality and the body, particularly when she is unaware of the scope of her mother's experiences and trauma. Because of her traumatic experience, Amparo cannot conceive of sexuality as pleasurable, let alone something with which her daughters should engage. As Lorena García states on Latina mothers' perceptions of their teen daughters' sexual behavior, "Within a larger societal context of patriarchal control over women's bodies, it [is] difficult for mothers to see their daughter as sexual subjects" (24). This is part of Amparo's inability to see her dead daughter Olga as anything but a virgin despite her daughter's adult age, and because of her presumption around Olga's virginity, it is the eldest daughter who is upheld as the "perfect Mexican daughter," a feat to which Julia does not aspire.

To contextualize Julia's struggle to give voice to the knowledge of her mother's rape and her sister's secrets that she can only articulate through self-inflicted violence, Tiffany Ana López's theory of "critical witnessing" as it applies to Latinx children's and YA literature is particularly helpful:

> To be a critical witness entails more than just telling or repeating a story or event. Rather, critical witnessing works from a story's impact as much as its intention as a means to spotlight the conditions that brought the story into being. . . . I am interested in reading Latina/o children's literature as a profound engagement with trauma theory that articulates and documents the ways Latina/o children are burdened by violence and haunted by cultural trauma, from the colonization of lands and bodies to the subjugation of minds and spirits, and the ways its authors map survival strategies.
>
> (López 206)

As López explains in her concept, children, especially children of Latinx immigrants like Julia, carry the traumatic legacy of their parents' lives that is passed down to them; for Julia, especially, this "burden" of her parents' history is punctuated by their deep silence surrounding what they have endured. Although speaking of Haitian American women's adolescent literature, Katharine Capshaw's analysis of trauma in relation to national identity is another useful lens by which to understand Julia's position, not as a migrant, but as a daughter of parents whose migration history is fraught with trauma that Julia negotiates through self-harm: "[characters] experience traumas of displacement and of physical/sexual violence. While their responses to a bifurcated identity are quite different, [they] must bear the weight of their own Haitian history" (86). Capshaw's assertion readily applies to Julia's identity as the daughter of undocumented Mexican immigrants, and in many ways, she must negotiate their invisibility within a system that also fails to see her as smart, worthy, or even American, for that matter. As Elia Michelle Lafuente notes in her discussion of YA literature and themes of adolescent identity in the context of nationhood, "The unsettled political and social context of these novels enhances the central theme of personal growth and discovery, culminating in the development of an identity on the border of two cultures" (34). For Julia, negotiating her ChicaNerd identity amid her parents' undocumented status as Mexican immigrants is a key aspect of belonging with which she must grapple throughout the text. In particular, Julia must process the emotional burden of the knowledge of her mother's rape that she suffered while crossing the border. While Julia does not experience rape, the knowledge of her mother's rape at the hands of a *coyote* (smuggler) causes her to "bear the weight" of her family's traumatic history of migration. Her attempted suicide is an embodiment of the trauma that is passed down from her family via a legacy of secrecy and silence.

What is missing from most of the novel is Amparo's admission to her daughter of what she has endured, learned only by Julia from her aunt's strained confession. The silence surrounding this traumatic event, uncovered only by Julia's pleas to her family, shows how, in the words of scholar Maya Socolovsky, "Silence, as a perpetrator of pain, struggles against attempts to recall and tell the past" (191). Amparo's refusal to speak of this trauma attests to Socolovsky's assertion, given that divulging this secret is in itself retraumatizing and painful. In the novel, the actual recollection of Amparo's rape is not spoken, rendering her experience unspeakable, as Laurie Vickroy explains: "What is not said or cannot be remembered is equally revealing of traumatic memories" (146). For Amparo, this unspeakable act, her rape, is instead expressed through hypervigilance over Julia's private life, what Julia at first interprets as mere evidence of her mother's backward, conservative ways. In Julia's ChicaNerd development, it is this fact of her mother's trauma that must come to the surface, but to get to this space of recognition and articulation, Julia undergoes a painful experience of her own, a suicide attempt.

Olga's sudden and violent death (she is hit by a bus) opens up the novel, and it is significant not only for its obvious plot detail, but its importance is also weighed by how it frames a number of thematic issues addressed in this chapter. Namely, Olga's death necessitates Julia's attempts to make sense of mortality; her identity and aspirations; and most importantly, it paves the way for her efforts to learn intimate facts about her family that are kept from her. For example, at Olga's funeral, Julia can only seemingly articulate her sister's demise through poetry, reflecting the ChicaNerd's poetic interests: "The only thing that makes sense to me is what Walt Whitman said about death: 'Look for me under your boot soles.' Olga's body will turn to dirt, which will grow into trees, and then someone in the future will step on their fallen leaves. There is no heaven" (5). While Julia's Whitmanesque lament seems cold and distant, it is important to note that these lines occur after she has vividly described her mother's mournful display of grief over her daughter's body at the funeral home. To make sense of something senseless, her older sister's brutal death at the prime of her life, Julia can only conjure the details of what she is experiencing through art. But in her admission that Whitman's philosophical renderings on death "make sense" to her, readers, in fact, wonder if this indeed does make sense to her at all. Julia is undoubtedly traumatized and numbed by Olga's death, but to distance herself from her mother's display—that is, to shield herself from becoming like her mother—Julia must recite poetry that appears to only offer a surface-level comfort. Sensing that Julia is being judged by mourners because of her lack of tears, she states, "Though my eyes haven't produced tears, I've felt the grief burrow in every cell of my body" (4). As Julia is aware, being the "perfect Mexican daughter" requires a public display of mourning, but her trauma manifests instead into a stoic demeanor that belies the intense grief she feels. Later in the novel, of course, the complex web of emotions, such as guilt, resentment, mourning, and loss transcends into self-harm, her attempted suicide.

As the opposite of the "perfect Mexican daughter," Julia feels like an outsider within her own family and extended kin network. In a telling example of Julia's feelings of outsiderness, shortly after Olga's death, Amparo suddenly informs Julia of her plans to host a quinceañera, which elicits in Julia a feeling of panic and dread: "But my family doesn't even like me. . . . They all think I'm weird, and you know that" (17). Amparo's declaration on the matter (Julia has no choice in something that has been decided for her) is, at best, odd, because of the timing so soon after Olga's death; at worst, this decision suggests Amparo's efforts to mold her daughter into her ideal version of what a Mexican daughter should be, given the pageantry and pomp surrounding many quinceañeras (Herrera, "Not-So-Sweet" 78). In an unsettling way, Amparo's sudden plans suggest her effort to mourn her daughter Olga through Julia, to throw a party she could never throw for her eldest daughter. Julia's objection to this stems not only from her feelings of alienation within her family but also her intuitive understanding that the party would be more for her dead sister than a celebration for her as the living daughter. Once again, Julia turns to art to capture her feelings of angst, displacement, and anxiety over not fitting in with her family:

> Sometimes I look at my books and tests, and the words all blur and swirl together. If I keep going like this, I'll never get into college. I'll end up working in a factory, marry some loser, and have his ugly children. After lying in bed for hours, I turn on the lamp and try to read. I've read *The Awakening* a million times, but I find it comforting. My favorite character is the lady in black who follows Edna and Robert everywhere. I also love the book because I'm so much like Edna—nothing satisfies me, nothing makes me happy.
>
> (19)

Julia's fear that she will be unable to escape a life of conformity is revealed in her signature humor and sarcasm, and although it may appear as a fleeting comment, her preoccupation with nagging thoughts that she will not make it to college is a recurring sentiment that she expresses throughout the novel. This dread undoubtedly reflects the first-generation status occupied by all the ChicaNerds, who do not take college admission for granted, unlike their privileged white counterparts, who are not burdened with the anxieties of economic stress, community access, and school support.

But what are we to make of her fascination with American literature so intimately tied to death, evident in her admiration of Whitman and Chopin? It is significant to note that Julia, unlike the character Gabi, for example, who uses Chicana feminist poetry as a model for her own poetic craft, identifies with 19th-century white writers—a marked departure from Gabi's burgeoning Chicana feminism. Julia's sassiness and sarcasm at first seem at odds with her interests in writers who would appear to have nothing to do with the realities of a working-class Chicana teenager from Chicago. Beyond that, though, is what her taste in literature suggests: most telling in her admission that her favorite character from *The Awakening* is the unnamed lady in black, who portends Edna's death—a demise that is symbolically fitting, given her resistance to late Victorian social decorum. How, exactly, is this novel "comforting"? Clearly Julia looks to dark subject matter for perceived comfort, indicative of her attempt to withdraw from the darkness of her own life. Julia too rejects gender expectations, so it is not surprising that she sees much of herself in relation to Edna Pontellier, but not two pages later in the book, this declaration of love for Chopin is contrasted with her rather humorous criticism of the well-known novel by the Mexican writer Laura Esquivel, *Como Agua Para Chocolate*—a snarky comment that appears shortly after she describes her long-standing aspirations to attend college, in contrast to Olga: "Olga was a good student, so I could never understand why she didn't want to go to a real college. I've been dreaming of going since I was little. . . . Olga was the perfect daughter—cooked, cleaned, and never stayed out late. Sometimes I wondered if she'd live with my parents forever like that sap Tita, from *Like Water for Chocolate*. Ugh. Such a terrible book" (20). Julia's disgust with the novel, though laugh-out-loud funny, is no doubt connected more to the novel's subject matter than it is to the writer's craft. The novel's great popularity among its Mexican (and non-Mexican readership, to be sure) makes Julia's statement even more biting. I raise these passages from the novel not to assert that Julia aspires to be *like* Chopin or Whitman, but I certainly believe that her criticism of "that sap Tita" stems from her beliefs that this character is traditional and passive, and the American characters she admires reflect her own desires of independence and freedom. Essentially, what Julia longs for is attainment of their writerly profession, and despite the character Tita's artistry in the kitchen, Julia is unable to interpret her as subversive, only sappy. The irony, of course, is readers of *The Awakening* question just how liberated Edna is if her only recourse from the constraints of 19th-century Victorian life is suicide.

Shortly after Olga's death, Julia begins a frantic search for answers to questions at which she is first unsure to ask. Olga's death comes at the same time that Julia is discovering her own sexual desires and her growing frustration over not being the "perfect Mexican daughter" that Olga is purported to be. To drive this point, Julia's search through her sister's room and laptop computer is at first a harmless fascination with uncovering the possibility of Olga's secret sex life. Part of Julia's almost manic obsession with searching for what is unknown to her is her rejection of the family's notion of privacy, especially her mother's refusal to understand this need to be alone: "When I tell her I need privacy, she laughs and tells me I've become too Americanized" (26). As in *Gabi*, where the ChicaNerd is accused of being "gringa," here Amparo also reduces Julia's request as evidence of her assimilation, which is supported by the research conducted by Lorena García. Regarding privacy, the Latina mothers García interviewed responded that "the idea of privacy for children and teenagers was an 'americano' or 'güero' notion" (23). Not surprisingly, then, Julia's daydreams involve an escape from Chicago, as she cannot imagine being both a writer and a Chicago resident. In her dreams, her desire to be a writer is captured in almost clichéd images: "In these dreams, I'm a famous writer who wears flamboyant scarves and travels all around the world, meeting fascinating people" (27). Julia's fantasies are significant not only for what they reveal—her aspirations of being a writer—but, in addition, for how they articulate a burning need to flee her hometown and reject a life of conformity she imagines will be her destiny if she does not escape.

"I Am Not Your Perfect Student to be Rescued": ChicaNerds, Peers, and White Teachers

With the exception of *Under the Mesquite*, which portrays the protagonist Lupita's relationship with her Chicano teacher, the novels examined in this book emphasize greatly the relationships that ChicaNerds cultivate with their white teachers, and *Mexican Daughter* is no exception. Because she is an aspiring poet, Julia's English teacher, Mr. Ingman, serves as her mentor and confidant, but as with Marisa's teacher, Mr. Ingman's encouragement of Julia's scholastic pursuits is rooted in white savior mythology. Nevertheless, Julia admires him, even as readers may express discomfort with the way he addresses her and her classmates in a lecture on the importance of learning standard English, for example:

> "See, I'm teaching you standard English, which is the language of power. What does that mean?" Mr. Ingman raises his eyebrows and looks around the room. "Anyone?"
> The room is silent. I want to answer, but I'm too embarrassed. . . .
> "It means that you will learn to speak and write in a way that will give you authority. Does that mean that the way you speak in your neighborhood is wrong? That slang is bad? That you can't say *on fleek* or whatever you kids are saying these days? Absolutely not. That form of speaking is often fun, inventive, and creative, but would

it be helpful to speak that way in a job interview? Unfortunately not. I want you to think about these things. I want you to think about words in a way you've never done before. I want you to leave this class with the tools to compete with the kids in the suburbs, because you're just as capable, just as smart."

(30–31, original italics)

Perhaps even more blatantly than Marisa's teacher, Mr. Ingman's sentiments only slightly veil his white savior racism—in particular, his belief that the students need him to teach "the language of power." In referring to their speech as mere "slang" rather than actual language with its own rhythms, rules, and nuance, Mr. Ingman is in effect encouraging assimilation at the expense of language loss. In his simplistic assertion that speaking standard English will give them "authority" to "compete with the kids in the suburbs," Mr. Ingman evades any discussion of how white supremacy, power, privilege, and authority will always be denied collectively to people of color even if some individual success stories are the exception. While the novel does not reference him, I am reminded of how throughout his presidency, President Obama was condescendingly referred to as "articulate" or "well spoken," a true master of speech, as if his talents were singular and exceptional. However, this unparalleled ability in oratory skills did not put an end to the racist vitriol flung at him and the First Family, which continued even after he left office. Will mastery at standard English prevent one from experiencing the pain of racism, as Mr. Ingman purports? As in the other texts, these exchanges affirm what scholar Connie Titone has said of white teachers' beliefs that what they do in the classroom with their students of color is necessary for their salvation and overall well-being (162). As a young student who loves literature and writing, Julia is at first captivated with her teacher's class, but we do witness moments in the text when she doubts or questions the advice he gives her—most pointedly, when he helps her in the college application process.

Although Julia admires her teacher for introducing her to the likes of Chopin and Whitman, she later acknowledges the limits to this affection, when she is forced to confront head-on his failure to understand why she would be reluctant to admit her parents' undocumented status in her college admission essays, a fact that he callously explains is necessary because "Admission committees love that stuff" (166). When she protests his advice, their subsequent exchange reveals Julia's internal conflict regarding her teacher; that is, while she admits discomfort with his white privilege, she also expresses appreciation for his mentoring:

> "But it's a secret," I say. "My parents told us we weren't supposed to tell anyone. What if I send in my application, and then the school calls immigration, and my parents get deported? Then what?"

"No one is going to deport them. That would be impossible."

"But they're illegal," I whisper.

"Undocumented," Mr. Ingman corrects me.

"My family call themselves ilegales or mojados. No one says *undocumented*. They don't know about being politically correct."

"It's a very stigmatizing word. I don't like it. Same with *illegal aliens*. That's even more repugnant." Mr. Ingman shudders as if the words feel venomous inside his body. . . .

Like my parents, I've always been suspicious of white people, because they're the ones who call immigration, who are rude to you at stores and restaurants, who follow you when you're shopping, but I think Mr. Ingman is different. No other teacher has ever been this interested in me.

"Okay, how do you know for sure that they won't get deported?" I insist one last time.

"Please, Julia. Trust me. I've helped dozens of students like you get into college. We're in Chicago, not Arizona. That doesn't really happen here. Not like that. No one is going to read your essay and track your parents down. Plus, have I ever lied to you?"

(166–68, original italics)

This exchange, while laden with Julia's apparent discomfort with revealing what is supposed to be private information, her parents' undocumented status, is troubling for a number of reasons. On the one hand, we see that Mr. Ingman, while purporting to be sympathetic and liberal, evident in his scolding of his student over her choice to use the word "illegal," in fact is quite willing to exploit her family's mixed immigration status as collateral to help her gain admission to elite colleges. Sánchez undoubtedly wants readers to grasp the complex layers of white liberal racism: in this case, Mr. Ingman's inability to see how disclosing her parents' undocumented status would incite fear and suspicion in Julia, to say nothing of how this would mean breaking her promise to her parents. His casual reassurance that deportation "doesn't really happen here" exudes not only his racial and class privilege, but it belies the fact that undocumented immigrants are targeted everywhere, even in supposedly "liberal" cities like Chicago. On the other hand, Julia's admission that "no other teacher has ever been this interested in me" complicates their relationship, making her willing to take his advice even at the expense of her family's trust. Yet she simultaneously states that she has had reason to distrust white people, and clearly Mr. Ingman is exactly those "white people," although he performs liberal-mindedness. His reference to "students like you"—that is, students of color—essentially tokenizes her as the student from the projects who can "make it," not unlike Marisa Moreno's awareness of being singled out as the "college girl from the *barrio*."

But Julia must also negotiate being "that student" among members of her family and community as well. Being the "smart girl," while positioning herself as a student who gains advice from teachers, also makes her a potential charity case or even suspect among her friends and classmates. At a family party, for example, Julia struggles to comprehend the unsolicited advice that her cousin and his wife give, individuals she identifies as being unique in her family: "There's no one in my family like them. No one has ever gone to a real college. I always want to ask them a million questions" (80). For Julia, these cousins represent everything she aspires to be: sophisticated, worldly, and college educated. What I find intriguing is that, like an earlier passage I cite in this chapter, Julia uses the descriptor "real" in her reference to college. Olga did not attend a "real" college, according to Julia; that is, she attended community college. Here, this sentiment is expressed again, which indicates that we are supposed to presume her cousins attended a university. Julia's problematic appropriation of elitist language is troubling, to say the least, but it also highlights the ways in which she has been exposed to these harmful views that relegate community colleges as "not real," in contrast to universities. Even as Julia lacks economic, gender, or racial privilege, she does benefit from adult attention, including family members and her teacher, who want to see her go to college. But what she also interprets is her cousin's appropriation of white savior language, as he tells her: "Well, listen, if you ever need help with your applications or have any questions, please let us know. We need more people like you in college" (81). Significantly, both Julia and her cousin adopt problematic language around salvation, elitism, and assimilation.

Yet even as she uses some of this language, she is also subjected to criticism from classmates, who accuse her of snobbery because of her language use and interest in literature, as one classmate tells her: "You're conceited. That's your problem. You think you're better than everybody. You think you're all smart, talking like a white girl and shit" (111). As I discussed at length in Chapter 1, ChicaNerds navigate peer pressure, white teachers, and family gender roles in ways that make their identity development and intellectual pursuits daunting and emotionally charged. Once again, as her classmate's comment suggests, being smart means being a white girl or at least trying to be one. These hurtful words, "talking like a white girl," are also almost verbatim the accusation that is hurled at Lupita, as I discussed in Chapter 4. Julia's interests and her intelligence make her suspect, but they also suggest the problematic view that intellectual Chicanas see themselves as superior to their classmates—a sentiment that the ChicaNerds do not ever express. The complicated space Julia inhabits in her family as the "weird" family member, coupled with her peer's attack, places her in a potentially uncomfortable realm of unbelonging. The ChicaNerd texts all expose the protagonists' weary battles to combat their community's preoccupation that intelligence or interest in school makes one gringa or assimilated.

Although the novel represents a tender and affirming relationship between Julia and her best friend, Lorena, their friendship also reflects Julia's feelings of isolation and outsiderness. In particular, Julia learns that her love of literature and art mark her as a weirdo or nerd to her friend, even as Lorena remains her closest friend. In art, Julia finds beauty, love, and validation, but museum trips are solitary activities: "I love art almost as much as I love books. . . . I always have to come to the museum alone, though, because no one will ever join me. I tried dragging Lorena once, but she just laughed and called me a nerd. I suppose I can't argue with that" (45). Significantly, Julia is not offended by her friend's teasing, suggesting that even as she acknowledges her distinct interests that set her apart from Lorena, she finds some affirmation in being called a nerd. Further, I find it revealing that in addition to agreeing with Lorena that she is a nerd, her sense of isolation is not due to this name-calling; instead, Julia desires to share her enthusiasm for the arts with family and friends. Interestingly, like Gabi, whose friend Cindy's pregnancy means that she will be unable to leave home to attend college, Julia also possesses academic advantages over Lorena, who decides to stay in Chicago to attend nursing school. Julia senses the differences between herself and her friend, but at first she is unwilling to consider the ways that her friend has not benefitted from mentorship and focalized teacher attention that steers her toward college attendance. I also point out this passage not to suggest that Julia is odd, nor that Lorena represents the more "typical" teenager because she cannot share her friend's enthusiasm. Rather, I insist on highlighting Julia's unabashed pleasure in the arts, even as she knows that she has nothing in common with her friend. This refusal to be self-conscious over her love of literature and art, I argue, makes her a ChicaNerd.

Reconciliation and Healing: College and Beyond

While a traumatic and painful event, Julia's suicide attempt, significantly, opens the possibility for reconciliation with her parents and confrontation with secrets, including the knowledge that her sister was pregnant at the time of her death. What happens after this moment occurs in rather quick succession: a hospital stay, an outpatient treatment, a trip to Mexico planned by her family to aid her in recovery, and her return to Chicago. What I find most telling in the novel's treatment of Julia's struggles with mental illness is the text's portrayal of therapy sessions that expose her vulnerability and pain, which she has long attempted to conceal from everyone around her.

Kimberley Reynolds's analysis of YA literature's representations of self-harm is a useful way of understanding Sánchez's novel that privileges Julia's experiences with depression and suicide attempt, which are undoubtedly connected to the maternal trauma she learns about when she visits her family in Mexico: "We have become accustomed to seeing narratives that feature characters who turn on themselves through the eyes, experiences, and accounts of girls. It is undoubtedly the case that most adolescent fictions that feature self-harming are centered on female subjects" (107). This is not surprising, considering that there has been an increase in literary representations of mental illness in texts for younger audiences, according to scholar Anastasia Wickham (10). In her study on representations of mental illness in young adult literature, Wickham states, "Questions of diagnosis notwithstanding, mental health is a common concern for adolescents and their families. As such, an investigation of mental illness taboos allows for a closer examination of perceptions that might stigmatize sufferers. To help with this, authors of young adult literature have begun to explore issues associated with mental illness" (11). While Reynolds and Wickham both address the significance of these themes in YA texts, however, their studies avoid discussing, for example, the specificities of adolescents like Julia, whose struggles with depression exist alongside her family's immigrant, racialized, and gendered identities. In asking how these books contribute to adolescent understanding of harmful patterns, such as self-inflicted violence or suicide attempts (107), Reynolds omits any question of how self-harm may in fact be intimately connected to racialized and gendered legacies of trauma, as is evident with Julia, who inherits her mother's traumatic rape and border-crossing. As Stringer reminds us, "Young adults can feel like outsiders and worry that they are not normal. Without a firm, stable identity, youths can have trouble separating confusion inside their head from the conflicting messages in the outside world" (Stringer 90). Julia's earlier dread over her mother's quinceañera plans is an example of this feeling of being an outsider or "not normal," or at least, so unlike her sister that she feels a distinct separation from her family unit.

But in her discussion of the novels by Sánchez and Quintero, Adrianna Santos argues, "issues like mental health, suicide, and sex, are confronted head-on by amplifying the voices of young women who are coming of age and in many ways, coming apart. What helps put them back together, though, is the acknowledgment of writing as a vehicle for self-making" (53). As Santos reminds us, Julia's "attempted suicide is not described until the last few pages of the novel. By withholding a description of the event itself, the text emphasizes the importance of Julia's healing process in coming to terms with what happened" (53). Further, although readers glimpse Julia's emotional struggles to situate herself within the family unit after Olga's death, we recognize her extreme efforts to ward off mental illness, seen in her relationships with her friends and her study of poetry. Beyond that, the novel's treatment of mental illness, healing, and recovery documents the text's staunch critiques of silence surrounding the pain suffered by young girls of color. When we recognize that Julia's battle with depression is rooted not only in her own individual struggles but also in her family's larger racialized and gendered experiences of trauma, we see how, in the words of Suzanne Bost, "Foregrounding pain . . . undermines the myth of self-reliance and demands more expansive ways of understanding individual agency" (5). Julia's depression is not merely a "natural" occurrence due to her outsider status within her home and school network; it is intimately connected to her family and community's experiences with pain that are seldom, if ever, acknowledged in mainstream culture.

Sánchez's raw and honest representation of Julia's struggles with depression and mental illness also function as the novel's attempt to confront the significant reality that Latina teenagers experience higher rates of depression than their peers in other ethnic groups, according to researchers (Piña-Watson and Castillo 309). In this light, the novel itself is a call to action on a number of fronts. On one hand, Sánchez's fictional portrayal of Julia's struggles with "normalcy" mirrors the research that points to Latina teens' struggles with depression, but additionally, the text also examines the empowered possibilities of seeking professional help. This fact should not be understated, given that research also finds that mental illness and depression continue to be stigmatized among Latinx populations (Mendoza, Masuda, and Swartout 209). Sánchez's creative decision to include Julia's therapy sessions in the novel confronts head-on the dangers of stigmatizing mental health, and in doing such, the writer also treats the subject of Latina/Chicana adolescent depression with compassion and empathy. Julia's therapy sessions may potentially demonstrate to teenage readers the healing, empowering, and uplifting possibilities of seeking help and communicating one's frustrations and fears.

The novel's central concern with Julia's healing is highlighted by the fact that there are several passages in the text that describe her individual therapy sessions, her experiences with group therapy, and her attempts to connect with her parents. In her first therapy session with the psychologist, Dr. Cooke, she expresses her growing feelings of depression that are largely due to her intense fear that the life she wants will never come to fruition: " 'I want to be a writer,' I finally say. 'I want to be independent. I want to have my own life. . . . I want to move away, go to college. I don't want to live in Chicago. I don't feel like I can grow here. My parents want me to be a person I don't want to be' " (217). For Julia, remaining in Chicago means the potential possibility that she will never achieve her dreams of college and being a writer, but beyond that, I suggest that these fears are tied to her anxiety that staying with her parents will trap her in a continuous cycle of silence and pain. Julia's articulation of these fears and her vocal expression of her artistic ambitions are also significant, as giving voice to her complex range of emotions, I suggest, is an expression of ChicaNerd feminism. To forge her own path as a ChicaNerd, Julia desires to separate from her family unit, even as she recognizes that leaving her home will cause her parents emotional pain that will only deepen the devastating loss of their eldest child.

Despite her family's initial reluctance at letting their daughter go, it is important to recognize that they do in fact accept her decision, even escorting her to the airport to see her off to college. In this simple but significant act, her parents symbolically carry themselves with her, much like we have seen in the other novels examined. In so doing, the novel focalizes the ChicaNerd's relationship with her parents as the core element of reconciliation and love that is foundational to her eventual departure for college. In her analysis of psychological recovery in Latina writings, Felicia Lynn Fahey posits that "the residual effects of ruinous historical events and the internalization of violent rhetoric or harmful cultural practices penetrate and mar relationships, thereby inhibiting intimacy" (xiii–xiv). But when Julia returns from her stay in Mexico with her family and the outpatient treatment center, one of her first conversations with her mother is an attempt at reconciliation: "I know I'm not the best mother sometimes. You're just so different, Julia. I've never known how to deal with you, and then after your sister died, I had no idea what I was doing. When I found out you were having sex, I was so scared you'd end up like your cousin Vanessa, alone and with a baby. I don't want you to have that kind of life" (284). The tense relationship throughout the novel between Julia and her mother is indicative of this strained effort to achieve intimacy, but instead their dialogue consists mainly of accusations, hurt feelings, and deep misunderstandings. But Amparo's solemn words resemble the words uttered by Marisa Moreno's mother, Patricia, who also expresses feelings of shame and inadequacy—that she has failed to mother her daughter properly. Julia's apology to her mother (285), like Marisa's heartfelt statement that Patricia "is the right kind of mother," functions as a reclamation of her family, in stark contrast to the outright rejection seen earlier in the text. Amparo's words are imperative for what they reveal: namely, her fears that her daughter will live a life that she associates with unhappiness, loneliness, and vulnerability. Although she admits to Julia, "I want you to have a good job and get married" (284), it is crucial that we acknowledge her mother's desire that her daughter will achieve a life of relative comfort and happiness. As we have seen in the ChicaNerd texts, the mothers want the best for their daughters, even if they do not always understand or agree with their headstrong daughters' decisions.

Although Julia's father is mainly silent throughout the text, Julia's discovery of his artistic talent, a fact she learns when she is in Mexico, provides a mode of connection that greatly impacts her ChicaNerd development. By discovering her father's artistry, Julia shifts her prolonged inability to see him as an anything but a silent, emotionally distant father. In her emotional statement to her father, "I wish you'd draw again, Apá. Maybe you can draw a picture of me sometime?" (338), Julia reclaims her father as an artist, even an inspiration for her own artistic talent. This moment, which occurs at the airport just moments before she departs for New York for college, symbolically connects the father to daughter, artist to artist, through an eventual acceptance rooted in love. As she learns, her father's traumatic witnessing of his wife's rape transcends into his inability to turn to art and his reluctance to share this fact about himself with his daughter. Going to Mexico, while it exposes Julia to her family's anguish, also introduces her to a genealogy of artistry that she did not know existed, enabling her to see her father as a silenced artist rather than simply a cold man.

In her eventual declaration that attending college and pursuing her dreams of writing is intimately connected to her family's history, Julia forges her ChicaNerd identity through a reclamation of them: "In some ways, I think that part of what I'm trying to accomplish—whether Amá really understands it or not—is to live for her, Apá, and Olga. . . . What a waste their journey would be if I just settled for a dull, mediocre life. Maybe one day they'll realize that" (339). In this deeply touching statement, Julia, like her ChicaNerd counterparts, acknowledges the responsibilities she feels for her immigrant family. As a first-generation Chicana student, Julia eventually learns that her college achievement, though due in large part to her own individual intelligence and hard work, is deeply connected to the sacrifices her family made, including traumatic experiences that Julia inherits. In her acknowledgment that she wants to "live" for her family, Julia reflects a communal, feminist, working-class reclamation of her immigrant family—what I classify as her ChicaNerd identity.

In the introduction to this chapter, I cited Erika Sánchez's description of her protagonist Julia as a "snarky" young woman, a character that publishers had a difficult time understanding or even liking. Such short-sighted views from the publishers to whom she had sent her manuscript are particularly dangerous, not only for their obvious racism, sexism, and classism, but also for simply reducing Julia to an unlikable character that demonstrates the erasure of her painful process of ChicaNerd identity development. By no means does Julia shed her snarky persona, nor does the novel in any way advocate for a loss of personality traits simply to gain admission to college. Rather, Julia's painful path—rebellion, trauma, loss, reconciliation—demonstrates her own unique journey that facilitates growth and ChicaNerd self-love and reclamation. This journey is still rocky, as evidenced by her admission that she continues to work through feelings of self-doubt about her performance in college: "Like the other day, I started worrying that I wouldn't do well in college because I'm just a broke-ass Mexican girl from a crappy neighborhood in Chicago" (329). While these feelings of doubt still persist, I interpret this statement as an honest, poignant, and vulnerable admission that in no way hampers the growth she has achieved. In this way, Erika Sánchez refuses to romanticize Julia's experiences with depression and loss as "part of her past," nor are all the loose ends neatly tied up. Instead, Julia's honest statement that she will fail in college suggests that her growth is far from over. With the love of her family and their history to guide her, Julia's ChicaNerd journey is shaped by and through the pain she and her family have endured. Through this cycle of loss, pain, and eventual reclamation, Julia embodies the resilience of a ChicaNerd.

6 "Tis the Life of a Misunderstood Teenage Poet"
ChicaNerd Poetics in *Gabi, A Girl in Pieces*

In an interview with scholar R. Joseph Rodríguez, Isabel Quintero says this of her protagonist, Gabi, from her novel *Gabi, A Girl in Pieces*: "The biggest obstacle for Gabi is realizing that she is fragmented, because she is trying to conform to everyone else's (family/friends/culture/boyfriends) expectations of who she should be and that the only way to become whole is to listen to herself and walk her own path" (183–84). Quintero's commentary on Gabi's struggles to conform or reject familial and societal expectations affirms what Roberta Seelinger Trites says about YA literature: "During adolescence, adolescents must learn their place in the power structure. They must learn to negotiate the many institutions that shape them: school, government, religion, identity, politics, family, and so on" (x). Gabi is no different; indeed, to some extent, all the ChicaNerds struggle with asserting themselves as autonomous beings as well as members of their families and communities. Gabi does indeed "walk her own path," as the author maintains. I identify this path as the eventual affirmation of ChicaNerd identity, where Gabi learns to accept and love herself while recognizing her agency as a young Chicana woman.

Written in diary format, *Gabi, A Girl in Pieces* chronicles Gabi Hernández's senior year of high school in the fictional town of Santa Maria de los Rosales, California—a period marked by traumatic events, such as her best friend's pregnancy as a result of rape; another close friend's rejection and abandonment by his family when he reveals he is gay; her mother's pregnancy; and finally, her father's death from a drug overdose. Gabi must also wrestle periodic fat-shaming and antiquated notions of sexuality voiced by Mrs. Hernández. *Gabi* addresses the many challenges that the protagonist must navigate to claim a ChicaNerd identity, and in the process, the novel rejects myths of Mexican female identity around stereotypes of overt sexuality; skin color as an indicator of "authentic" Mexican identity/colorism; and family struggles, such as her mother's pregnancy, her father's drug overdose, and her younger brother's behavioral problems. In my discussion of the novel, I examine in depth the significance of sexuality and fat-shaming that serve as major elements that Gabi must contend with as she carves her own path as a ChicaNerd poet and student who aspires to attend the University of California, Berkeley. As I will discuss at length, the majority of the conflicted messages that Gabi receives around maintaining her virginity and losing weight come from her mother, a complicated figure who also encourages her daughter to perform well academically. Gabi's ability to withstand her mother's criticism, combined with her astute analysis of sexual, gendered double standards that police Chicana adolescent sexual curiosity, reveals her resilience and her ability to find strength in poetic creativity.

Gabi, a self-identified "short, plump . . . and super light-skinned" Chicana, develops her growing sense of ChicaNerdiness in spite of such emotional upheaval (Quintero 14), laying claim to the writer's acknowledgment that the character must "walk her own path." As scholar Amy Cummins writes in her discussion of the novel, the text represents "academic agency," which "denotes the actions of asserting one's right to education, gaining access to formal education, and using education for self-chosen purposes" (43). Embracing her autonomy and identity as a "misunderstood teenage poet" (Quintero 110), Gabi cultivates her creative nerdiness through her use of highly personal and emotional material as poetic subject matter—in particular, using this poetic lens to voice staunch critiques of sexual double standards around the Chicana body that prohibit young women like Gabi from freely expressing themselves as sexual beings. Unlike the "typical" science or math nerd, Gabi's writing talent offers a seldom seen aspect of nerd identity.

Sex, Mothers, and the ChicaNerd

In my previous scholarship on Chicana mother/daughter feminist literature, I examined the complexities of maternal relationships that are both empowering and a potential source of strife and contention (*Contemporary Chicana Literature*). While I acknowledge that this work focalized "adult" Chicana mother/daughter literature, it is useful to examine how Chicana feminism has theorized the mother-daughter relationship, as this can also shed light on Gabi's process of developing a ChicaNerd identity amid her loving but frustrating relationship with her mother. This text, along with Sánchez's *I Am Not Your Perfect Mexican Daughter*, which I discussed in Chapter 5, centers the at-times fraught maternal relationship that proves to be the most challenging aspect of ChicaNerd self-love and empowered declaration. While to some extent all the ChicaNerd protagonists must navigate their nerdiness amid normal adolescent confusion about sexuality and their changing bodies, these two novels most explicitly chart the ChicaNerd path in connection to their growing sociopolitical consciousness as young women who must determine their bodily autonomy against their mothers' perspectives. As I will discuss throughout this chapter, the maternal relationship factors greatly into how Gabi perceives herself as a ChicaNerd poet who yearns to use her poetic craft to critique rigid standards of gender that police adolescent female sexuality and the fat Chicana body. Rather than entangle herself in constant fights with her mother, Gabi learns to use poetry as an outlet to vocalize a distinct, youthful ChicaNerd feminism.

In Gloria Anzaldúa's seminal text *Borderlands/La Frontera: The New Mestiza*, the famed Chicana theorist argues that Chicanas must maneuver conflicting messages from their families, particularly their mothers, regarding sexuality and power. According to Anzaldúa, Chicana mothers teach their daughters to reinforce a familial structure of patriarchy that maintains their oppression, which she defines as cultural tyranny:

> Culture is made by those in power—men. Males make the rules and laws; women transmit them. . . . Through our mothers, the culture gave us mixed messages: *No voy a dejar que ningún pelado desgraciado maltrate a mis hijos.* And in the next breath it would say, *La mujer tiene que hacer lo que le diga el hombre.* Which was it to be—strong, or submissive, rebellious or conforming?
> (38–40, original italics)

No doubt influenced by Anzaldúan thought, Quintero's novel features many instances where Mrs. Hernández both encourages her daughter to pursue education while also maintaining problematic views on virginity as akin to possessing value. According to Anzaldúa, mothers teach their daughters to live within a family system of patriarchy that discourages autonomy, sexual freedom, or deviation from a heteronormative identity. Through this mothering, Chicana daughters learn their symbolic "place" within a family structure that values them based on their acquiescence to patriarchy and their proximity to heterosexuality. As cultural transmitters, according to Anzaldúa, mothers like Mrs. Hernández may love their daughters and even demonstrate affection or cariño, but in these "mixed messages," the dominant lesson that is passed down indicates that it is virginity, more so than educational success, that determines one's status within the family. I do not mean to suggest that Gabi's mother does not wish for her daughter's educational attainment, but it is important to note that her mother expects that her daughter will achieve higher education *while* not breaking the "rule" of engaging in premarital sex.

Gabi's mother encourages her academic pursuits, believing that a smart Mexican daughter is preferable to a "disgraceful" American one. In fact, Gabi astutely critiques the many struggles faced by Chicana daughters who must battle their Mexican parents' problematic views on gender and sexuality, which, in the case of Gabi's mother, are also tied to accusations of whiteness. Significantly, Mrs. Hernández's warnings to her daughter reflect her anxiety that Gabi will become "more white" and therefore "less Mexican" if she loses her virginity. While the educational research I cited in Chapter 1 has positioned accusations of "acting white" among student-to-student relations as a result of educational segregation that has failed to serve children of color, Gabi's major source of white shaming comes from her mother. Rather than admonish her daughter for being too smart and therefore "too white," Mrs. Hernández instead frames sexual curiosity and sexual activity as a determining factor of one's attempt at whiteness. This is supported by research conducted by scholar Lorena García, who investigated Latina teen sexuality to combat existing stereotypes about them. In the interviews she conducted with Latina mothers and their adolescent daughters regarding sexuality and virginity, she found that Latina mothers "drew upon perceptions of racial differences between white women and themselves in terms of sexual behavior and attitudes as a way to assert to their daughters the importance of maintaining a gendered identity that was grounded in their identities as Mexican and Puerto Rican women" (45). As García points out, these mothers

> utilized this particular discursive strategy to mark the sexual boundary for their U.S.-born daughters and to assert control over their daughters' sexual behavior through their ability to question their daughters' racial/ethnic authenticity, indicating that these mothers understood their daughters' emerging sexuality through the lens of gender and race.
>
> (45)

In questioning Gabi's allegiance to Mexicanidad, as García's research underscores, Mrs. Hernández shames her daughter as a way to control (or at least attempt to control) what she sees as the dangers of emulating white girls' supposed sexual behavior. To further drive this point, on the novel's opening page, Gabi sardonically refers to the antiquated and sexist "advice" her mother transmits: "Ojos abiertos, piernas cerradas" (7), words that Gabi is unable to refute "because she'll think I'm bad. Or worse: trying to be White" (7). Within this consejo, a young girl may only prevent pregnancy simply by "keeping her legs closed" and eyes open, but as Gabi understands, this supposed advice serves only to deny and inhibit sexual desire and sexual autonomy. Gabi's critique of her mother's problematic advice also hints at her own confusion over why her mother refuses to engage in a healthy conversation about sex. In a humorous twist, Gabi does indeed "keep her eyes open"; that is, she identifies problematic assertions, refusing to deny what she observes or to remain silent on ideologies she deems unjust.

When Gabi's best friend, Cindy, reveals her pregnancy, for example, Mrs. Hernández blames this fact on being too *"gringa"*: "Being Mexican-American is tough sometimes. Your allegiance is always questioned. My mom constantly worries that I will be too Americana. This morning we were talking about Cindy, and my mom [started] saying crazy things like, 'The reason Cindy is pregnant is because she was hanging out *con esa gabachilla* Diana'" (34, italics mine). Although it is later revealed that Cindy's pregnancy is a result of rape, and not consensual sex, Mrs. Hernández's views do point to troubling binaries of sexuality that presume virginity among Chicana girls and promiscuity among "*gabachillas*." Gabi's constant battles with her mother's contradictory, problematic messages that reinforce archaic binaries of the "good" (passive) Mexican daughter and the "loose," disrespectful American/white daughter demonstrate the significance of the Mexican mother's role in the shaping of her Chicana daughter's identity-formation (Herrera, *Contemporary Chicana Literature* 29). Gabi herself struggles to make sense of Cindy's pregnancy, fearing that her best friend "had just become another statistic: Hispanic Teen Mom #3,789,258" (11). Much as Marisa Moreno and her boyfriend grapple with his younger sister's teenage pregnancy, Gabi expresses fear and even revulsion that this may jeopardize her friend's future. While she vows to support her friend, she is uncomfortable with how Cindy's pregnancy may reinforce the long-standing racist, sexist stereotypes that reduce all young Chicanas to potential teen mothers. Gabi's discomfort with her friend's pregnancy because of its proximity to the Chicana teen mother stereotype to some extent points to the relative privilege she possesses as a ChicaNerd who is expected to excel academically and defy existing stereotypes. Unlike Cindy, who is not encouraged to pursue higher education, Gabi is mentored by a teacher and academically supported by her mother, even as her mother reinforces archaic notions of female sexuality. Of course, Gabi utters these statements before she is aware of her friend's victimization.

In Gabi's curiosity about sex, the novel additionally calls for a rejection of the stereotype of nerds as asexual and incapable of expressing sexual desire. In the novel, being a ChicaNerd does not negate her legitimate sexual curiosity. Gabi's mother, in her questioning accusation to her daughter, "Oh, que [sic] te crees? Americana? We don't do things like that" (106), reflects anxiety over Gabi's Americanness. Although Mrs. Hernández alternates between use of the terms "gabacha" or "Americana," she in fact conflates them, despite her daughter's US birth which, of course, makes her "American." For Mrs. Hernández, the "we" represents Mexican-descent women, regardless of the location of their birth; in this binary of "us" and "them," she expresses her desire that her daughter be more "Mexican," which she constructs as inherently restrained in the expression of sexuality. Gabi must confront head-on her mother's troubling views on female sexuality when she processes the reality of rape culture that perpetuates victim blaming rather than systemic change around female bodily autonomy and sexual violence against women.

After learning that a popular classmate has raped her best friend, Gabi unleashes onto her diary to voice her rage over the casual uttering of "boys will be boys"—what she refers to as a "load of bullshit" (229) that not only normalizes sexual violence but simultaneously degrades women of all ages for expressing interest in sex. Displaying sexual desire, Gabi learns, means that young women will be reduced to objects who are "asking for it"—that is, guilty for their own victimization and rape. She further lashes against this by writing in her diary, "Remember how your mother warned you that boys only want one thing from you? Well, it's not your straight A's or your excellent drawing skills or your extensive knowledge of action films. It's the thing you have guarded (hint: it's between your legs) your whole life from everyone" (230). While Gabi does not explicitly call it such, she is alluding to what feminist scholars term "rape culture," which is defined as "a complex set of beliefs that encourages male sexual aggression and supports violence against women . . . a society where violence is seen as sexy and sexuality as violent" (qtd in Marshall 49). Essentially, Gabi's enraged diary entry becomes an ode to Chicana feminism and its rejection of rape culture that does not value Chicana intellect, only their bodies, but this value-placing on bodies in itself is a facade, since Gabi comes to learn that it is the heterosexual Chicana body, in its deference to patriarchy, that is expected. Certain bodies are valued, as Gabi critiques in her diary, particularly those who also meet unrealistic standards of appearance and weight. Her friend's victimization also confirms to her that regardless of weight, size, or race, women's bodies are always potentially at risk for rape. As Gabi realizes, ChicaNerds like herself who possess talent in writing or art are invisible. In her refusal to be silenced or marginalized, however, Gabi's diary, though private, can be a read as a staunch and vocal example of ChicaNerd feminism that defiantly resists sexual and racist double standards.

Gabi's curiosity and assertiveness around sexuality demonstrate that "adolescent fiction depicting sexually active adolescents signals an underlying shift in how the social categories of childhood, adolescence and adulthood are conceived" (Kokkola 9). Her desire to engage in sexual activity, although in some part due to how the loss of virginity is shaped as a "rite of passage" in mainstream culture (Trites 84), may be read as a desire for her to enact sexual and bodily control on her own terms. Gabi's feelings of shame and preoccupation with her friend's pregnancy show how "the construction of adolescence as a period of strife, uncertainty, angst and fluidity all serve to support beliefs in the purity of childhood and the stability of adulthood. The price for imposing these beliefs on the adolescent is largely paid for by the teenage population, who are treated as delinquent deviants when they express their carnal desires" (Kokkola 37). This fear of being treated as "delinquent deviants," to borrow Kokkola's words, instead manifests in Gabi's negotiation of her mother's anxieties about "turning white." Gabi desires an honest, open conversation with her mother about sexual desire, but her mother's resistance to this frankness means that Gabi can only use the privacy of her diary to imagine the "QUESTIONS I WOULD LIKE TO ASK MY MOTHER BUT AM AFRAID TO BECAUSE SHE WILL PROBABLY THINK I AM: A) BAD, B) WHITEWASHED, AND/OR C) ALL OF THE ABOVE" (147, original caps). In a powerful fashion, the novel normalizes teen sexual desire and humanizes Gabi. Although Gabi at times humorously chides herself in a self-deprecating manner, the novel is compassionate in its treatment of a girl who expresses curiosity about sex and who struggles with maternal shaming and internalized guilt.

Chicana feminist scholars have long critiqued these gender and sexual dynamics within patriarchal Chicanx families (Hurtado 386), and women scholars of color have additionally examined the ways in which white women are viewed by immigrant families as "sexually immoral," in contrast to first-generation young girls of color (Espiritu 416). In an essay that examines themes of rape and sexual violence in Chicana literature, prominent Chicana scholar María Herrera-Sobek claims that Chicana writers insert these themes in their fictional works to offer a "denunciation of the subordinate status of these women at various levels: societal, individual and familial" (246). Thus, Gabi's desire to attend UC Berkeley is unwelcome news to Mrs. Hernández, who "is always going on about how good Mexican girls stay home and help their families when they are in need and how that differentiates us from other people. Kind of wishing I was other people right now if that is what is going to determine my Mexicanness at the moment" (83). Gabi not only challenges her mother's assertions that she is "acting white," but she also questions how this attack also misclassifies her as a "lesser" Mexican. Within Mrs. Hernández's frame of reference, one cannot be both American and Mexican—that is, Chicana. Instead, one is Mexican or white, and what determines one's identity on the ethnic spectrum is one's sexual restraint. Quintero's novel thus demonstrates the particular challenges faced by first-generation Chicana teenagers in relation to their parents' constricting gender norms around sexuality.

On Loving the Fat ChicaNerd Body

In Chicana fat activist Virgie Tovar's 2018 feminist publication *You Have the Right to Remain Fat*, the writer recalls vivid memories from her childhood when she lovingly and adoringly celebrated her fat, brown girl body:

> When I was a little girl, my favorite part of the day was when we got home from errands or preschool. . . . I would stop at the end of the little hall, where the calico-cat-colored rug met the linoleum of the dining room. I would spread out my arms and legs as far as I could. And I would jiggle. My thighs and belly, my cheeks and my whole body would wobble. I would turn my head in circles. I liked

that everything moved and undulated. My body was like the water in the bathtub or the water at the community pool, which I loved so much in the summer. My body was like that water, a source of relief and fun, a place I could jump into and be held. It felt good. Oh, it felt so good.

(7–8)

As she describes just a few lines after this cherished memory, however, Tovar's unabashed bodily self-love is short lived. While her preschool days were marked by this corporeal, joyful celebration, the next 20 years of Tovar's life were spent hostage to diet culture, fatphobia, and fat-shaming, that attacked her fat, brown, female body as unworthy and inferior. In her fierce critique of rampant fat bigotry that dehumanizes fat women, especially fat women of color, Tovar reclaims her "right to be fat." Playfully yet subversively reappropriating mainstream rhetoric around "American" (read: white men's) notions of freedom, Tovar in fact rejects assimilationist ideology, instead advocating for fat women to reclaim, embrace, and emphatically celebrate their bodies in a defiant move that refuses admission in a system that fails to see fat women as fully human in the first place.

Tovar's feminist reclaiming of her fat, brown, female body, as she writes, is a feat in and of itself, considering the stigmas surrounding bodies that do not abide by the Western ideal. According to sociologist Samantha Kwan, who studies societal views of weight and size, the normalization of thinness leads to what she describes as "body privilege," which gives unearned benefits to those who possess this standard of physicality:

fat intersects with other signifiers, such as gender and race, to influence everyday interactions, thereby acknowledging how networks of power work in complex, multiple, and seemingly innocuous ways—namely, through interactions and self-surveillance. Like structures that privilege whiteness, cultural and social structures privilege the thin, or at least what has been deemed a "normal"-sized body. . . .

The thin body is such a coveted social standard that it is an unchallenged norm.

Meanwhile, those without privilege must negotiate daily interactions, sometimes feeling shame, guilt, and anger because of their bodies. In short, body privilege allows its possessor to avoid physical and emotional injury.

(146–47)

According to Kwan, while fatness denotes a lack of body privilege, when we factor in gender and race, we see that these additional identities further mark certain bodies as "other," even grotesque. Gabi's diary entries reveal not only her frustrating attempts to lose weight, to no avail, but they also show her growing critique over the pressure she faces to alter her body that is deemed unattractive and not good enough. In YA literature especially, these concerns are commonly expressed because "The heteronormative nature of twenty-first-century-Western culture means that young women are consistently scrutinized, by them and by others, regarding their physical attractiveness, particularly to men. . . . The types of female figures considered attractive, however, vary depending on specific cultural and historical contexts" (Johnston 312). Gabi expresses embarrassment at her fat Chicana body, particularly at times when this interferes with her ability to partake in "normal" adolescent pastimes, such as shopping: "I don't want to be fat for many reasons, mostly because it's embarrassing climbing stairs and having little old ladies rush by you while you have to pause and catch your breath. Also, there's lots of clothes I'd like to buy. It seems like when you go to the store, the only clothes that are on sale are skinny girl clothes while big girl clothes are regular price or super expensive" (170). Gabi's internalized shame over clothes shopping reflects the findings of Kwan's research on fat women's navigation of public space, which revealed the fear that the public space of the shopping mall or clothing store renders them "invisible" (149). For Gabi, however, what she fears is not only invisibility but hypervisibility in spaces where her size is potentially a source of scorn or ridicule.

Although Virgie Tovar's audience is mainly adult women, her refreshing and critical call for bodily love in many ways conjures Gabi's quest to develop empowered ChicaNerd identity around her fat body. Gabi's process of claiming a poet-nerd identity goes hand-in-hand with learning to reject harmful messages, mainly voiced by Mrs. Hernández, that seek to undermine her self-love and acceptance. Although Gabi loves her mother, their relationship is often marked by her mother's hurtful comments about Gabi's weight. As Gabi facetiously writes in her diary, "When she says, 'No comas tanto. You're getting fatter than a pregnant woman,' she's not so wonderful. But when she says, 'She loves to read. She has a 3.75. Mira, le dieron otro certificado. . . ,' she's the best" (26). On the one hand, her mother decries Gabi's weight, suggesting fatness should be regarded as a source of shame. In a sense, her mother reproduces social stigmas around fatness rather than nerdiness, which would seem to reinforce patriarchal ideologies that value virginity and thinness. As Beth Younger claims in her analysis of YA texts, "Contrary to popular belief, young women affected by social pressure to be thin are not just white girls but increasingly include young women from other ethnic groups" (48). For Gabi, however, reclaiming her body equates to an acceptance of herself as a ChicaNerd. Gabi critically recognizes that to love herself is a challenging task because of the conflicting messages that surround her, those mainly voiced by her mother.

To develop a sense of subjectivity and agency, Gabi must learn to love not only her fat body, but her fat and *nerdy* Chicana body. Younger's study of YA literature has found that these texts will often "valorize the contemporary ultra-thin standard of beauty" (46). But it is significant to note that Gabi refuses to relinquish her bodily self-love to attain what she sees as unrealistic, sexist, and racist expectations of conformity. For example, in María Alicia Garza's analysis of what she describes as "super-sized women" in Chicana literature, she argues that "By writing the body, Chicana authors reappropriate the body politic—the one defined by both Chicano and Anglo cultures—in order to reconstruct a body that is unencumbered by cultural values that favor male domination over women's bodies" (137). As Garza argues, representations of the fat female body in Chicana literature reflect the writers' knowledge that these bodies are positioned as the "other" within mainstream and Chicanx cultures (138). Garza's observations are supported by Mrs. Hernández's constant admonishments that her daughter lose weight. Her mother's pride in Gabi's intellect contradicts these views, leaving Gabi feeling rightfully confused and frustrated. Significantly, though, Gabi's critical perspective as a "plump" and nerdy Chicana is privileged by the novel's use of an intimate diary structure, subversively giving voice to a character that is expected to remain silent and unassuming. Through her diary, and later, through poetry, Gabi discovers power in using creative means to find agency and voice as a ChicaNerd.

Further, Gabi's possession of light skin serves as a significant factor in her daily navigation of Chicana nerdiness. As a light-skinned Chicana, Gabi rejects the problematic accusation that she "does not look Mexican": "My skin is there for all the world to see and point at and judge. [*Güera*]. Casper. Ghost. Freckle Face. Ugly. Whitey. White girl. Gringa. I've been called all of those names. Skin that doesn't make me Mexican *enough*" (35, italics mine). Gabi's feelings of rejection, particularly due to her mother's fat-shaming, are also complicated by her appearance, which does not affirm, but rather challenges widespread myths about Mexican identity. Although the possession of light skin has often been equated to privilege in Latinx communities, as scholar Sandra D. Garza attests, Gabi's lighter skin affirms the fact that "skin color and the physical body largely mediate our relationships with society, marking insiders and outsiders in the global, national, and local arenas" (39). Gabi is thus rendered a "white girl" by her Chicanx peers without knowledge of her own sense of identity as a Chicana, and by voicing accusations she demonstrates her critiques of using skin color as a basis to measure her Chicanisma. What I also find significant is that Mrs. Hernández's assertions regarding being gringa, in fact, have nothing to do with her daughter's light skin. Although in her well-known essay, "La Güera," the Chicana playwright/theorist/poet Cherríe Moraga has critically examined the ways in which she as a light-skinned Chicana was encouraged to "pass" as white, in Quintero's novel, we have quite the opposite. Mrs. Hernández instead uses sexual promiscuity as a marker of whiteness rather than skin color. Still, Gabi's possession of a fat body further prevents her from gaining full access to the communities surrounding her.

Like Marisa, who painfully and honestly captures her raw feelings in her UT essay, Gabi must also learn to articulate her pain as a mode of reclaiming an empowered identity. When combined with her poetic interests, her light skin makes her more susceptible to problematic notions of authenticity as they pertain to phenotype. Gabi's fat, light-skinned body makes her a target of criticism that seeks to negate her quest for self-acceptance, but "pushing back against ethno-national patriarchal ideologies inflected by misogyny and preoccupied with much more than race and gender, in Gabi one finds an irreducibly complex intersectional singular subjectivity" (Ellis 17). Most important, though, Gabi learns to embrace poetry as a means to combat fat-shaming, accusations of not being "Mexican enough," and familial struggles—namely, her father's drug addiction: "I'm finding out that I really like poetry. It's therapeutic. . . . I've always liked poetry, but I didn't realize how powerful it could be" (83–84). In this regard, Quintero's compassionate construction of Gabi as a ChicaNerd who learns to love her body, is a direct contrast to the tendency in YA literature to represent fatness as "outside of the norm and often the result of deeper psychological problems. . . . It is rare for a young adult novel to portray fat, or even a little extra weight, as beautiful—or even as an alternative standard of beauty" (Quick 54). Gabi learns that poetry is an effective tool to vocalize both joy and pain. This achievement of voice through poetry highlights the empowered possibility of cultivating and claiming a Chicana poetic nerd identity to combat cultural, familial, and social isolation.

Reclaiming ChicaNerd Poetics: On Being a Chicana Poet

For Gabi, writing poetry alone does not suffice in the construction of a nerd identity. Additionally, with the mentorship of her high school English teacher, Gabi learns to read her deeply personal poetry aloud "in that underground coffee shop/with the older crowd/who are cooler than me," as she writes in her poem about the experience of her first public reading (139). By performing her poetry, Gabi learns the power of adopting a ChicaNerd poet identity, something she was not sure she could claim. In claiming herself as an artist, she witnesses the healing and affirmation that poetry can provide, particularly the significance of emulating Chicana poets who validate her right to create art. Sonia Alejandra Rodríguez's analysis of Latinx children's and young adult literature's representation of healing and transformative acts aptly describes Gabi's process of claiming the artist identity, much like the characters Rodríguez discusses, who "use creativity and imagination to challenge and transform the different forms of violence they experience in their lives" ("Conocimiento" 9). As I discussed earlier in the chapter, Gabi's use of poetry and diary writing to combat violence and incite healing is most vivid in her staunch critiques of sexual violence and gendered double standards. According to scholar Amanda Ellis, Gabi's poetry writing shows how she "pens her way out of shame, homophobia, lurking sexual violence, and grief by embracing who she is through her writing" (15). Speaking of her father's addiction, her college aspirations, and bodily love, Gabi addresses her audience:

> Offer it up for sale there
> my fat girl words
> in my fat girl world
> take it I say,
> you want it?
> I got it here for you,
> all of this for all of you.
> (140)

Rejecting cultural notions of shame and modesty that attempt to stunt her aspirations and self-love, Gabi hurls out her "fat girl words" to insist on visibility and autonomy. Rather than hide behind her body, as her mother encourages, Gabi dares to love herself, inserting herself within the public space of open mic readings to speak her truth. Moreover, Gabi learns to identify with Chicana poets, such as Sandra Cisneros, and adopts this writer's well-known poem "Loose Woman" as a mantra: "That's the kind of woman I want to be when I grow up" (149). In radical Chicana feminist poetics, Cisneros's poem rewrites the misogynistic alignment of female sexual agency with "looseness," stating, "They say I'm a beast./And feast on it. When all along/I thought that's what a woman was" (Cisneros 1–3). As Aída Hurtado argues, "To love oneself as woman is . . . a revolutionary act. The reclaiming of self has come for Chicana feminists through self-love—not narcissistic, selfish involvement but as a political act of valuing what patriarchy has devalued" (416). Cisneros's poetry directly communicates to Gabi the subversive power and strength of radically loving one's body that others see as flawed, deficient, or excessive.

By accepting Cisneros as a powerful role model, Gabi looks for cultural, gender, class, and bodily affirmation embedded within the tradition of Chicana feminist poetry. Voicing pain through poetry "helps heal wounds/Makes them tangible" and is thus an act of burgeoning Chicana feminist agency (141). The importance of Gabi's discovery of Chicana poetry cannot be underestimated, as Larissa M. Mercado-López explains in her analysis of Chicana adolescence: "Chicana feminist youth literature can have serious implications for young Chicana readers living in the in-between spaces of childhood and adulthood" (5). This feminist poetry not only affirms the reality of Gabi's transition from teenager to adult, but it plants the seeds of ChicaNerd poetic critique that are fundamental to her sense of self-love and autonomy. Moreover, Gabi comes to learn the subversive act of inscribing herself into her poetry, stating, "I can't stop writing. . ./I write about my brother./I write about me./I write about my mom./I write about my dad" (141). By writing about herself and her family, Gabi embodies a ChicaNerd feminist poetic that reclaims one's authentic, lived experiences as necessary elements for creativity. Rather than separate her reality as a ChicaNerd from her art form, Gabi learns to use her poetic craft to amplify her Chicana voice. Like Marisa, who must speak harshly but honestly in her UT essay as a step toward empowering subjectivity, so too Gabi must unleash the suffering she has experienced as a ChicaNerd through poetry. Reading her poetry aloud gives her the space to openly claim her nerdiness. While Cisneros's poetry teaches her the subversive power of ChicaNerd bodily self-love, Chicana poetic muses also affirm her right to create poetry that directly honors her bicultural, lived experiences. When Gabi's teacher, Ms. Abernard, assigns the task of creating poetry that weaves multiple languages, using Cisneros and the work of the late Chicana poet Michele Serros as prominent examples of poets who regularly code-switched in their work, Gabi expresses shock that this is possible: "Before we read their poetry, I didn't even know you could use two languages in a poem. I thought they either had to be in English or in Spanish. Turns out I was wrong" (67). The Chicana poetry she reads instills Gabi with a sense of pride in her cultural and linguistic heritage, validating her existence in a way literature has not done before. Essentially, Chicana poets give Gabi permission to speak her truth through the use of code-switching, including subject matter that weaves in cultural signifiers, such as "chicharrones," as Gabi humorously notes in relation to a Serros poem (67). In her admiration of their poetry, Gabi understands intuitively the significance of adopting women of color muses who have paved the way for her, as a young, "plump" ChicaNerd to create art.

While *What Can(t) Wait* at times featured a tense relationship between Marisa and her white teacher, Ms. Ford, it is noteworthy that *Gabi, A Girl in Pieces* depicts Gabi's teacher, Ms. Abernard, in a distinctly different way. For example, it is Ms. Abernard who introduces Gabi to poetry by Cisneros and Serros, and it is this same teacher who encourages her to perform her poetry at open-mic sessions. Ms. Abernard also cultivates Gabi's talent in alternative creativity when she assigns Gabi's class to create 'zines as part of their final class project. As Amanda Ellis explains in her discussion of Gabi's 'zine, the novel's cover is depicted again in the text, representative of Gabi as a "girl in pieces": "A significant pictorial source of Gabi's deepest self-projections, the collage is composed of revealingly asymmetrical images of dismembered body parts on torn papers. Each piece creates a central (albeit distorted) body" (18). My analysis of the novel does not privilege a discussion of Gabi's 'zine making, but her teacher's willingness to assign activities that foster independent creativity is significant in Gabi's development of ChicaNerd subjectivity. Much as Gabi learns that her culture, community, and unique linguistic repertoire should be used as vital sources of creative inspiration, she likewise learns to centralize her body as 'zine subject matter. In this act, Gabi rejects bodily shame and stigmas that encourage invisibility. Prominently displaying her body is a subversive mode of ChicaNerd feminism. This same teacher encourages Gabi's application to UC Berkeley because "Ms. Abernard said a lot of famous poets have made their home there, and that it has a poet-friendly community" (84). Although Ms. Abernard's encouragement similarly conveys a message of leaving home, as we saw with Ms. Ford's eager hope that Marisa leaves Houston for Austin, it is significant to note that Ms. Abernard pushes Gabi to claim a poet identity. I reference this important distinction not because I wish to undermine the significance of having unsympathetic white teachers, but to show the disparate experiences of having "white saviors" versus "white teachers."

However, despite Gabi's progression toward youthful Chicana feminism, her distinct version of ChicaNerd identity, the novel presents us with a powerful revelation near the conclusion that threatens to jeopardize all that Gabi has worked hard to achieve. By including this plot detail in the narrative, I suggest that Quintero is attempting to show how Gabi's process of empowerment is ongoing, as she must confront the reality of her best friend's rape, which compels her to reject everything she has been taught about sexuality and agency. Although Gabi's empowered ChicaNerd declaration coincides with the end of her senior year of high school and her excitement over gaining admission to her dream school, her college admission is threatened when she lashes out at her friend's rapist, German, in a rush of anger. In her defense of her friend, Cindy, Gabi's anger also manifests as rage against rape culture in which her mother and other women in her family are complicit. Using her own 'zine assignment with Ms. Abernard as the avenue in which to voice this staunch critique, Gabi questions why young women are "labeled slut[s]" (204). Gabi's art is then didactic and Chicana feminist in its refusal to remain silent against a culture that vilifies and dehumanizes young women. When we consider Gabi's critiques of rape culture, sexual double standards, and weight stigmas, all of which occur within the realm of poetry, diary entries, and the 'zine, we witness Gabi's painful, but cathartic, realization that art is a powerful avenue in which to vocalize her strong beliefs.

Gabi's rejection of rape culture is evident in her attack against Cindy's rapist. When German describes Cindy as "begging for it" (260), Gabi refuses to restrain herself, as she describes in her diary: "I don't know how long I was on top of German slapping him around. I do know that eventually I was pulled off by security. My mother was called and charges were pressed" (261). The novel does not glorify Gabi's attack as rightful vengeance, but it is important to note that the text exposes the limits of "good girl" behavior, or gendered codes of conduct that dictate female passivity. In this light, actions like Gabi's, though rooted in solidarity with her violated friend, are narrowly framed as evidence of hyperemotionality rather than as justified acts of rage against rape culture that refuses to confront the casual treatment of male sexual violence. As punishment for defending her friend, Gabi is suspended from school and barred from attending and participating in traditional high school rites of passage, including "grad night" and the high school graduation ceremony. Gabi's suspension exposes the ways in which "students are taught that there are consequences for disobeying rules just as there are legal consequences for breaking laws," according to Sonia Alejandra Rodríguez (64). As I discussed in Chapter 1, Gabi's suspension must be read alongside the historical tendency to define young girls of color as inherently deviant and "bad." The high school's underlying threat to reveal her suspension to UC Berkeley not only potentially threatens her college admission and jeopardizes her future, but it marks her as a "criminal," reinforcing the tendency to unjustly categorize Chicanx students as criminalized threats to the school's social order (S. Rodríguez 65). Gabi's status as an honors student and aspiring college student is temporarily revoked, revealing the shaky foundation on which Gabi stood in the first place. As a Chicana student who must navigate a racist and sexist educational system, her "goodness" is always precarious; even in her defense of her friend, she is criminalized in a way the rapist student is not. We are also left with an uncomfortable truth and unresolved conclusion: Cindy's rapist is left unaccountable for his assault, a chilling but all-too-realistic warning that Quintero undoubtedly wants to emphasize to her adolescent readers. While readers may undoubtedly empathize with Gabi's suspension, the novel's unsettled treatment of German—he is essentially left off the hook for rape—is a frustrating glimpse into the reality of rape culture that overwhelmingly fails to punish, much less prevent, male sexual violence.

In Isabel Quintero's complex narrative around a ChicaNerd who enjoys having sex for the first time, eating tacos, and writing Chicana poetry that emulates Chicana feminist poetics, *Gabi, A Girl in Pieces* gives a seldom seen representation of Chicana adolescence. At long last, Gabi arrives at a place of profound love and self-acceptance, despite her community's messages that she must alter herself to achieve praise. Gabi's ChicaNerd path entails not only her negotiation with racist and sexist ideologies that position young women of color as incapable of intelligence and creativity; further, she must also navigate the dangerous terrain of fatphobia and rape culture, at times articulated by her mother. But in her mother's encouragement that she attend college, Mrs. Hernández is a complicated figure in her own right, demonstrating Quintero's insistence that readers uncover the subversive possibilities of Chicana mother/daughter relationships.

Most important, rather than separate from her Chicana heritage, Gabi seeks to be both a nerd *and* a Chicana, powerfully claiming her right to do so. Gabi learns that creating poetry is an empowering, cathartic, and joyful act that allows her to voice strong opinions in ways she is not typically allowed to do in her everyday surroundings. Similar to *What Can(t) Wait*, Gabi at last achieves acceptance by her mother when she informs her of her admission to UC Berkeley. Much as Marisa's mother serves as her daughter's guide, Mrs. Hernández tells Gabi: "*Pues, esta siempre es tu casa*" (279, italics mine). Like Marisa, Gabi learns to see her mother's affection as a source of pride, and this maternal acceptance and love provides her with a model of Chicana agency she may otherwise not have claimed. In the end, Mrs. Hernández does not serve as an obstacle to college achievement; instead, Gabi is reminded of the loving *casa* Mrs. Hernández has cultivated for her children, a haven to which she can always return. Although Gabi expresses frustration with her mother, she must also voice the necessity of maternal support so as to leave home. Gabi learns to successfully navigate her mother's contradictory messages on gender roles, choosing to love her mother and to reclaim her maternal relationship as a powerful tool in the development of ChicaNerd agency. Like the title of the novel, Gabi must pick up the pieces of her home life that surround her, with all the positive *and* negative connotations they entail, but in her refusal to reject her mother, family, hometown, or heritage, she embodies the often messy but necessary path that leads to ChicaNerd empowerment.

7 To Be or Not to Be

Shakespeare, College, and Chicana Feminist Consciousness in *Ghosts of El Grullo*

Existing scholarship on Patricia Santana's writing has largely examined her 2002 debut novel, *Motorcycle Ride on the Sea of Tranquility*, a text that centers the narrative around the Chicana protagonist, Yolanda Sahagún, as she psychologically and emotionally struggles with the return of her Vietnam veteran brother, Chuy, whose drastic changes coincide with her own coming of age. In *Ghosts of El Grullo*, the sequel to *Motorcycle Ride*, we are reintroduced to the same characters, but the time frame spans Yolanda's senior year of high school through college graduation. Yolanda's emerging college life forms the basis of the plot, but additionally, her mother's death, which occurs in Yolanda's first year in college, means that she must return to her mother's story—excavate the origins of her own ChicaNerdiness—to attain her college degree and continue to graduate school. Like Lupita, who must complete her high school year after her mother's death, Yolanda also suffers the loss of her mother at a moment in her life when she is embarking on her college experience. For Yolanda, as is the case for Lupita, the process of constructing and claiming a ChicaNerd identity entails the added burden of negotiating the depths of mourning, anguish, and loss over a mother who factored greatly in her college acceptance and achievement.

I have deliberately chosen to conclude this book with a chapter on Santana's understudied novel, the sequel to *Motorcycle Ride*. Though there is also a lack of literary scholarship on the first novel, this text has remained the achievement for which Santana is known.[1] And while it may seem odd that I have chosen to write on the sequel, which spans Yolanda's college years rather than the high school days of *Motorcycle Ride*, I will explain my rationale. As I stated in the introduction to the book, the texts I have examined all feature unique Chicana protagonists who must navigate a precarious path to ChicaNerd identity formation and self-acceptance as nerdy Chicana subjects. Essentially, I see all the texts leading up to Santana's novel, almost a glimpse of what college life will entail for the Chicana teenagers. Yolanda is also several years older than the rest of the protagonists I examine, but in ending this book with her, I suggest that the ChicaNerd path may continue into adulthood.

To be sure, Yolanda's college experience is far from idealistic or romantic; it is during her first years of college, after all, that she loses her mother to cancer while being away from home for the first time in her young life. But losing her mother, I argue, serves as the foundation on which Yolanda carves her adult ChicaNerd identity, one which she initially expresses through her love of literature, particularly Shakespearean poetry, and which later transcends into a deep-seated Chicana pride that is influenced by her new knowledge of Mexican and Latin American literature she studies in college. Yolanda's newfound Chicana pride is inspired by and through her mother's own history as a young woman from the town of El Grullo, Jalisco, México, a landscape that Yolanda eventually visits to excavate the maternal source of her own ChicaNerd path. This desire to uncover the truths of her mother's early life—in short, to unearth her ChicaNerd origins—binds all the texts together. In many ways, all the protagonists are looking for something, searching for answers, or otherwise attempting to understand their positionality within the contexts of their families, communities, and schools. This is most pronounced in *Ghosts of El Grullo*, a novel that insists that ChicaNerds look inward—that is, look at their own families, especially their mothers, to uncover their nerd lineage. It is only when Yolanda finds the answers she seeks, and indeed, by asking more questions along the way, that she can attend graduate school as a ChicaNerd adult.

Coming of Age: Becoming Chicana in Patricia Santana's Novels

Both *Motorcycle Ride* and *Ghosts* trace Yolanda's development of Chicana consciousness within a specific period of American history that influenced the rise of Chicanx activism—namely, the years during and after the Vietnam War. In *Motorcycle Ride*, Yolanda's brother, Chuy, with whom she previously had a close relationship, returns to their San Diego home after serving in battle, and his strange behavior, newly formed violent tendencies, and emotional distance from the family all point to his trauma as a psychologically wounded veteran of war. Alongside his traumas, which Yolanda struggles to understand, the novels examine what it means to be a young Chicana amid such political upheaval surrounding this deeply unpopular war. Yolanda learns to negotiate her own sense of gender and racial consciousness in a family that she loves but finds flawed as she recognizes the gender subordination she faces as a daughter. As John Alba Cutler argues in his discussion of *Motorcycle Ride*, "She begins to understand her nascent sexuality via modes of oppression that are unquestioned traditions in her home, and which are emblematized in Chuy's pathological behavior" (602–3). In her confusion over her beloved brother's emotional and physical estrangement from their family, including the surprising, brutal sexual attack he commits upon a Chicana, a friend of the family, Yolanda becomes conflicted not only with his behavior but in her knowledge that she as a young woman must bear the brunt of male sexual and physical violence. Nadia Avendaño makes a similar assessment to Cutler's argument, stating, "The Chicana protagonist becomes a conscious subject as opposed to a passive object who, through the act of questioning and interpreting her socio-cultural context, gains a new understanding of herself and her place in the world as a Chicana" (67).

This process of "questioning and interpreting her socio-cultural context" largely occurs within the confines of her home environment as she examines her father's behavior, her parents' marriage, and the male privilege bestowed upon her older brothers. One of the primary struggles she faces throughout both *Motorcycle Ride* and *Ghosts* is carving a space for herself within her Chicanx patriarchal family, a unit that becomes more fragmented after their mother's death. Without their mother as the emotional anchor, Yolanda initially extracts herself from her father in particular while maintaining close ties with her siblings: "Yolanda's rebelliousness and growing feminist consciousness has its communal counterparts that convey a sense of closeness to her family as well as her ethnic community without annulling the more individualistic or feminist counter narratives" (Avendaño 69). Like the rest of the ChicaNerd protagonists examined in this study, Yolanda's path toward an empowered declaration of self-love entails rebellion and resistance to the many factors that constrain her, "inimical to an independent and authentic female identity" (Eysturoy 19). For many of the protagonists, rebellion is part of their ChicaNerd journey, particularly in *Ghosts* and *Mexican Daughter*. Her mother's death, however, forms the basis of Yolanda's process of uncovering her own ChicaNerd legacy and, in doing so, teaches her how to reunite with her father and even forgive him while not compromising her Chicana feminist consciousness and her right to study literature in college and attend graduate school.

The process of ChicaNerd agency first begins at home, early in *Ghosts*, when Yolanda informs her father that she will not commute to school at UC San Diego but will instead live in the dorms. Much as Lupita's father at first is reluctant to permit his daughter to live away at school, as we saw in *Under the Mesquite*, Yolanda's father, Lorenzo, similarly is displeased upon learning this news, although his anger at Yolanda's defiance is much more visible, as he accuses her of "abandoning" her family (23). At this baseless accusation, Yolanda protests: "I get good grades in school. I win scholarships and awards and honors. What? Don't you trust me? What do I have to do to make you trust that I'm mature and can take care of myself in this big world? Why is it my brothers can go and live on their own when they're not married, but we can't?" (23–24). Yolanda's adamant protest not only is indicative of her ability to interpret her father's sexism that is not so subtly hidden beneath his fear that she will abandon her family; in addition, what I find even more significant is Yolanda's reference to her high academic achievement as the basis of the defense she launches. As a ChicaNerd who has excelled, indeed, surpassed in school, Yolanda argues that this fact alone proves her maturity and trustworthiness. In addressing her family's gender double standard that allows her single older brothers to leave home without objection, Yolanda is astute enough to recognize that even her academic performance does not protect her from her father's machista whims. What is more, Yolanda protests the false premise that leaving home for school denotes an act of selfishness, and in this way, we are reminded of the multiple ways in which ChicaNerds must assert their right to attend college without being unfairly accused of abandoning their families or relinquishing their responsibilities as daughters.

Yolanda further drives her challenge to her father's machista stance by invoking her "American" right to rebel, as she argues to Lorenzo: "The problem is just that, that we kids *don't* talk back to you enough, don't question your old-fashioned rules. We live in the United States of America, Papá" (24, original italics). By alluding to her Americanness, Yolanda chastises her father's views as inherently out of date, and thus, Mexican—an identity from which she wants to distance herself. Lorenzo's accusation that Yolanda's words are tantamount to "una falta de respeto" (24)—that is, a lack of respect—denote a specific cultural code of conduct that defines respect as obedience to the paternal authority, no matter how unfair the rules may be. Yolanda's defiance to her father's position affirms Eysturoy's assertion that the Chicana protagonist, "through the interactions with the social and cultural environment, and therefore also with the traditions of her ethnic heritage . . . gains an understanding of her individual self as a woman and as a Chicana" (26). Like all the ChicaNerds, Yolanda frequently wrestles with hostile racial climates but also home environments that are governed by patriarchy. In her rather naïve insinuation that the United States somehow tolerates rebellion, regardless of what historians may know to be true, Yolanda equates restriction, confinement, and obedience with Mexican culture. To some extent, all the Chicana protagonists confront the limitations of this myth, as their racialized identities as young women of color reveal that unequal power structures are a reality in the United States as well. However, while Yolanda initially attributes her rebellion to a so-called fact of "United States of America" life, a quintessential American pastime, her college experience introduces her to an identity that she will eventually cultivate as she grows up: Chicana—that is, a ChicaNerd.

But this battle over living on campus does not include Yolanda's mother, Dolores, who in fact serves as her ally, even an accomplice to her plans. Dolores's savvy but subtle resistance to her husband's sexism is most evident in how she succeeds in making Lorenzo approve of their daughter's college living arrangements. In a humorous passage a few pages after Yolanda's protest to her father's denial, Yolanda describes a seemingly impromptu home visit from her favorite teacher and vice principal, but one that is actually arranged by Dolores and unknown to Lorenzo, as they all meet to discuss the importance of allowing Yolanda to live in the campus dorms:

> In all of this, my mother was quiet, deferring to my advocates and not wanting my father to suspect that she was in on this. Then he turned to look at her. "Well, Dolores," he said. "Our daughter has proven herself to be a mature, responsible student, all right. Why, look at her grades! And as these two very intelligent ladies have just mentioned, she will be able to study better with the library nearby. The Newman Center is a very good thing too. Yes, yes, I absolutely agree with these women. *Por cierto que* I've felt this way all along, but Dolores, I want you to feel comfortable with this, too." We all turned to look at my mother who sat quietly with her hands folded on her lap. "Well, Lorenzo, if you are sure...." "Yes, yes," he said, nodding his head, smiling at the beautiful Ms. Tagore. "Of course, yes. I think it is the best thing for our Yoli." "Well then," she said with just the right amount of hesitation, "it is fine with me." And as my father reached for the coffeepot to refill Ms. Tagore's cup—when in my life have I ever seen my father serving a woman coffee?!—my mother glanced at me and winked.
>
> (34, original italics)

I refer to Dolores as Yolanda's accomplice to her daughter's ChicaNerd resistance to patriarchy because of her creative, humorous, and uncanny ability to sway Lorenzo in a way that makes it appear that she is passively waiting for her husband to make the decision. While it would seem that Dolores merely defers to her husband's patriarchal authority, given that ultimately it is Lorenzo who appears to give his approval, I suggest we read Dolores's actions as far more subversive. Dolores's performance of demureness, combined with her mischievous wink to Yolanda, demonstrate the unique ways in which she has learned to defend her female children in a manner that belies the strategy needed to commit such acts. Lorenzo's blustery words of pride over his daughter's good grades, which he earlier ignores when Yolanda reminds him of such, are humorous precisely because he is clueless to his wife's covert defiance to his authority. It is Dolores's savviness, evident in her ability to gather a collective group of women to advocate for Yolanda—not Lorenzo's permission—that enables Yolanda to move in the dorms. I insist on defining Dolores's actions as subversive to shed light on how she models to her ChicaNerd daughter the creative means of resisting gender oppression the only way she can, by supporting her daughter's achievement of independence and agency.

While Yolanda is at first excited about what university life will entail, the novel pays particular attention to her feelings of being an outsider, of not belonging within a university setting that she knows was not created with working-class women of color in mind. At her first campus party, Yolanda struggles with how to respond to classmates' questions about where she will spend her spring break, thinking to herself, "Should I tell them my spring break was going to be spent in a barrio of mainly poor Mexicans with a few immigrant Germans, Poles, and Swiss sprinkled about? Should I tell them I lived in a modest—no, I wouldn't say ramshackle—house with a bedroom I'd shared my whole life with four other sisters?" (64). Rather than mere embarrassment, Yolanda's reluctance to tell her peers the truth of her barrio neighborhood, observed in her false description of her hometown as "kind of an off-the-beaten-path resort on the Pacific Ocean" (64), should instead be interpreted as her attempt to shield herself from her classmates' pity and scorn. Yolanda inherently knows that her privileged classmates would undoubtedly pity her as a working-class Chicana daughter of Mexican immigrants. This knowledge forms the core of her feelings of unbelonging—commonly known as imposter syndrome, her feelings that she has no business occupying the privileged realm of higher education. Yolanda's discomfort and anxiety expose the reality that first-generation students of color must also navigate the tricky social terrain of university life, in addition to the classroom setting.

In fact, these intense feelings of unbelonging are more pronounced a few paragraphs later, when some of the partygoers offer her a hit off a marijuana joint, which frightens her, as she describes: "I was thinking that maybe Elton John was right, and I should have just stayed on the farm, forgot all this highfalutin university stuff because this was not my world and never would be my world" (65). For Yolanda, the marijuana itself is not the cause of her fear, but rather, succumbing to the drug-induced high unearths feelings of inadequacy that were absent up to this point. In short, Yolanda feels like a fraud, and her inability to casually enjoy the weed she has been offered, in contrast to her privileged classmates, reveals the anxiety that accompanies being a first-generation, working-class young woman of color in the early 1970s. Yolanda herself admits that she feels more at ease "studying on the seventh floor—the Library of Congress *Ps* of language and literature" (61). As a ChicaNerd, it is within the safe walls of the university library that she feels confident and secure, not at the beach party surrounded by white students whose entitlement affords them the privilege of belonging. Yolanda's trepidation that she will lose control over herself if she succumbs to the potent marijuana unearths her intense fear over this social aspect of university life, a landscape that she does not understand in the same way she comprehends the academic components of college. Because Yolanda is the first in her family to live on campus, these feelings of inadequacy at first appear to be a shock, given that she unknowingly believed that the biggest struggle of college attainment would be her father's stubbornness to her request to be a dorm student. Yolanda's high school academic experience does not prepare her for the reality of isolation that accompanies many first-generation college students of color, let alone during the early 1970s, a period of time in which Chicanx students were rarely encouraged to pursue higher education.

Brown and Proud: MEChA and ChicaNerdiness

If campus parties lead to feelings of imposter syndrome and discomfort, Yolanda finds a sense of belonging and empowerment as a ChicaNerd through her newfound involvement with her university MEChA chapter. In a humorous twist of irony, the younger Yolanda in the first novel of the two-part series, *Motorcycle Ride*, often pokes fun at her eldest sister, Carolina, who joins the activist group during her first year at San Diego State University. In *Ghosts*, Carolina teases her younger sister for earlier mocking her Chicana political ideals. This transformation from British literature enthusiast to proud Mechista activist does not occur until Yolanda is in college, and while she recalls memories of her older sister's political consciousness, she also juxtaposes her sister's activism with her own initial passion for the "greats" of British and American literature, as she describes in one memory of a family trip to their parents' hometown of El Grullo, Jalisco:

> I had brought along enough reading material: Shakespeare, Chaucer, English and American modern short stories. I was preparing myself for an academic career in British literature, planning on participating in the education abroad program in England where I would probably live indefinitely. (I could already imagine my high school counselor saying, "Oh my, you read the complete works of Shakespeare by the age of thirteen? A precocious child, indeed!")
>
> (164)

While at the age of 13 the young Yolanda mocks her older sister, the college-aged Yolanda recalls this memory to demonstrate her transformation from Anglophone enthusiast to Chicana rebel. As a young teen, Britain itself is the source of enlightenment, knowledge, and empowerment, and Mexico represents all that is backward because of its symbolic association with her parents: "My love affair with Mexico: my ambivalent, passionate love-hate relationships with my parents' *tierra*. At times this affair played out like a romance novel; at times it played out like a Gothic mystery. Mexico equals Mami; Mexico equals Papi. And so, good Doctor Freud, where was my place in this equation?" (174, original italics). In her literary mind, Yolanda can only describe her feelings toward Mexico in genre-specific terms. As a ChicaNerd who longs to study literature and enter academia, however, Yolanda is at first unable to locate her intellectual curiosity within her Mexican culture and Chicana identity. Yolanda feels an intimate connection to Mexico, but this land does not form the basis of her lifelong journey, which is why she can only think of it through feelings of ambivalence. Joining MEChA, however, shifts Yolanda's perspective so that she is later able to travel to Mexico to understand her mother, and thus, the source of her ChicaNerd identity. Although she does not fully belong in Mexico, it is MEChA that teaches her that she can be of both Mexican and American descent—that she can be from "ni de aquí, ni de allá," neither from here nor there, as the common Chicanx expression goes. Overturning feelings of not belonging, she finds through MEChA a term that captures the complex web of being countryless: Chicana, or what I call a ChicaNerd.

Yolanda's interest in MEChA stems from a sense of isolation as one of the few Chicanx students on her college campus, but in addition to that, joining the group serves as her attempt to chart her own Chicana subjectivity in contrast to the confining home environment in which she was raised. As a 13-year-old Chicana bookworm, Shakespeare and the like were sources of knowledge, but as a conscious ChicaNerd college student, MEChA becomes key to her transformation: "I was hungry for enlightenment, for knowledge and for a view of the world beyond the sheltered perimeters of my Palm City. I wanted to see the world with new eyes, but I wanted to see it with people who came from a place like mine. And without MEChA, I sensed I would be too lonely and alienated to see the light" (72). Essentially, Yolanda is attempting to locate a home, one in which her newfound Chicana consciousness can grow. In her parents' home, where her subordination is determined by her gender and birth order, Yolanda is frustrated with the gender politics of her Mexican family, which contrast the liberties she gains from the activist group. While Chicana historians have long exposed the Chicano Movement's own brand of patriarchy, Yolanda is unwilling to express any critique of a group that has provided for her a space of ethnic solidarity that is absent from the campus at large.[2] Not surprisingly, her self-imposed Chicana identity is at odds with Lorenzo, who not only mocks her for what he sees as her naïveté, but in doing so, reveals his own nationalistic, anti-indigenous sentiments on Mexican heritage:

> "I'm a Chicana," I announced to my mother and father one weekend near the end of my first year in college.... "*You* are Mexicans," I said pointing to one then the other with my authoritarian, know-it-all finger, "but I'm a Chicana." "What do you mean you're a Chicana?" my father said. "No, Yolanda, you are *not* a Chicana; you're a Mexican, the daughter of Mexican parents. I've heard about those *disque* 'Chicanos'—a bunch of rabble-rouser *politiquillos*. People

who don't know what they are, so they make up some word that sounds like 'chicanery'—*una chicanada*. Do you have any idea what that word means?" I could tell my father was trying to be reasonable, though his face was already turning red as he picked up his tortilla and then put it back down and then picked it up again, his rolled tortilla getting colder by the second. "A 'chicanada' is a trick, a deception. . . ." "Maybe to you," I said, "but to me the word 'Chicano' comes from the Meshica Indians, from the word 'Meshicanos,' or 'Mexicans.' . . ." "Ah, so you're saying that you, with your blue eyes and white skin, are part of the Meshica tribe," he said, now chuckling. "*Vaya*, a little *indita* in our family."

(70, original italics)

While this passage reflects Yolanda's humorous, though self-righteous proclamation that she is distinct from her parents, those backward Mexicans, which readers are undoubtedly expected to critique, her father's outright anger at his daughter's newfound identity is rather crucial. In his sarcastic reference to Yolanda's fair skin and eyes, Lorenzo mocks his daughter's allegiance to an indigenous heritage that is celebrated by MEChA. As scholar Lourdes Alberto discusses, Yolanda's claim to Mexican indigenous lineage was part and parcel of the Chicanx revolutionary ideology of the late 1960s and '70s: "Mesoamerican history became crucial in engendering Chicano political thought and identity, serving as a counternarrative to the oppressive experience of Mexican Americans in the United States" (107). In Yolanda's case, laying claim to "Meshica" heritage derives from her sense of isolation and alienation she experiences as a first-generation Chicana college student. But the irony of this Chicanx cultural nationalism, as Alberto points out, is that this rhetoric of indigenism in fact constructs indigenous subjects as "a myth of origin, but . . . unimaginable as contemporary subjects" (114). By harking to a distant, indigenous past, the lives of actual present-day indigenous peoples are seldom visible within this imaginary, thus continuing the process of erasure that privileges mestizo and even light-skinned Mexican people, despite attempts to the contrary.

Lorenzo's casual utterance of a common anti-indigenous epithet, "indita," reflects the racial privilege bestowed upon him in Mexico, even as his status as a working-class immigrant in the United States relegates him to an impoverished outsider. As a light-skinned Chicana, much like Gabi Hernández, Yolanda undoubtedly experiences the privilege of racial passing, but her unique experiences of isolation on an elite university campus—that is, her gendered *and* racialized experience as a first-generation Chicana college student—is unknown to Lorenzo, who uses skin color as the basis to determine ethnic and national identity. While we as readers are encouraged to dissect Yolanda's passionate, if shortsighted, proclamation that fails to account for her light-skin privilege,

I also point to her attempts to carve a place of loving acceptance as an empowered ChicaNerd.

Yolanda's craving for a home where her nerdiness can thrive is met by her kinship with the Mechistas, the group she identifies as her "real passion" (231). Significantly, Yolanda finds a way through MEChA to merge her newfound political ideology with her enthusiasm for her nerdy school subjects like literature and philosophy. In her craving for "direction and enlightenment in my young university student mind" (232), Yolanda finds a space for literary nerdiness within MEChA. Despite the limitations of patriarchal cultural nationalism, it is through this organization that Yolanda unites these facets of her life that give her meaning, such as antiracism and nerdiness:

> What I found in MEChA was a much-needed family of friends on campus who reminded me of home and Palm City—Concha, Rosario, Cristina, Enrique, Raúl, José Luis, Chito, Poli—friends who contributed to my ever-growing vocabulary, a litany of words that constituted a new kind of prayer for me, words such as "cultural nationalism," "Marxist Leninism," "oppression," "exploitation," and "dialectical materialism...." Craving answers to my own raison d'etre, I gobbled these words and concepts and philosophies with the ravenous hunger of a vulnerable and naïve apprentice.
>
> (232)

Though Yolanda refers to herself as "vulnerable and naïve," I insist that we interpret her passion for activism as an empowered means of achieving ChicaNerd agency. In naming her new friends, Yolanda equates them to Chicanx kin, demonstrating her search for an adopted family who shares her political views. Significantly, her activism fuels her knowledge, and by studying philosophy and literature, she gains the tools to understand her positionality as a first-generation working-class Chicana student. Through MEChA *and* nerdiness, Yolanda finds a space of belonging that empowers her to assert her right to study and learn as a nerdy Chicana subject.

Tracing a Maternal ChicaNerd Legacy

Much as Yolanda must learn to connect her passion for literature to her newfound sense of Chicana consciousness, she must similarly excavate her mother's story to make sense not only of her motherlessness, but to come to an empowered state of ChicaNerd agency that unites all facets of her life: her family, love of literature, and Mexican heritage that is no longer a source of shame but the loving root of her identity. If Dolores's presence in Yolanda's young life is crucial to her sense of ChicaNerd self, her mother's death leaves her with many unanswered questions about her own future, her father's role in her life, and her academic pursuits. Like Lupita, whose mother's death propels her from a pained artist and later to an emerging ChicaNerd poet whose maternal memories fuel this empowerment, Yolanda similarly must wrestle with intense grief over the reality of Dolores's absence; further, Dolores's death casts anguish and fear that she has missed something of her mother's life that can potentially shed light on her feelings of unbelonging and confusion over the future.

To further mark the connection between maternal death and the protagonist's feelings of loss and even aimlessness, which are healed only upon excavating her mother's story, the novel's sections are separated with passages from the Mexican writer Juan Rulfo's famed novel *Pedro Páramo*—a work that Yolanda is introduced to in a Latin American literature class. The writer's immediate appeal to her is upon discovery that Rulfo originated from her parents' home state of Jalisco, but beyond that, her love for his novel has much to do with how she seeks answers about her mother's life within the pages of this haunting text, as she admits: "When she died, I dropped my French, poli sci, and chemistry classes. The only class I didn't drop was the contemporary Latin American lit class. I couldn't. I needed to hold on to Juan Rulfo, have him near me. He had become my friend and my guide. . . . In truth, he was my connection to Mamá and the world she came from" (111). What I find rather revealing about Yolanda's admission about the comfort the novel brings her is not only the strangeness of the book's subject matter but also how she searches for answers within the pages of a fictional work to learn about her mother's world rather than learn from her father, a living being. But as a fictional work that delves into themes of fragmentation and the unconscious, using it to look for clues into her mother's past is rather odd. The uncanniness of this admission also harks back to my discussion in the earlier chapter—namely, Julia's fascination with the literature of death that only increases with time. As I discussed, Julia's admiration for this literature signals her initial inability to communicate with her parents about the tragedy of her sister's shocking death. Yolanda's intense love for Rulfo's novel speaks volumes of a young daughter's struggles to articulate the pain of a mother's death during a time when the daughter is seeking answers to what her future holds, connecting her more perhaps to Lupita than Julia. Both *Under the Mesquite* and *Ghosts of El Grullo* capture the complicated process by which the protagonists negotiate their ChicaNerd paths that are riddled with insecurities and doubt over identity and social consciousness following their mothers' deaths. Although scholars have long pointed to the ways in which Western culture has associated mothers with death, otherness, and decay and the dead mother as a powerful force with which living daughters must grapple (Goodwin and Bronfen; Rubenstein), the dead mothers in the novels by García McCall and Santana instead function as empowering sources of memory, inspiration, and creativity on which to chart a

ChicaNerd path. Yolanda's painful process of recovering and excavating what I refer to as her ChicaNerd legacy, a lineage of Chicana nerdiness, entails returning to her parents' town of El Grullo.

Yolanda admits that she "inherited" a love of reading from her mother (120), and this fact connects both mother and daughter in a ChicaNerd legacy that Yolanda attempts to uncover by visiting her mother's sisters in El Grullo. In her sudden decision to flee to Jalisco, Yolanda conveys her desire to dig up remnants of her mother's story that she believes she will discover within the walls of her mother's family home:

> This is what happens, then, with the death of your mother, that moment you realize you were her daughter and didn't know her very well, and she is no longer alive for you to get to know. You are compelled to know her story, to put the bits of anecdotes together, to walk the corridors of her childhood house, peruse the library with its yellowed, musty books and find something of your mother in every nook and cranny of her home. . . . Your mother is gone, and you are left with a father you love and you hate, with siblings you adore who get on with the daily chores of life, but who have your mother present in ways you cannot surmise.
>
> (120)

Significantly, Yolanda goes to the source of her mother's story, El Grullo, rather than the San Diego home of her own childhood and adolescence, revealing her innate desire to metaphorically travel back in time, to learn of her mother before she became Mami. In her reference to the family library that houses the "yellowed, musty books," Yolanda points to their shared connection—their love of books that is passed down from Dolores to Yolanda (120). It is this very symbol of ChicaNerd identity—the library—that most fascinates Yolanda, as evidenced in her decision not to drop her Latin American literature class, as she hopes to find answers of her mother's life within the pages of a novel she adores. Although speaking of Victorian fiction, Dever's analysis of representations of the death of the mother is apt, particularly is it reflects Yolanda's impromptu visit to Jalisco to uncover pieces of her mother's past: "Victorian dead-mother plots facilitate a number of cultural processes, functioning most prominently, perhaps, as a means of addressing the question of origins in terms at once physical and psychological" (6). I do not classify *Ghosts* as a dead-mother text, but Dever's argument may certainly describe Yolanda's desire to uncover and learn of her mother's life prior to her migration. In asking "Who is my mother?" Yolanda is trying to answer the other pointed question, "Who am I?" The disappointment she feels upon her return home from El Grullo—that is, the reality that she has learned very little of her mother's early life—does, however, teach Yolanda that memory may function as a powerful mode of filling in the gaps of her maternal lineage: "So, for now, most of my mother's history lay quietly hidden . . . leading me to conjure in my mind, from my own memories, the rest of her stories. The need to know and understand her life seemed suddenly, desperately connected to my need to know and understand, little by little, my own" (131). While the large body of Chicana literature holds many examples of daughters who yearn to discover hidden stories of their dead mothers' histories,[3] texts like *Ghosts* and *Under the Mesquite* question what it means to lose a mother during the complicated period of adolescence, especially when the Chicana protagonists must also work through gendered and racialized meanings of Chicanisma. Yolanda's growing consciousness, her own identity-formation, which is still in the making, is punctuated by her disappointment that she must rely solely on memory. Memory, however, functions as a significant ChicaNerd strategy of resistance, a refusal to forget.

Although Yolanda returns to El Grullo in the hopes of finding answers to questions she does not yet even know to ask, the visit instead functions as a reminder to return to memory, to recall Dolores's words and actions on which to build her present and future. Going back to El Grullo, the source of her mother's origins, in actuality serves as a winding return to home, to San Diego and college. Dolores's fundamental role in Yolanda's ChicaNerd subjectivity cannot be underestimated, as it she who teaches her daughter to recognize her family and home as creative sources of inspiration, even in the intense frustration they cause her daughter, as Dolores implores her daughter before her death:

> "You are a part of another world, *mi'ja*," she said, smiling, gesturing with a nod ahead at the road. "You are going to go places I never went. I can see that already. All I ask," and here she looked earnestly at me, as if she wanted to be sure I memorized this request, "is that you not forget where you come from and that you respect your childhood home. You never know when you might want to return, looking for a familiar, loving face."
>
> (75)

In her passionate but gentle plea to her daughter that she remember the home space she has cultivated for her children, Dolores's words embody what Chicana education scholar Dolores Delgado Bernal calls "pedagogies of the home"; although unknown to Yolanda at the time, her mother's advice describes what Yolanda must do to thrive as an emerging academic, to excavate the maternal knowledge amid the college environment of the early 1970s where few role models for educational attainment exist. As Delgado Bernal explains, pedagogies of the home refer to

> The communication, practices and learning that occur in the home and community, what I call pedagogies of the home, often serve as a

cultural knowledge base that helps Chicana college students negotiate the daily experiences of sexist, racist, and classist microaggressions. Pedagogies of the home provide strategies of resistance that challenge the educational norms of higher education and the dominant perceptions held about Chicana students.

(624)

Dolores's death impels Yolanda to remember her mother as a source of knowledge that her mainstream academic education will not recognize. Though no longer alive to serve as a calming, reassuring presence in her daughter's life while she navigates the treacherous waters of academe, Dolores's quiet cultivation of Chicana feminist resistance lives within Yolanda. In recalling her mother as "the one who handed us the pencil or the microphone; she was the one who set the stage on which our stories came alive. The behind-the-scenes person, both discreet director and enthusiastic audience in our lives, this was Mamá" (45), Yolanda pays homage to her mother as a teacher, both storyteller and listener, the source of her own ChicaNerd subjectivity that she would be otherwise unable to achieve. What I find significant in not only Dolores's words but also Yolanda's own description of her mother are the ways in which academic achievement and love of learning are both intimately connected to the role of the mother. Like the rest of the ChicaNerd protagonists, the maternal relationship provides both loving affirmation *and* resistant, feminist, and working-class knowledge to thrive within academic settings that are dangerous for women of color.

In a touching connection that harks back to both *What Can(t) Wait* and *Under the Mesquite*, early in the novel Dolores insists on purchasing a satchel for Yolanda before she embarks on her new college life. While a seemingly minor detail in the novel, the gift symbolizes Dolores's own former identity as a student, a maternal connection traced by a satchel that Yolanda finds outdated, old-fashioned, and ugly:

> On my bed sat a small duffel bag with my clothes for the weekend and the Fedmart satchel that Mamá had bought me. She didn't just buy it for me; no, she *insisted* I get it, clear in her mind that this was what I would need to carry notebooks and pencils to my classes. I didn't have the heart to tell her I would never use it.... How could I explain to Mamá that the satchel was dorky? I didn't. I accepted it, and as soon as I was on campus, I headed for the bookstore to buy myself a regular backpack like all the students.
>
> (48, original italics)

As a first-generation college student, Yolanda resists any reminders of her family as she embarks on an unfamiliar setting, and buying a new backpack "like all the students" is indicative of her attempts to seamlessly blend into the campus—that is, assimilate—at least until she earns membership in MEChA. But in addition to finding the satchel "dorky," Yolanda rejects the bag because of her perception that the bag is too Mexican, more appropriate for her mother than for her as a Chicana college student: "(Maybe these briefcase contraptions were used in Mexico, I thought, and maybe romantic suitors slipped love letters into their pockets, but not here)" (48). Prior to her mother's death, Yolanda works hard to achieve distance from her mother, whom she loves but finds frustrating. The satchel, although lovingly purchased by Dolores for her college-bound daughter, represents the past, Mexico, an antiquated time—in short, all that Yolanda initially believes has nothing to do with her contemporary reality as a Chicana university student.

However, after Dolores's death, the satchel becomes symbolic of things far more sinister for Yolanda than merely her mother's old-fashioned taste. Although Dolores's gift to her daughter, much like Patricia Moreno's gift to Marisa, serves as a maternal offering of love and encouragement to succeed in college away from home, Yolanda is unable to reconcile the bag's meaning to her mother—a parting gift for her daughter—to her own interpretation of it. For Yolanda, the bag holds the painful reminders of her mother's victimization to the patriarchal control imposed by Yolanda's father, Lorenzo—what she interprets as a lifetime of martyrdom and sacrifice:

> I took one last look at the items in the bag: the little booklet on the rhythm method, the prayer pamphlet my mother read in her last days titled *Quince Minutos con Dios*, and her favorite rose petal rosary. Then I buckled the satchel shut and in one strong, vicious swoop, tossed it over the pier and into the ocean. I'd had it with this religion. What good did fifteen minutes with God do my mother? What good did a lifetime of saintliness do her? Here, God, keep your rose petal rosaries and your fifteen minutes—cram them up your ass, if you will. I had no use for God, or for his smug cohorts and silly prayers.
> (133)

Although the items that Yolanda references belong to her mother, not to her, she tosses out what she interprets as symbols of female repression and self-sacrifice. Yolanda resents religious items that dictate a particular type of womanhood that she resists and does not want for herself. Yolanda flings what she sees as symbols of her mother's martyrdom, eliminating any semblance of religiosity, to distance herself from a patriarchal institution that she sees as culpable in her mother's victimization. In ridding herself of the satchel and Catholic documents in the most dramatic fashion, throwing them off the San Diego pier, Yolanda flings these items altogether into the ocean, where they will end up as castaways or perhaps even be eaten by marine animals. Merely throwing them away is unacceptable for Yolanda, who visualizes throwing the objects into the ocean as one final, sweeping gesture. In this almost violent act, she is symbolically and with much effort, flinging the weight of the past, making sure that where the items land, they will be irretrievable.

In Yolanda's seething but critical questions, "What good did fifteen minutes with God do my mother? What good did a lifetime of saintliness do her?," Yolanda takes Catholicism and Mexican patriarchy to task, aligning the novel's critique of female martyrdom with Chicana literature's long history of challenging this unrealistic expectation for Chicana and Mexican women, particularly women who are mothers.[4] As scholar Yvonne Yarbro-Bejarano explains, "Catholicism in its institutionalized form . . . indoctrinates women to accept suffering and sacrifice as their lot" (*The Wounded Heart* 12). In Yolanda's rage against Catholicism, she is also questioning the role of Marianismo in what she interprets as her mother's passivity. Marianismo, according to María Herrera-Sobek, refers to the Christian ideology that aligns mothers with the pain and suffering of Mary (*The Mexican Corrido* 8), emphasized in the Mexican expression "La mujer mientras más sufrida es, más buena es" (Huaco-Nuzum 263), which translates to "The more a woman suffers, the better she is." Although in both *Motorcycle Ride* and *Ghosts* Dolores's strength is conveyed in subtle ways, Yolanda's intense grief over her mother's death prohibits her from seeing her mother as anything but her father's victim. In many ways, her trip to El Grullo functions as a desperate attempt to discover something rebellious about her mother, a shocking secret, perhaps, something to explain her life in the United States that is marked by a marriage to a volatile man, bearing seven children, and poverty. Yolanda's major source of struggle, however, is to uncover her mother's strength—most notably, her significant role in shaping her own ChicaNerd identity. Grief, compounded by an aching longing for her mother, however, erases the many memories she holds of her mother's subtle power and important role as the family's anchor.

The novel's ending, as Yolanda has decided to accept UCLA's English graduate program offer, coincides with her maternal aunts' visit to San Diego on Dolores's birthday—a sentimental gesture that is symbolic of the text's insistence on highlighting the significance of female relationships in her path to college and beyond. But perhaps even more compelling is Yolanda's decision to forgive her father, whom she sees as culpable in her mother's perceived lifetime of sacrifice. As Yolanda learns, forgiveness *is* strength, what she will need to propel her toward graduate school success without her mother's steady presence. Choosing to forgive her father enables her to recall what she has been at pains to deny, "the good memories: My father working on the house's plumbing, calling out to whichever daughter was around. . . . Or assembling all of us at the kitchen table for the monthly lessons of multiplication tables—*dos por cuatro son . . . cinco por ocho son*—so that we wouldn't be burros in the classroom" (276). It is only when she discovers the grace that accompanies forgiveness that she may attend graduate school, a decision that she had previously been debating. While the novel remains critical of Lorenzo's many flaws, I insist on uncovering Yolanda's growth as a ChicaNerd who is at last able to shed the intense resentment she had long harbored toward her father. As a feminist and socially conscious young woman, Yolanda chooses to forgive her father for his absence following Dolores's death, demonstrating her ability to show compassion for her flawed but loving father. In so doing, Yolanda embarks on graduate school life with the strength of maternal memory that she will need to carve an empowered future.

Patricia Santana's fictional portrayal of Yolanda Sahagún's painful but liberating path through college to graduate school during the mid-1970s illuminates the struggles facing our Chicana foremothers, who attended college during a politically and racially charged time. To be sure, our current political and social landscape remains anything but tranquil, but Yolanda's attendance at UCSD during a period in which few women of color gained admission to colleges and universities is significant. As a Chicana daughter of Mexican immigrants, her decision to live in the campus dorms was only one of the myriad struggles that Yolanda faced. Further, the 1970s remains a crucial moment in Chicanx history, a time in which Chicanx students defined what it meant to be brown, to be a student, in a country that refused (and refuses) to see them as human, much less American. Yolanda is a fictional character, but Santana's authentic, complex persona may be read as the antecedent to the contemporary, real-life Julias, Marisas, Lupitas, and Gabis of the world. Santana's novel allows us to imagine the racialized, gendered path of ChicaNerds from the past who fought for their inherent right to study, create, and learn. Yolanda's road is timeless, however, as her quest to attend college and graduate school, much like the rest of the ChicaNerd protagonists, is daunting because of her working-class, first-generation identity—a reality we continue to face in the present day. Negotiating the politics of MEChA, her mother's death, and her family dynamics, Yolanda's achievement of empowered ChicaNerd identity entails loss and mourning. Tracing a maternal ChicaNerd legacy, Yolanda learns to uncover memory and her mother's strength to guide her in the next chapter of her life. No longer the devoted Shakespearean, Yolanda discovers the power of Chicana feminism to honor her mother, love her father, and ultimately, to claim nerdiness for herself.

Notes

1. See also scholarship by Theresa Delgadillo, Belinda Linn Rincón, and Ariana Vigil, which examines the role of gender and sexuality in Chicanx/Latinx literary representations of war and violence. Full citations listed in Works Cited.

2. See, for example, the most recent anthology of Chicana historical writings, *Chicana Movidas: New Narratives of Activism and Feminism in the Movement Era*. Full citation in Works Cited.
3. See, for example, Lorraine López's *The Gifted Gabaldón Sisters* or Reyna Grande's *Dancing With Butterflies*, among others.
4. See Ana Castillo's collection of essays, *Massacre of the Dreamers*, or Sandra Cisneros's essay "Guadalupe the Sex Goddess," for example.

Conclusion
Reflections From a (Grown-up) ChicaNerd: Or, Why I Wrote This Book

In her 2019 essay "A Mirror in Hand, but Make It Spanglish," Isabel Quintero describes one of the first interviews she gave after the publication of her celebrated novel, *Gabi, A Girl in Pieces*. As Quintero recalls, the interviewer registered shock at her writing success, given that she was, after all, "only" the daughter of Mexican immigrant parents: "What the interviewer was covertly asking was, 'How'd that happen? How come you like learning and thinking, when you come from people who don't?' No, my parents do not have a formal education, and yes, they worked with their hands, but why couldn't they also be critical thinkers or be lifelong learners? Isn't that part of what being an 'intellectual' is?" ("A Mirror" 124). Quintero's legitimate anger at the interviewer's shortsighted (to say nothing of it being racist and classist) question affirms what her novel does best—in fact, what all the novels I examine in this book do exceptionally well. With their validating, compassionate, and critical representations of Chicanx communities and families that value and support their ChicaNerd kin, the novels insist that we expand and challenge existing ideologies around intellect and intelligence. In exposing this interviewer's limited understanding of Chicanx communities, Quintero also questions why her community is narrowly understood as incapable of expressing intellect, as if Chicanxs and intellect are incompatible sides of a coin. While the ChicaNerds I examine all aspire to traditional markers of success—college attainment—they do so while legitimizing and reclaiming their Chicanx families as fundamental to their sense of agency, identity, and social consciousness as brown and nerdy subjects. The writers normalize intellectual curiosity in our communities while also affirming multiple ways of knowing. Like Quintero, I demand that we recognize and see ourselves as learners, intellectuals, and thinkers—to proclaim to the world, "This is what a nerd looks like."

In the introduction to this book, I began by describing what it felt like to be a shy, quiet Chicana nerd bookworm in high school. To understand why Chicana young adult literature holds a special place in my nerdy, brown girl heart, I have to begin with high school, a time in my life that most days than not I would prefer not to think about. High school would be the time when I most understood and felt that I was an outsider and a nerd, and it would take me many years before I began to look back on that history through a more reflective lens, when the memories would not cut so deeply. To look back is still painful, and perhaps it will always be so, but what accompanies that pain is a deep sense of compassion and empathy for my younger self and for other ChicaNerds who may also find solace within the pages of Chicana young adult novels. Fueling this compassion I feel for ChicaNerds is a commitment I have to demonstrate empowering, resistant strategies to give a voice to our stories, our histories, and our lives. This literature is vital for young readers, indeed, for all people, but especially for those whose environments reduce them to the margins, where systemic and social structures silence and erase them.

I would be hard-pressed to deny that much of the impetus to embark on this study comes from a desire to speak of my lived experiences, as well as my colleagues', as nerdy Chicana subjects who struggled to excel in high school and beyond while staunchly defending our brown girl identities. I have used this book as a cathartic attempt to make sense of my own ChicaNerd history, relishing in writing about fiercely intelligent, at times frustrating, characters who remind me of the pains of growing up Chicana when there are so few realistic and sympathetic images of us in mainstream culture. But this is not a work of nonfiction or autobiographical writing, as is obvious, but a literary analysis of Chicana young adult fiction that utilizes multiple disciplines to account for representations of ChicaNerd protagonists. That I have been able to find a wealth of Chicana young adult literature attests to the significance of this understudied field in which we have much still to do. In each of the protagonists, I see glimpses of my twin sister, my friends, and myself. In Yolanda Sahagún, I recall my early love of literature, but I also remember being uncomfortably aware that the literature I studied was far removed from the world I knew that surrounded me. As a child, I had a talent for spelling bees, much like Luz Ríos. Like Gabi, Julia, and Lupita, I wrote stories, longed to travel and study, and read profusely to learn about the world beyond me, locations I could not visit but could only imagine in my mind. Marisa's caretaking responsibilities resembled mine, for it was while attending college and graduate school that I helped raise my niece, and as much as I loved my goddaughter, I struggled to dedicate time to my academic work when my family relied on me to not shun these obligations. As a ChicaNerd myself, these protagonists mirror my experiences in uncanny ways, and when I first read these novels, I knew I had found a home in them. The literature validated me in ways I had never been before. I felt *seen*.

This affirmation I find in Chicana YA literature is a long time coming. Growing up, I had few examples of positive and empowered ChicaNerds who could teach me what it meant to bask in nerdiness. In print, on television, or in film, I could never imagine that it was possible for someone like me to unite Chicana consciousness with love of learning and community, encapsulated in a name I would later call a ChicaNerd. It is no wonder that even today, even as the body of Chicana YA literature continues to grow, students like mine cannot yet fathom that nerdy interests are legitimate, valid, and unabashedly Chicana. In fact, when I declare to my students, "What can I say? I'm a nerd," typically prompted during a particularly intense class session when the literature I teach gets me fired up, my students usually laugh, at first surprised that this professor of theirs would admit to such a thing. I do this intentionally. By vocalizing this identity I claim, I insist on declaring to them that one can be a Chicana and a nerd, and by making this proclamation to them while plastering a big smile on my face, I show them the joy, pleasure, power, and love that comes from claiming this identity. I know of no other way to be, so I live in this ChicaNerd body of mine, showing my students the possibility of nerd self-love. Over time, this passionate declaration inspires my nerd-in-hiding students to finally vocalize their nerdy experiences in a way that does not shame but empowers. But even as I powerfully and lovingly call myself a ChicaNerd, I admit that from time to time, I am still plagued with doubts about my right to exist and to continue researching within the privileged and predominantly white (male) space of academia. Academia is a space I may occupy but one in which I am not welcome, as I am made painfully aware of on almost a daily basis. The reality is that when you are a woman of color in academe, you are forever an outsider.

As a Chicana academic who has earned tenure and promotion, I realize that I occupy a space of privilege that few members of my community will ever achieve. This privilege, however, comes at a cost. In her recent essay in the *Chronicle of Higher Education*, literature scholar Marlene Daut narrates the racist and sexist hostility she experienced in her tenure-track position while she attempted to go up the ranks in academe. Her powerful words are downright chilling in their truth: "The larger point I want to make, however, is that while my promotion to full professor might signal hope . . . it is not a sign of progress for black women. . . . In short, my promotion happened—like those of all the black women before me—not because times have changed, but because I beat the odds." Daut's survival within a system that at times openly despises women academics of color is not lost on me, a Chicana who has similarly wrestled not only with invisibility but with vicious attempts from white women and male Chicano colleagues to eliminate me from a profession that was not designed for women of color. As a full professor, I hold a prestigious rank, but like Daut, I also "beat the odds," meaning the space I occupy is a lonely, terrifying one. Stories similar to Daut's are revealed in the groundbreaking collection *Presumed Incompetent: The Intersections of Race and Class for Women in Academia*, a text regularly assigned in higher education settings because of its importance in exposing the racialized, gendered, and classed realm of academia. It is no wonder I am so drawn to essays like Daut's and to collections like *Presumed Incompetent*, whose voices legitimize the pain I've experienced on my path in higher education. I have been told by colleagues that I am "lucky" to hold a position and title I have worked hard to achieve, and this path was quite literally paved with my sweat and tears, given that I have had to dodge racist and sexist attacks while somehow managing to publish, serve the university, and teach and advise my students. The latest research shows that in the United States, less than 1 percent of full professors are Latina, according to the National Center for Education Statistics. At my institution alone, a campus that has been designated as a Hispanic Serving Institution, "Hispanic" faculty account for a little over 13 percent of the faculty population, although there is no data on the specifics according to rank and gender (Fresno State Office of Institutional Effectiveness). Our Latinx student population, however, is close to 50 percent. It goes without saying that I am most likely one of the few Chicana professors my students will ever encounter along their academic journeys. Even at my Hispanic Serving Institution campus, I am an outsider. Like the ChicaNerds I study, my experience as a first-generation, working-class Chicana faculty member means I continue to navigate an unfriendly climate of racism, sexism, and even ageism. Despite my professor status or even my age, the truth is that my somewhat youthful appearance, short stature, name, and appearance all combine to make my presence always suspicious, possibly there by some mistake or more than likely affirmative action, or because someone "gave" me this job, as I have been told.

This in-betweenness I navigate extends beyond the campus and into my personal life. My mother often expresses concern that I read too much, that I work too hard, that I overextend myself. When I tell her I know of no other way to live, that books are my world, and without my books, I feel empty, she sighs in her loving way, for she adores, but does not always understand this daughter of hers. Isn't it always that way between mothers and their ChicaNerd daughters? When I showed my mother the article that would set the foundation for this book, the 2017 *The Lion and the Unicorn* publication "Soy Brown y Nerdy," she read it cover to cover, as she always does. As usual, she praised me over the phone but then protested, "¡pero tú no eres una nerd!" While my mom was sincere in her compliments, and indeed, I cannot recall a time when she has not supported my writing and research, one thing was clear: as much as she enjoyed the article, she was still a bit uncomfortable with my adamant embracing of the nerd identity. Her "pero tú no eres una nerd" comment was undoubtedly meant to comfort me, but I did my own protesting and told her that yes, in fact, I was "una nerd," a ChicaNerd, to be exact. But where did this come from? Why was my mother hell-bent on shielding her youngest child from an identity that I not only claim but one that I wear with pride? No matter what my article argued, my mother could still not separate what she knew about nerd (outsider, outcast, victim of bullying) and what she saw in me today, a happy person with supportive friends, no longer an outcast, or so she believes. My mother did not want to associate me with anything remotely resembling a Steve Urkel or Geek Squad member, just another reject who is the butt of everyone's jokes. For her, to see me as a nerd meant to see me as an object of scorn and ridicule, a torment she does not wish upon anyone, let alone her own daughter.

Or, maybe "nerd" reminds her too much of that other cruel name, "la tontita," what my father called me when I was a child—"A joke," he claimed. Come on, he's just kidding. As a young girl, I was undeniably the payasa of my family, the clown who told corny jokes and danced silly jigs to make my mother and siblings laugh. Because of my ready smile and good-natured personality, traits that my mother nurtured and loved about me, my father associated these qualities with stupidity—hence, "la tontita," the stupid one, the not-so-smart Cristina. My mother was angered at this name, and she defended me as much as she could, but the name stuck until my father's departure years later. Nerd. Tontita. To my mother, how could these terms hold any value beyond their meanness? I cannot redeem "tontita," for no matter how you slice it, the name is a vicious attack against anyone, especially a young Chicanita like I was that was hurled at me for simply existing in my fun-loving, book-reading body. But perhaps after reading this book, my mother will come to understand why I need to vocalize my ChicaNerdiness, to call forth an identity that I align with profound love, joy, and above all else, resistance. To combat the many stereotypes and injustices placed on smart and intellectually curious Chicanitas, as I discussed at length in Chapter 1, the ChicaNerd identity is vital, necessary, and powerful. This book is my attempt to tell a different kind of story about those whom we call nerds.

Why Representation Matters: ChicaNerds on the Page and in Life

When I was in high school over 20 years ago, I never would have imagined that I would one day write a book that unabashedly proclaimed that there was something empowering or resistant about being a nerd. All around me, I witnessed the opposite: there was nothing liberating about being a nerd. No way. Being a nerd, as I was at the time, was downright isolating, even scary. It meant always being a potential victim of bullying or living an invisible adolescent experience. Among many, two instances that I remember vividly stand out, for they remind me of the pain and stigma that has long been associated with being a nerd.

One night during our sophomore year, my twin sister, Elena, and I decided to attend our high school's football game, a rare occurrence, but we ventured out, excited about the possibility of going somewhere together. About halfway through the game, however, our excitement turned to trepidation, then anxiety, and then an intense desperation to flee as soon as possible because for no reason we could determine, a handful of classmates began throwing empty soda cans at our backs. At first, we ignored these girls, thinking optimistically and even foolishly, "Maybe the cans slipped out of their hands." But soon we realized that the girls were intentionally launching the cans at us, deliberately trying to cause us harm and embarrassment in front of the other spectators who packed the stadium bleachers. This was no accident. We were targeted. But why? What had we done to these girls, one of whom we had known since the fourth grade? Though we never admitted this to each other, Elena and I knew the reason, but we were too ashamed and too hurt to speak this aloud. We were targeted because we were nerds. And although we were Chicana, like our classmates, our presence at the football game, our mere existence, it could be said, incited anger and aggression in these girls who refused to see us as one of them. We were Chicana, but we weren't *really* Chicana, were we? How could we—quiet bookworms that we were—be Chicana, one of them? But there was more. We trespassed on what those girls undoubtedly saw as their turf, the prized football field bleachers. We did not belong in a space that was designated for the cool, popular kids, everything we were not. The girls' bullying and meanness won out, for Elena and I never attended a football game alone for the duration of our time in high school.

Another moment, this time in our sophomore year math class, a boy we knew said to our best friend (in front of Elena and me, no less), "You know, you'd be popular if you didn't hang out with the twins." These words stung, of course, but more painful was the expression on our friend's face, the stunning realization that our friend was actually contemplating the possibility of popularity and adoration, if only we weren't holding her back. According to this cruel boy's thinking, our existence as "not the right kind of Chicana" meant popularity was never a possibility—simply out of the question—but as a white girl, our friend had potential were it not for her friends, those nerdy twins. As her friends, we had little social capital to offer, but as a white girl who had chosen to befriend these quiet Chicana twin sisters, she had clearly sacrificed much, and it pained us to admit that she may have felt that she was "stuck" with us—the nerdy, unpopular, quiet Chicana girls who were lost in the crowd.

I recall these moments, though difficult as they remain to this day, to emphasize the ways in which "nerd" and "Chicana" have been disparate aspects of identity that I have been at pains to unite in my creation of the term "ChicaNerd." These two moments of outsiderness, of bullying, made clear a number of realities within the social, racial, gender, and class dynamics of my high school community. As a quiet Chicana who liked to read and who seldom spoke in class, popularity was out of the question, and this meant I occupied an odd place among my peers. I was not welcomed among the white, middle-class students, but even among my Chicana classmates, I was rarely acknowledged as one of them. I did not belong anywhere. The few friends I had were a mixture of white girls and girls of color who existed on the periphery of our large high school student body where cliques ruled. Unlike my older brothers, who were popular, athletic, and handsome, few people knew my sister or me. In fact, when classmates learned that we were not only related to these handsome young men, but that—gasp!—we were their younger sisters, this realization was usually met with outright shock. As I knew back then and as I know today, when you are rendered invisible, proving that you exist becomes a daily struggle. But as the ChicaNerds and I know, merely existing is not enough. ChicaNerds and all nerds of color deserve to embody their nerdiness, to wear it proudly and fiercely, to take up space, not hide behind it. I am reminded of the powerful concluding scene in the film adaptation of Josefina López's play *Real Women Have Curves*. Like a true ChicaNerd, Ana confidently walks along the busy New York City streets on her first day as a Columbia University college student, defiantly and powerfully making herself at home. A smart, vocal, and passionate young woman, Ana's intelligence and determination, coupled with the love of her family, combine to make her the kind of ChicaNerd we should all strive to be. If nothing else, I hope this book insists on the right of ChicaNerds to survive while powerfully thriving among their books and nerdiness and loving themselves while doing so.

While representation is important, it is not enough. Representation alone will not change the systemic reasons that make claiming a ChicaNerd identity challenging in the first place. Although I never intended that this book would necessarily be used for educators, maybe it was naïve to think so. If anything, the research I cited in Chapter 1 shows that it is educators who play an instrumental role in shaping students' perceptions of academics, who factor greatly in whether students dream about college and beyond. Indeed, our educational system as a whole affects children of color in ways we can only imagine. As products of this unequal school system, it is no wonder that many of my classmates internalized the dangerous myth that smart teens of color were not really "down," which meant, they were really white. Until we undo the violence of white supremacist patriarchy, young ChicaNerds will continue to be silenced, erased, and invisible. It is my hope that we hear more ChicaNerd stories that defiantly and emphatically resist racist, sexist, and classist tropes that deem our narratives unworthy.

I have not lost all hope, for in the world of stand-up comedy, I accidentally stumbled upon ChicaNerd kin. In her February 9, 2017, appearance on Conan O'Brien's show, the Chicana/Tejana comedian Cristela Alonzo graced the Los Angeles studio audience stage with her signature comedic jabs at white people and politics, including self-deprecating remarks about her romantic flops. As I listen to and watch her, what do I notice about her appearance? Is she wearing a cardigan sweater over a tee shirt that reads "Equal Pay Now," a reference to the continued fight for equal pay for women? And jeans? Are those Converse shoes I spot on her feet? Watching her on the stage, I naturally laugh at her jokes, for she is undeniably, wickedly funny. But I realize that along with appreciating her humor, what captures my rapt attention is her outfit that is so reminiscent of my daily attire of tee shirt, cardigan, jeans, and tennis shoes. To top it off, her eye glasses and vibrant-red lipstick culminate the nerdy-chic look. By donning a political tee shirt underneath a fancy-looking cardigan, but pairing those items with faded jeans and pearls, Cristela's fashion sense could be described as eclectic. However, in her strategic decision to adorn clothing items that match her progressive politics, Cristela is unapologetically declaring to viewers: "This is what a nerd looks like." Is it any wonder that I audibly gasped and then laughed when I studied her outfit, for she reminded me . . . of me!

Cristela Alonzo often casually describes herself as a nerd on her social media platforms and in her stand-up routines. On her Twitter feed, it is not uncommon for her to use this descriptor in lighthearted but validating ways. For example, in a tweet dated February 20, 2019, she posted a photo of herself with a Super Mario Brothers coffee mug, calling herself a "classy nerd." In an earlier one, she cited a photo of the popular Texas Congressman Beto O'Rourke, describing herself as a "cool nerd." I know a nerd when I see one, and it is clear to me that she takes genuine pride in claiming this aspect of her identity. What does it mean for a Chicana comedian to use her public platform to vocalize to her followers and the world that she is a nerd? For me, this is a refreshing, empowering, and subversive way to broadcast the brown, Chicana female body as a nerd, an identity we have been too comfortable aligning with white maleness. Cristela's words mean something to me. While it is possible that she is simply calling it like she sees it, perhaps not thinking too much about it, I call attention to how her seemingly casual usage of "nerd" to describe herself is profoundly meaningful and impactful for women of color and especially for Chicanas like myself. For nerds of color everywhere, especially young women nerds of color, we cannot underestimate the importance of seeing someone like us on the stage and on the page. ChicaNerds like Yolanda, Luz, Lupita, Julia, Gabi, and Marisa are all around us, if we choose to see them. In the years ahead, I have no doubt that more Chicana YA writers will publish books with characters like the ChicaNerds I adore. Until then, I will continue trying to live up to the mantra of Bomba Estéreo's brilliant song "Soy Yo," if I were only half as cool as the nerdy, delightful protagonist from their video.

Works Cited

Acevedo, Elizabeth. *The Poet X*. HarperTeen, 2018.
Alamillo, Laura, Larissa M. Mercado-Lopez, and Cristina Herrera, eds. *Voices of Resistance: Interdisciplinary Approaches to Chican@ Children's Literature*. Rowman and Littlefield, 2017.
Alberto, Lourdes. "Nations, Nationalisms, and *Indígenas*: The 'Indian' in the Chicano Revolutionary Imaginary." *Critical Ethnic Studies*, vol. 2, no. 1, 2016, pp. 107–27.
Aldama, Frederick Luis. "Introduction: The Heart and Art of Latino/a Young People's Fiction." *Latino/a Children's and Young Adult Writers on the Art of Storytelling*, edited by Frederick Luis Aldama. U of Pittsburgh P, 2018, pp. 3–25.
Alexander, Joy. "The Verse-Novel: A New Genre." *Children's Literature in Education*, vol. 36, no. 3, 2005, pp. 269–83.
Anderegg, David. *Nerds: Who They Are and Why We Need More of Them*. Jeremy P. Tarcher/Penguin, 2007.
Anzaldúa, Gloria. *Borderlands/La Frontera: The New Mestiza*. Aunt Lute, 1987, 1999.
Atkinson, Yvonne, and Michelle Pagni Stewart. "Do Dick and Jane Still Live Here? Reading Children's Literature as Ethnic Literature." *Ethnic Literary Traditions in American Children's Literature*, edited by Yvonne Atkinson and Michelle Pagni Stewart. Palgrave Macmillan, 2009, pp. 1–7.
Avendaño, Nadia. "The Chicana Subaltern and the Ethnic Female *Bildungsroman* in Patricia Santana's *Motorcycle Ride on the Sea of Tranquility*." *Letras Hispanas*, vol. 9, no. 1, 2013, pp. 66–75.
Balderrama, Francisco, and Raymond Rodríguez. *Decade of Betrayal: Mexican Repatriation in the 1930's*. U of New Mexico P, 2006.
Barajas, Heidi Lasley, and Jennifer L. Pierce. "The Significance of Race and Gender in School Success Among Latinas and Latinos in College." *Gender and Society*, vol. 15, no. 6, 2001, pp. 859–78, www.jstor.org/stable/3081906
Basu, Balaka, Katherine R. Broad, and Carrie Hintz, eds. *Contemporary Dystopian Fiction for Young Adults: Brave New Teenagers*. Routledge, 2014.
Baxley, Traci P., and Genyne Henry Boston. *(In)Visible Presence: Feminist Counternarratives of Young Adult Literature by Women of Color*. Sense Publishers, 2014.
Beauvais, Clémentine, and Maria Nikolajeva, eds. *The Edinburgh Companion to Children's Literature*. Edinburgh UP, 2017.
Bernal, Dolores Delgado. "Learning and Living Pedagogies of the Home: The Mestiza Consciousness of Chicana Students." *Qualitative Studies in Education*, vol. 14, no. 5, 2001, pp. 623–39, doi:10.1080/09518390110059838.

Works Cited

Bernal, Dolores Delgado, C. Alejandra Elenes, Francisca E. Godínez, and Sofía Villenas, eds. *Chicana/Latina Education in Everyday Life: Feminista Perspectives on Pedagogy and Epistemology*. State U of New York P, 2006.

Bettie, Julie. *Women Without Class: Girls, Race, and Identity*. U of California P, 2003.

Black Girl Nerds, www.blackgirlnerds.com. Accessed 1 July 2019.

Boffone, Trevor, and Cristina Herrera, eds. *Nerds, Goths, Geeks, and Freaks: Outsiders in Chicanx and Latinx Young Adult Literature*. UP of Mississippi, 2020.

Bost, Suzanne. *Encarnación: Illness and Body Politics in Chicana Feminist Literature*. Fordham UP, 2010.

Bronfen, Elisabeth. *Over Her Dead Body: Death, Femininity, and the Aesthetic*. Routledge, 1992.

Brown, Amy. "Waiting for Superwoman: White Female Teachers and the Construction of the 'neoliberal savior' in a New York City Public School." *Journal for Critical Education Policy Studies*, vol. 11, no. 2, 2013, pp. 123–64.

Brown, Christia Spears, and Campbell Leaper. "Latina and European American Girls' Experiences with Academic Sexism and their Self-Concepts in Mathematics and Science During Adolescence." *Sex Roles*, vol. 63, no. 11–12, 2010, pp. 860–70.

Brown-Guillory, Elizabeth, ed. "Introduction." *Women of Color: Mother-Daughter Relationships in 20th-Century Literature*. U of Texas P, 1996, pp. 1–19.

Bucholz, Mary. "The Whiteness of Nerds: Superstandard English and Racial Markedness." *Journal of Linguistic Anthropology*, vol. 11, no. 1, 2001, pp. 84–100.

———. "'Why Be Normal'? Language and Identity Practices in a Community of Nerd-Girls." *Language in Society*, vol. 28, no. 2, 1999, pp. 203–23.

Cadden, Mike. "The Verse Novel and the Question of Genre." *The ALAN Review*, vol. 39, no. 1, 2011, pp. 21–27.

Camacho, Michelle Madsen and Susan M. Lord. *The Borderlands of Education: Latinas in Engineering*. Lexington, 2013.

Canales, Viola. *The Tequila Worm*. Wendy Lamb Books, 2005.

Capshaw, Katharine. "Trauma and National Identity in Haitian-American Young Adult Literature." *Ethnic and Literary Traditions in American Children's Literature*, edited by Michelle Pagni Stewart and Yvonne Atkinson. Palgrave Macmillan, 2009, pp. 83–96.

Carlone, Heidi B. and Angela Johnson. "Understanding the Science Experiences of Successful Women of Color: Science Identity as an Analytical Lens." *Journal of Research in Science Teaching*, vol. 44, no. 8, 2007, pp. 1187–1218.

Carrillo, Juan F., and Esmeralda Rodriguez. "She Doesn't Even Act Mexican: Smartness Trespassing in the New South." *Race Ethnicity in Education*, vol. 19, no. 6, 2016, pp. 1236–46.

Castillo, Ana. *Massacre of the Dreamers: Essays on Xicanisma*. Plume, 1994.

Chávez, Denise. *Loving Pedro Infante*. Washington Square Press, 2001.

Chesney-Lind, Meda, and Katherine Irwin. *Beyond Bad Girls: Gender, Violence and Hype*. Routledge, 2008.

Cisneros, Sandra. "Guadalupe the Sex Goddess." *Goddess of the Americas/La Diosa de las Américas*, edited by Ana Castillo. Riverhead, 1996, pp. 46–51.

Coats, Karen. *The Bloomsbury Introduction to Children's and Young Adult Literature*. Bloomsbury Academic, 2018.
Conchas, Gilberto Q. *The Color of Success: Race and High-Achieving Urban Youth*. Teachers College Press, 2006.
Covarrubias, Rebecca, and Stephanie A. Fryberg. "Movin' on up (to College): First-Generation College Students' Experiences with Family Achievement Guilt." *Cultural Diversity and Ethnic Minority Psychology*, vol. 21, no. 3, 2015, pp. 420–29, http://dx.doi.org/10.1037/a0037844
Crew, Hilary S. *Is It Really Mommie Dearest? Daughter-Mother Narratives in Young Adult Fiction*. Scarecrow Press, 2000.
@cristela9. "NEW MUG ALERT! Having tea in my pipe mug because I'm a classy nerd. Mug from @thinkgeek." *Twitter*, 20 Feb. 2019, 5:41 pm, https://twitter.com/cristela9/status/1098397306758414336
@cristela9. "This is the kind of thing I do in my free time. . . 'cause I'm a cool nerd. @BetoO'Rourke posted this on his IG . . . I had to rewrite the lyrics to #Metallica's 'Unforgiven.' FYI: mid-terms in TEXAS. . .@RepBetoO'Rourke (Pass it on)." *Twitter*, 27 July 2018, 12:11 pm, https://twitter.com/cristela9/status/1022922438235975681?lang=en
Cruz, Cindy. "Toward an Epistemology of a Brown Body." *International Journal of Qualitative Studies in Education*, vol. 14, no. 5, 2001, pp. 657–69, doi:10.1080/09518390110059874.
Cummins, Amy. "Academic Agency in YA Novels by Mexican American Women Authors." *Gender(ed) Identities: Critical Readings of Gender in Children's and Young Adult Literature*, edited by Tricia Clasen and Holly Hassel. Routledge, 2016, pp. 42–58.
Cummins, Amy, and Myra Infante-Sheridan. "Establishing a Chicana Feminist *Bildungsroman* for Young Adults." *New Review of Children's Literature and Librarianship*, vol. 24, no. 1, 2018, pp. 18–39, https://doi.org/10.1080/13614541.2018.1429128
Cutler, John Alba. "Disappeared Men: Chicana/o Authenticity and the American War in Viet Nam." *American Literature*, vol. 81, no. 3, 2009, pp. 583–611.
Daut, Marlene. "Becoming Full Professor While Black." *The Chronicle of Higher Education*, 28 July 2019, www.chronicle.com/article/Becoming-Full-Professor-While/246743?cid=wcontentgrid_hp_9. Accessed 30 July 2019.
Day, Sara K. *Reading Like a Girl: Narrative Intimacy in Contemporary American Young Adult Literature*. UP of Mississippi, 2013.
Delgadillo, Theresa. "The Criticality of Latino/a Fiction in the Twenty-First Century." *American Literary History*, vol. 23, no. 3, 2011, pp. 600–24.
Delpit, Lisa. *"Multiplication Is for White People": Raising Expectations for Other People's Children*. The New Press, 2013.
Dennihy, Melissa. "Talking the Talk: Linguistic Passing in Danzy Senna's Caucasia." *MELUS*, vol. 42, no. 2, 2017, pp. 156–76, https://doi.org.hmlproxy.lib.csufresno.edu/10.1093/melus/mlx208
Dever, Carolyn. *Death and the Mother from Dickens to Freud: Victorian Fiction and the Anxiety of Origin*. Cambridge UP, 1998.
Driscoll, Catherine. *Girls: Feminine Adolescence in Popular Culture and Cultural Theory*. Columbia UP, 2002.
Eburne, Jonathan P., and Benjamin Schreier, eds. "Introduction: Working in on Nerds, Wonks, and Neocons, This Year and to Come." *The Year's Work in Nerds, Wonks, and Neocons*. Indiana UP, 2017, pp. 1–26.

Ellis, Amanda. "Chicana Teens, Zines, and Poetry Scenes: *Gabi, A Girl in Pieces* by Isabel Quintero." *Nerds, Goths, Geeks, and Freaks: Outsiders in Chicanx/Latinx Young Adult Literature*, edited by Trevor Boffone and Cristina Herrera. UP of Mississippi, 2020, pp. 15–30.

Espinoza, Dionne, María Eugenia Cotera, and Maylei Blackwell, eds. *Chicana Movidas: New Narratives of Activism and Feminism in the Movement Era*. U of Texas P, 2018.

Espiritu, Yen Le. "We Don't Sleep Around Like White Girls Do: Family, Culture, and Gender in Filipina American Lives." *Signs*, vol. 26, no. 2, 2001, pp. 415–40, https://www.jstor.org/stable/3175448.

Eysturoy, Annie O. *Daughters of Self-Creation: The Contemporary Chicana Novel*. U of New Mexico P, 1996.

Fahey, Felicia Lynne. *The Will to Heal: Psychological Recovery in the Novels of Latina Writers*. U of New Mexico P, 2007.

"Fast Facts: Race/Ethnicity of College Faculty." *National Center for Education Statistics*, https://nces.ed.gov/fastfacts/display.asp?id=61. Accessed 25 July 2019.

Fine, Michelle, and Lois Weis. *Silenced Voices and Extraordinary Conversations: Re-Imagining Schools*. Teachers College Press, 2003.

Flores, Alma Itzé. "A Chicana Mother-Daughter Spiritual Praxis." *The Chicana Motherwork Anthology: Porque Sin Madres No Hay Revolución*, edited by Cecilia Caballero et al. U of Arizona P, 2019, pp. 195–211.

Flores-González, Nilda. *School Kids/Street Kids: Identity Development in Latino Students*. Teachers College Press, 2002.

Fraustino, Lisa Rowe, and Karen Coats, eds. "Introduction: Mothers Wanted." *Mothers in Children's and Young Adult Literature*. UP of Mississippi, 2016, pp. 3–24.

Fregoso, Rosa Linda. "Homegirls, Cholas, and Pachucas in Cinema: Taking over the Public Sphere." *California History*, vol. 74, no. 3, 1995, pp. 316–27, www.jstor.org/stable/25177514. Accessed 12 July 2017.

García, Alma, ed. *Chicana Feminist Thought: The Basic Historical Writings*. Routledge, 1997.

García, Lorena. *Respect Yourself, Protect Yourself: Latina Girls and Sexual Identity*. New York UP, 2012.

García, Marilisa Jiménez. "Side-by-Side: At the Intersections of Latinx Studies and ChYALit." *The Lion and the Unicorn*, vol. 41, no. 1, 2017, pp. 113–22, https://doi.org/10.1353/uni.2017.0008

Garza, María Alicia. "Writing Large: Super-sized *Mujeres* in Chicana Literature." *Letras Femeninas*, vol. 26, no. 1–2, 2000, pp. 137–55.

Gilmore, Dorina K. Lazo. "Minority Mama: Rejecting the Mainstream Minority Model." *Mothers in Children's and Young Adult Literature*, edited by Lisa Rowe Fraustino and Karen Coats. UP of Mississippi, 2016, pp. 96–112.

Gonick, Marnina. "Between 'Girl Power' and 'Reviving Ophelia': Constituting the Neoliberal Girl Subject." *NWSA Journal*, vol. 18, no. 2, 2006, pp. 1–23.

———. "From Nerd to Popular? Re-figuring School Identities and Transformation Stories." *Seven Going on Seventeen: Tween Studies in the Culture of Girlhood*, edited by Claudia Mitchell and Jacqueline Reid-Walsh. Peter Lang, 2005, pp. 46–62.

González, Bárbara Renaud. *Golondrina, why did you leave me?* U of Texas P, 2009.
González, John Morán, ed. *Cambridge Companion to Latina/o American Literature.* Cambridge UP, 2016.
González, Rigoberto. *The Mariposa Club.* Tincture, 2009, 2010.
González, Tanya, and Eliza Rodríguez y Gibson. *Humor and Latina/o Camp in Ugly Betty: Funny Looking.* Lexington Books, 2015.
Goodwin, Sarah Webster, and Elisbeth Bronfen, eds. *Death and Representation.* Johns Hopkins UP, 1993.
Grande, Reyna. *Dancing with Butterflies.* Washington Square Press, 2009.
Griffin, Christine. "Good Girls, Bad Girls: Anglocentrism and Diversity in the Constitution of Contemporary Girlhood." *All About the Girl: Culture, Power, and Identity*, edited by Anita Harris. Routledge, 2004, pp. 29–43.
Guerrero, Aurora, director. *Mosquita y Mari.* Wolfe Video, 2013.
Gutíerrez y Muhs, Gabriella, et al., eds. *Presumed Incompetent: The Intersections of Race and Class for Women in Academia.* Utah State UP, 2012.
Harris, Adam. "Harvard Won This Round, but Affirmative Action Is Weak." *The Atlantic*, 2 Oct. 2019, www.theatlantic.com/education/archive/2019/10/harvard-wins-affirmative-action-case-plaintiff-will-appeal/599281/. Accessed 11 Oct. 2019.
Harris, Anita, ed. *All About the Girl: Culture, Power, and Identity.* Routledge, 2004.
Hernández, Jo Ann Yolanda. *White Bread Competition.* Piñata Books, 1997.
Herrera, Brian Eugenio. " 'But Do We Have the Actors For That?' Some Principles of Practice for Staging Latinx Plays in a University Theatre Context." *Theatre Topics*, vol. 27, no. 1, 2017, pp. 23–35, https://doi.org/10.1353/tt.2017.0004
Herrera, Cristina. "Cinco Hermanitas: Myth and Sisterhood in Guadalupe García McCall's *Summer of the Mariposas.*" *Children's Literature*, vol. 44, 2016, pp. 96–114.
———. *Contemporary Chicana Literature: (Re)Writing the Maternal Script.* Cambria Press, 2014.
———. "Not-So-Sweet *Quince*: Teenage Angst and Mother-Daughter Strife in Belinda Acosta's *Damas, Dramas, and Ana Ruiz.*" *Voices of Resistance: Interdisciplinary Approaches to Chican@ Children's Literature*, edited by Laura Alamillo, Larissa Mercado-López, and Cristina Herrera, Rowman and Littlefield, 2018, pp. 77–90.
———. "Seeking Refuge *Under the Mesquite*: Nature Imagery in Guadalupe García McCall's Verse Novel." *Children's Literature Association Quarterly*, vol. 44, no. 2, 2019, pp. 194–209.
Herrera-Sobek, María. *The Mexican Corrido: A Feminist Analysis.* Indiana UP, 1990.
———. "The Politics of Rape: Sexual Transgression in Chicana Fiction." *Chicana Creativity and Criticism: New Frontiers in American Literature*, edited by María Herrera-Sobek and Helena María Viramontes. The U of New Mexico P, 1996, pp. 245–56.
Huaco-Nuzum, Carmen. "Orale Patriarchy: Hasta cuando corazón will you remain el gallo macho de mi familia?" *The Chicana/o Cultural Studies Reader*, edited by Angie Chabram-Dernersesian. Routledge, 2006, pp. 261–68.

Hughey, Matthew W. *The White Savior Film: Content, Critics, and Consumption*. Temple UP, 2014.

Hurtado, Aída. "The Politics of Sexuality in the Gender Subordination of Chicanas." *Living Chicana Theory*, edited by Carla Trujillo. Third Woman Press, 1998, pp. 383–428.

James, Kathryn. *Death, Gender and Sexuality in Contemporary Adolescent Literature*. Routledge, 2009.

Johnston, Jeremy. "'Maybe I am Fixed': Disciplinary Practices and the Politics of Therapy in Young Adult Literature." *Children's Literature Association Quarterly*, vol. 44, no. 3, 2019, pp. 310–31.

Jones, Heather. "Being Weird and Black Doesn't Mean You're Interested in Being White." *Wear Your Voice: Intersectional Feminist Media*, 18 May 2016. Web. 22 July 2016.

Keeling, Kara K., and Scott T. Pollard, eds. *Critical Approaches to Food in Children's Literature*. Routledge, 2009.

Kendall, Lori. "Nerd Nation: Images of Nerds in US Popular Culture." *International Journal of Cultural Studies*, vol., 2, no. 2, 1999, pp. 260–83.

———. "'White and Nerdy': Computers, Race, and the Nerd Stereotype." *Journal of Popular Culture*, vol. 44, no. 3, 2011, pp. 505–24.

Kinney, David A. "From Nerds to Normals: The Recovery of Identity among Adolescents from Middle School to High School." *Sociology of Education*, vol. 66, no. 1, 1993, pp. 21–40.

Kokkola, Lydia. *Fictions of Adolescent Carnality: Sexy Sinners and Delinquent Deviants*. John Benjamins Publishing Company, 2013.

Kwan, Samantha. "Navigating Public Spaces: Gender, Race, and Body Privilege in Everyday Life." *Feminist Formations*, vol. 22, no. 2, 2010, pp. 144–66.

Ladish, Lorraine C. "In Best-selling 'I Am Not Your Perfect Mexican Daughter,' Erika Sánchez hits crucial chord." *NBC News*, 7 May 2018. Nbcnews.com

Lafuente, Elia Michelle. "Nationhood, Struggle, and Identity." *Contemporary Adolescent Literature and Culture: The Emergent Adult*, edited by Mary Hilton and Maria Nikolajeva. Ashgate, 2012, pp. 33–45.

Larkin, Susan. "Awash in Illusion: The Search for Identity and Agency in Adolescent Literature." *Broadening Critical Boundaries in Children's and Young Adult Literature and Culture*, edited by Amie A. Doughty. Cambridge Scholars Publishing, 2018, pp. 160–72.

Leaper, Campbell, Timea Farkas, and Christia Spears Brown. "Adolescent Girls' Experiences and Gender-Related Beliefs in Relation to Their Motivation in Math/Science and English." *Journal of Youth and Adolescence*, vol. 41, no. 3, 2012, pp. 268–82.

Lesnik-Oberstein, Karín, ed. *Children's Literature: New Approaches*. Palgrave Macmillan, 2004.

Lipkin, Elline. *Girls' Studies*. Seal Press, 2009.

López, Laura Marie. *Confronting Predators and Shadow Beasts: Representations of Working-Poor Chicanas in Contemporary Young Adult Literature*. Diss. University of Texas, San Antonio, 2012. UMI, Ann Arbor, 2012.

López, Lorraine. *The Gifted Gabaldón Sisters*. Grand Central Publishing, 2008.

López, Tiffany Ana, ed. "Introduction." *Growing Up Chicana/o*. Avon Books, 1993.

———. "Reading Trauma and Violence in U.S. Latina/o Children's Literature." *Ethnic and Literary Traditions in American Children's Literature*, edited by Michelle Pagni Stewart and Yvonne Atkinson. Palgrave Macmillan, 2009, pp. 205–26.
López, Vera, and Meda Chesney-Lind. "Latina Girls Speak Out: Stereotypes, Gender and Relationship Dynamics." *Latino Studies*, vol. 12, no. 4, 2014, pp. 527–49, doi:10.1057/lst.2014.5.
Marshall, Elizabeth. *Graphic Girlhoods: Visualizing Education and Violence*. Routledge, 2018.
Mathison, Ymitri, ed. "Introduction: Growing Up Asian American in Young Adult Fiction." *Growing Up Asian American in Young Adult Fiction*. UP of Mississippi, 2018, pp. 3–21.
McCall, Guadalupe García. *All the Stars Denied*. Lee and Low, 2018.
———. *Shame the Stars*. Tu Books, 2016.
———. *Under the Mesquite*. Lee and Low, 2011.
McCallum, Robyn. *Ideologies of Identity in Adolescent Fiction: The Dialogic Construction of Subjectivity*. Routledge, 1999.
McLennan, Rachael. *Adolescence, America, and Postwar Fiction: Developing Figures*. Palgrave Macmillan, 2009.
Medina, Carmen. "When *Jerry Springer* Visits Your Classroom: Teaching Latina Literature in a Contested Ground." *Theory Into Practice*, vol. 40, no. 3, 2001, pp. 198–204, https://doi.org/10.1207/s15430421tip4003_8
Medina, Meg. *Yaqui Delgado Wants to Kick Your Ass*. Candlewick Press, 2013.
Mendoza, Hadrian, Akihiko Masuda, and Kevin M. Swartout. "Mental Health Stigma and Self-Concealment as Predictors of Help-Seeking Attitudes among Latina/o College Students in the United States." *International Journal for the Advancement of Counselling*, vol. 37, no. 3, 2015, pp. 207–22.
Mercado-López, Larissa M. "Entre Tejana y Chicana: Tracing Proto-Chicana Identity and Consciousness in Tejana Young Adult Fiction and Poetry." In *Voices of Resistance: Interdisciplinary Approaches to Chican@ Children's Literature*, edited by Laura Alamillo, Larissa M. Mercado-López, and Cristina Herrera. Rowman and Littlefield, 2018, pp. 3–15.
Millán, Isabel. "Contested Children's Literature: Que(e)ries into Chicana and Central American *Autofantasías*." *Signs: Journal of Women and Culture in Society*, vol. 41, no. 1, 2015, pp. 199–224, doi:10.1086/681919.
Moraga, Cherríe. "La Güera." *Loving in the War Years: Lo que nunca pasó por sus labios*, edited by Cherríe Moraga. South End Press, 2000.
Moya, Paula M. L. "Resisting the Interpretive Schema of the Novel Form: Rereading Sandra Cisneros's *The House on Mango Street*." *Bridges, Borders, Breaks: History, Narrative, and Nation in Twenty-First Century Chicana/o Literary Criticism*, edited by William Orchard and Yolanda Padilla. U of Pittsburgh P, 2016, pp. 121–38.
Museus, Samuel D., and Peter N. Kiang. "Deconstructing the Model Minority Myth and How It Contributes to the Invisible Minority Reality in Higher Education Research." *New Directions for Institutional Research*, no. 142, 2009, pp. 5–15.
Neseth, Hans, Todd Savage, and Rachel Navarro. "Examining the Impact of Acculturation and Perceived Social Support on Mathematics Achievement

Among Latino/a High School Students." *The California School Psychologist*, vol. 14, no. 1, 2009, pp. 59–69.

Nikolajeva, Maria. *Power, Voice and Subjectivity in Literature for Young Readers*. Routledge, 2010.

Noble, Diana J. *Evangelina Takes Flight*. Piñata Books, 2017.

Ochoa, Gilda. *Academic Profiling: Latinos, Asian Americans, and the Achievement Gap*. U of Minnesota P, 2013.

Opam, Kwame. "On 'The Good Place,' Chidi Redefines the Black Nerd." *The New York Times*, 24 Sept. 2019, www.nytimes.com/2019/09/24/arts/television/the-good-place.html?fbclid=IwAR2vk75LRzmE3MkMBzmQh4f29nLwvLo5sXbWUTAQo74_RJwZT5rFmrlybU. Accessed 25 Sept. 2019.

———. "Transformational Caring: Mexican American Women Redefining Mothering and Education." *Latina/Chicana Mothering*, edited by Dorsía Smith Silva. Demeter Press, 2011, pp. 104–19.

Ortner, Sherry B. "'Burned Like a Tattoo': High School Social Categories and 'American Culture'." *Ethnography*, vol. 3, no. 2, 2002, pp. 115–48.

Payne, Marissa. "At age 26, Ravens' John Urschel retires from NFL to pursue PhD in math at MIT." *Washington Post*, 27 July 2017.

Pérez, Ashley Hope. *Out of Darkness*. Carolrhoda Lab, 2015.

———. *What Can(t)Wait*. Carolrhoda Lab, 2011.

Pérez, Celia C. *The First Rule of Punk*. Viking, 2017.

Pérez, Emma. *The Decolonial Imaginary: Writing Chicanas Into History*. Indiana UP, 1999.

Piña-Watson, Brandy, and Linda G. Castillo. "The Role of the Perceived Parent-Child Relationship on Latina Adolescent Depression." *Child and Adolescent Social Work Journal*, vol. 32, no. 4, 2015, pp. 309–15.

Pomerantz, Shauna, and Rebecca Raby. "'Oh, She's *So* Smart': Girls' Complex Engagement with Post/Feminist Narratives of Academic Success." *Gender and Education*, vol. 23, no. 5, 2011, pp. 549–64, doi:10.1080/09540253.2010.538014.

———. *Smart Girls: Success, School, and the Myth of Post- Feminism*. U of California Press, 2017.

Quick, Catherine S. "'Meant to be Huge': Obesity and Body Image in Young Adult Novels." *The ALAN Review*, vol. 35, no. 2, 2008, pp. 54–61, https://doi.org/10.21061/alan.v35i2.a.8

Quintana, Alvina. *Home Girls: Chicana Literary Voices*. Temple UP, 1996.

Quintero, Isabel. *Gabi, A Girl in Pieces*. Cinco Puntos, 2014.

———. "A Mirror in Hand, but Make It Spanglish." *English Journal*, vol. 109, no. 1, 2019, pp. 123–26.

Ramírez, Pablo C., and Margarita Jiménez-Silva. "The Intersectionality of Culturally Responsive Teaching and Performance Poetry: Validating Secondary Latino Youth and Their Community." *Multicultural Perspectives*, vol. 17, no. 2, 2015, pp. 87–92, doi:10.1080/15210960.2015.1022448.

Reid, Korin. "Gender, Race, and Stereotypes in 'Scorpion,' 'Silicon Valley' and 'The Big Bang Theory'." *Model View Culture: A magazine about technology, culture and diversity*, 27 Apr. 2015. Accessed 10 Sept. 2016.

Reynolds, Kimberley. *Radical Children's Literature: Future Visions and Aesthetic Transformations in Juvenile Fiction*. Palgrave Macmillan, 2007.

Rincón, Belinda Linn. *Bodies at War: Genealogies of Militarism in Chicana Literature and Culture*. U of Arizona P, 2017.

Rodríguez, R. Joseph. *Teaching Culturally Sustaining and Inclusive Young Adult Literature*. Routledge, 2019.

Rodriguez, Sarah L., et al. "Becoming *La Ingeniera*: Examining the Engineering Identity Development of Latina Undergraduate Students." *Journal of Latinos in Education*, 2019, pp. 1–20.

Rodríguez, Sonia Alejandra. "Conocimiento Narratives: Creative Acts and Healing in Latinx Children and Young Adult Literature." *Children's Literature*, vol. 47, 2019, pp. 9–29.

———. "School Fights: Resisting Oppression in the Classroom in Gloria Velásquez's Latina/o Young Adult Novel *Juanita Fights the School Board*." *Children's Literature in Education*, vol. 49, no. 1, 2018, pp. 61–72.

Román, Elda María. "Jesus, When Did You Become So Bourgeois, Huh? Status Panic in Chicana/o Cultural Production." *Aztlán: A Journal of Chicano Studies*, vol. 38, no. 2, 2013, pp. 11–40.

Rubenstein, Roberta. "House Mothers and Haunted Daughters: Shirley Jackson and Female Gothic." *Tulsa Studies in Women's Literature*, vol. 15, no. 2, 1996, pp. 309–31.

Sáenz, Benjamin Alire. *Aristotle and Dante Discover the Secrets of the Universe*. Simon and Schuster, 2012.

Sánchez, Erika. *I Am Not Your Perfect Mexican Daughter*. Alfred A. Knopf, 2017.

Santana, Patricia. *Ghosts of El Grullo*. U of New Mexico P, 2008.

———. *Motorcycle Ride on the Sea of Tranquility*. U of New Mexico P, 2002.

Santos, Adrianna M. "Broken Open: Writing, Healing, and Affirmation in Isabel Quintero's *Gabi, A Girl in Pieces* and Erika L. Sánchez's *I Am Not Your Perfect Mexican Daughter*." *Nerds, Goths, Geeks, and Freaks: Outsiders in Chicanx/Latinx Young Adult Literature*, edited by Trevor Boffone and Cristina Herrera. UP of Mississippi, 2020, pp. 45–59.

Saxton, Ruth O. *The Girl: Constructions of the Girl in Contemporary Fiction by Women*. St. Martin's, 1998.

Serrato, Phillip. "Promise and Peril: The Gendered Implications of Pat Mora's *Pablo's Tree* and Ana Castillo's *My Daughter, My Son, The Eagle, The Dove*." *Children's Literature*, vol. 38, 2010, pp. 133–52.

Socolovsky, Maya. "Narrative and Traumatic Memory in Denise Chávez's *Face of an Angel*." *MELUS*, vol. 28, no. 4, 2003, pp. 187–205.

Soto, Gary. *Nerdlandia*. Puffin Books, 1999.

Stringer, Sharon A. *Conflict and Connection: The Psychology of Young Adult Literature*. Boynton/Cook Publishers, 1997.

Suhr-Sytsma, Mandy. *Self-Determined Stories: The Indigenous Reinvention of Young Adult Literature*. Michigan State U, 2019.

Téllez, Michelle. "Mi Madre, Mi Hija y Yo: Chicana Mothering through Memory, Culture and Place." *Chicana/Latina Mothering*, edited by Dorsía Smith Silva. Demeter Press, 2011, pp. 57–67.

Titone, Connie. "Educating the White Teacher as Ally." *White Reign: Deploying Whiteness in America*, edited by Joe L. Kincheloe, Shirley R. Steinberg, Nelson M. Rodríguez, and Ronald E. Chennault. St. Martin's Griffin, 1998, pp. 159–75.

Tomasetto, Carlo, Francesca Romana Alparone, and Mara Cadinu. "Girls' Math Performance Under Stereotype Threat: The Moderating Role of

Mothers' Gender Stereotypes." *Developmental Psychology*, vol. 47, no. 4, 2011, pp. 943–49.

Tovar, Virgie. *You Have the Right to Remain Fat*. Feminist Press, 2018.

Trites, Roberta Seelinger. *Disturbing the Universe: Power and Repression in Adolescent Literature*. U of Iowa P, 2000.

———. *Twenty-First Century Feminisms in Children's and Adolescent Literature*. UP of Mississippi, 2018.

———. *Waking Sleeping Beauty: Feminist Voices in Children's Novels*. U of Iowa P, 1997.

Valenzuela, Angela. *Subtractive Schooling: U.S.-Mexican Youth and the Politics of Caring*. State U of New York P, 1999.

Vega, Desiree, James L. Moore, III, and Antoinette H. Miranda. "In Their Own Words: Perceived Barriers to Achievement by African American and Latino High School Students." *American Secondary Education*, vol. 43, no. 3, 2015, pp. 36–59.

Vickroy, Laurie. *Trauma and Survival in Contemporary Fiction*. U of Virginia P, 2002.

Vigil, Ariana. *War Echoes: Gender and Militarization in U.S. Latina/o Cultural Production*. Rutgers UP, 2014.

Villa, Raúl Homero. *Barrio-Logos: Space and Place in Urban Chicano Literature and Culture*. U of Texas P, 2000.

Villenas, Sofía. "Pedagogical Moments in the Borderlands: Latina Mothers Teaching and Learning." *Chicana/Latina Education in Everyday Life: Feminista Perspectives on Pedagogy and Epistemology*, edited by Dolores Delgado Bernal, C. Alejandra Elenes, Francisca E. Godínez, and Sofía Villenas. State U of New York P, 2006, pp. 147–59.

Walker, Sheila J. *African American Girls and the Construction of Identity: Class, Race, and Gender*. Lexington Books, 2018.

Ward, Janie Victoria, and Beth Cooper Benjamin. "Women, Girls, and the Unfinished Work of Connection: A Critical Review of American Girls' Studies." *All About the Girl: Power, and Identity*, edited by Anita Harris. Routledge, 2004, pp. 15–27.

Weheliye, Alexander G. "Post-Integration Blues: Black Geeks and Afro-Diasporic Humanism." *Contemporary African American Literature: The Living Canon*, edited by Lovalerie King and Shirley Moody-Turner. Indiana UP, 2013, pp. 213–34.

White, Barbara A. *Growing Up Female: Adolescent Girlhood in American Fiction*. Greenwood Press, 1985.

Wickham, Anastasia. "It Is All in Your Head: Mental Illness in Young Adult Literature." *Journal of Popular Culture*, vol. 51, no. 1, 2018, pp. 10–25.

Wissman, Kelly. "'Spinning Themselves into Poetry': Images of Urban Adolescent Writers in Two Novels for Young Adults." *Children's Literature in Education*, vol. 40, no. 2, 2009, pp. 149–67.

Yarbro-Bejarano, Yvonne. "Sexuality and Chicana/o Studies: Toward a Theoretical Paradigm for the Twenty-First Century." *The Chicana/o Cultural Studies Reader*, edited by Angie Chabram-Dernersesian. Routledge, 2006, pp. 224–32.

———. *The Wounded Heart: Writing on Cherríe Moraga*. U of Texas P, 2001.

Younger, Beth. "Pleasure, Pain, and the Power of Being Thin: Female Sexuality in Young Adult Literature." *NWSA Journal*, vol. 15, no. 2, 2003, pp. 45–56.

Zentella, Ana C. "TWB (Talking while Bilingual): Linguistic Profiling of Latina/os, and Other Linguistic Torquemadas." *Latino Studies*, vol. 12, no. 4, 2014, pp. 620–35, http://dx.doi.org.hmlproxy.lib.csufresno.edu/10.1057/lst.2014.63.

Zepeda, Gwendolyn. *Houston, We Have a Problema*. Grand Central Publishing, 2009.

Index

academic achievement: barriers to 40; familial support for 28
academic profiling 29–30
Acevedo, Elizabeth 71
achievement gap 29
acting white 75–77, 107–8, 111; see also "trying to be white"
activism 47–48, 51–52, 122, 127, 130
affirmative action 44
African American girlhood 33
African American YA writers 9
Alarcón, Norma 8, 66
Alberto, Lourdes 129
Aldama, Frederick Luis 11–12
Alexander, Joy 71
Alonzo, Cristela 16, 145–46
Anderegg, David 22
anthologies 11–12
Anzaldúa, Gloria 79, 107
appropriateness of Chicana college aspirations 56, 61
artistic resistance path 52–53
Asian Americans 29–30
Asian American YA literature 10
assimilation pressure 71, 77–79, 95, 135
Atkinson, Yvonne 12
"at risk" label 20, 34–35
authenticity claims 76–77
autonomy 116
Avendaño, Nadia 123

Barajas, Heidi Lasley 28–29
belonging 126
Benjamin, Beth Cooper 33–34
Bernal, Dolores Delgado 133–34
Bettie, Julie 68
Beyond Bad Girls (Chesney-Lind and Irwin) 35

bildungsroman study 72
birthright citizenship 51
black nerds 23–25
black/white relations 56–57
blerd (black nerd) 16
bodily self-love 111–12, 114
body privilege 112
Bomba Estéreo 19, 23
Borderlands/La Frontera (Anzaldúa) 107
Bost, Suzanne 101
Brown, Amy 57
Brown, Christia Spears 57–58
Brown-Guillory, Elizabeth 90
Bucholtz, Mary 22, 23, 25–26
bullying 43, 45–46, 144

Cadden, Mike 71
Canales, Viola 41–42
Capshaw, Katherine 91
Carrillo, Juan F. 27–28
Catholicism 136
Chesney-Lind, Meda 34, 35, 66
Chicana adolescents: fictional portrayals of 2; as intelligent subjects 6
Chicana *bildungsroman* study 72
Chicana cholas 35
Chicana feminism 2, 41, 67, 94, 106, 110, 118; see also ChicaNerd feminism
Chicana feminist knowledge production 52
Chicana identity: fluidity of 8; stereotypes 3
Chicana nerds *see* nerds
Chicana YA texts: benchmark anthologies 11–12; as established genre 2–3; expanding existing nerd

discourses 16; literary canon 11–13; women nerds of color 25–26
ChicaNerd feminism 52, 80, 82, 101–2, 107, 110, 118; *see also* Chicana feminism
ChicaNerd identity 2; combatting myths 11; fatness 113; high school setting for 6; library and 132; maturity and honesty in 64; shaped around rebellion 89; *see also* nerds
Chicano Movement 47–48
Chicanx community: "at risk" label plaguing 35; as complex 46; high expectations for girls 13–14, 39; sexism within 48; solidarity in 40, 46; support from 38, 47–48
Chicanx cultural heritage 17
Chicanx revolutionary ideology 129
Coats, Karen 10
coconut (derogatory slur) 45, 54n4
code-switching 117
colonization 42
color-blind society myth 56–57
community obligations 48
computer savviness 21
Conchas, Gilberto Q. 29
Covarrubias, Rebecca 60
Crew, Hilary S. 90
critical witnessing theory 91
Cruz, Cindy 73–74
Cummins, Amy 7, 72, 77, 79–80, 106
Cutler, John Alba 128

Daut, Marlene 141
Decolonial Imaginary, The (Pérez) 51–52
deportations 50–52
depression 100–1
Dever, Carolyn 81, 132
Dinnihy, Melissa 78
double standards 84, 106, 110, 116, 118, 124
Driscoll, Catherine 31

Eburne, Jonathan P. 22–23
educational stereotypes 26–31
education/educational attainment: academically segregated environments 27; deficit ideology 28–29; denial of equal access 41; equal access myth 63; ethnic isolation in honors classes 20–21; ethnicity intersecting with gender 57–58; familial support 28; myths around 73; parents' refusal to support 59; as priority 7; racism in 44; racist textbooks 42; school-kid identity 31; STEM domains 57–58; white teachers 4; *see also* teacher/student dynamic
education studies 31
Ellis, Amanda 116
emerging writer, thematic use of 71–72
engineering identity development 58–59
ethnic identity 77
ethnic isolation 21
Eysturoy, Annie 72

Fahey, Felicia Lynn 102
families: children's education myth 73; as educational models 69; education support from 67; gender double standard 123–24
family achievement guilt 60–61
Family Matters (television show) 24–25
family obligation 47, 64, 140
fathers: connecting with daughters 102–3; gendered double standards of 84–85; machista stance 124; sexist attitude 60, 65, 85, 123–24; strong presence of 81–82; *see also* families; mothers; parents; patriarchy
fatness 112, 118
female nerds, in popular culture 23–26
first generation student of color 60–63, 69, 93–94, 103, 126–29, 134–35
Flores, Alma Itzé 10–11
Flores-González, Nilda 30–31
forgiveness, as strength 136–37
Fraustino, Lisa Rowe 10
Fregoso, Rosalinda 35
Fryberg, Stephanie A. 60–61

Gabi, A Girl in Pieces (Quintero) 89; overview 15, 105–6; protagonist's struggle 105; sexual curiosity 109–11; teen pregnancy 108–9; white shaming 107–8
García, Lorena 90–91, 95, 108
García McCall, Guadalupe *see Under the Mesquite* (García McCall)

Index

Garza, María Alicia 114
Garza, Sandra D. 114
gender bias in institutions 34
gendered double standards *see* double standards
gendered obligations/expectations 41, 46–47, 71, 84, 89
gender expectations 14–15
gender subordination 111, 122, 128
Ghosts of El Grullo (Santana) 15, 121
girlhood studies 31, 32–33
girl power rhetoric 32, 36
Girls' Studies (Lipkin) 32
Gonick, Marnina 26, 31
González, Rigoberto 9, 36n4
González, Sarai 19
good girl ideology 35, 66, 89–95
Good Place, The (television show) 24–25
Google classroom exercise 26–27, 34
Griffin, Christine 33
Guerrero, Aurora 55–56

Haitian American women's adolescent literature 91
Harper, William Jackson 24–25
Harris, Anita 32–33
Harvard University 44
Hernández, Jo Ann Yolanda *see White Bread Competition* (Hernández)
Herrera, Brian Eugenio 79
Herrera-Sobek, María 111, 136
hipsters 22–23
home spaces: as ChicaNerd identity foundation 83; as first classroom 73; pedagogies of the home 133–34
House on Mango Street, The (Cisneros) 40
Hughey, Matthew W. 56–57
Hurtado, Aída 69, 116

I Am Not Your Perfect Mexican Daughter (Sánchez) 14–15
idealized motherhood 68–69
identity negotiation 45–46
immigration 96–97
imposter syndrome 6, 126
Indigenous YA literature 12
Infante-Sheridan, Myra 7, 72, 77, 79–80
institutionalized racism 38, 41, 50
internalized racism 29

Irwin, Katherine 35
isolation 65, 89, 99, 115, 127–29

Jiménez García, Marilisa 11, 12
Jones, Heather 24

Kendall, Lori 21–22
Kwan, Samantha 112

Lafuente, Elia Michelle 91
Lazo Gilmore, Dorina K. 10
Leaper, Campbell 57–58
light-skinned Chicana 17, 106, 114–15, 129–30
light-skin privilege 129–30
linguistic passing 78–79
linguistic profiling 76–77
linguistic terrorism 79
Lipkin, Elline 32, 35
López, Josefina 145
López, Laura 10
López, Tiffany Ana 1, 31, 91
López, Vera 34, 66

male-centered novels 9
male nerds of color 21
male sexual violence 119, 123
Marianismo 136
Mariposa Club, The (González) 36n4
Marshall, Elizabeth 5
mass deportations 50–52
maternal loss 80–82, 86
maternal nerd legacy 15, 39
maternal relationships: as empowerment source 89–90; in *Gabi, A Girl in Pieces* 106; as guiding force 10–11; significance of loss 80–82; support and 120; in *White Bread Competition* 49; *see also* mother/daughter relationships
McCall, Guadalupe García 70
McLennan, Rachael 7, 32
MEChA chapter 127–30
Mechista activism 127–30
Medina, Carmen 75
mental illness 99–101
Mercado-López, Larissa M. 42, 86, 116–17
meritocracy myth 31–32
Meshica heritage 129
Mexican/Chicanx history, women's role in 51–52

Mexican identity 15, 76, 78, 86, 105, 114
Mexican immigration families *see* families
Misadventures of Awkward Black Girl (Rae) 36–37n6
mobility, importance of 68
model minority myth 29–30
Moraga, Cherríe 114
Mosquita y Mari (film) 55–56
mother/daughter pedagogies 10–11
mother/daughter relationships: author's story 142–43; not idealizing 83–84; strained efforts 102; *Under the Mesquite* 74, 83–84; *What Can(t) Wait* 68; *White Bread Competition* 49–53; *see also* maternal relationships; mothers
motherlessness 80–82, 130–31
mothers: academic achievement 134; as cultural transmitters 107; as educational models 69; loss of 80–82; role of 134; white shaming daughters 108; *see also* fathers; parents
Motorcycle Ride on the Sea of Tranquility (Santana) 5, 121, 122
multiple narrative voices 40–41

national identity 91, 129
nerd identity 9, 21
Nerdlandia (Soto) 37n8
nerds: asexual stereotype 109; as betrayal to ethnicity 20; black 16, 23–25; blerd 16; classifying characters as 6–7; cool identity of 22–23; defined 13; description of 2; labeling 20; lacking athletic prowess 22; male nerds of color 21; outsiderness and 22–23; stereotypes of 6, 7; traditional attire 22–23; visibility of 23
nerd visibility, power of 19
Nightly Show, The (Comedy Central series) 16
novels in verse 40–41

Obama, Barack 96
obligation: to community 48; to family 47, 64, 140; gendered 46–47, 89
Ochoa, Gilda 29–30

Opam, Kwame 24
oppression: as cultural tyranny 107; food as tool for 45–46; systemic 41–43
otherness 44
outsiderness 22–23, 59, 93, 99, 126, 144–45

parental hierarchy 84
parents: as educators 73–74; fear of intellectual achievement 65; gender/sexuality views 107; refusal to support educational pursuits 59; *see also* families; fathers; mother/daughter relationships; mothers
patriarchy: home environments governed by 124; resistance to 125; *see also* fathers
pedagogies of the home 133–34
Pedro Páramo (Rulfo) 131
peer pressures 25–26, 98
peer relationships 20–21, 75, 89
Pérez, Ashley Hope 3–4; *see also What Can(t) Wait* (Pérez)
Pérez, Emma 51–52
Pierce, Jennifer L. 28–29
poet identity 115–17
poetry: code-switching 117; as empowering 120; voicing pain through 116
Poet X, The (Acevedo) 71
Pomerantz, Shauna 32
"Post-Integration Blues" (Weheliye) 23–24
power structures 57, 71–72, 105, 124
Presumed Incompetent (Gutíerrez y Muhs et al.) 141–42
privacy 94–95
protagonists: Betty Súarez 25; community support for 39–40; defined 3; defining themselves 7; familial support for 39–40; feelings of loss 130–31; *Gabi, A Girl in Pieces* 105; snarky voice 88, 103; *Under the Mesquite* 3; *What Can(t) Wait* 3; *White Bread Competition* 3; as writers 72
psychological recoveries 102

queer Chicano masculinities 9
Quintero, Isabel: "A Mirror in Hand" 139; *see also Gabi, A Girl in Pieces* (Quintero)

Raby, Rebecca 32
racial hierarchy 45–46
racial profiling 29
racism: continued legacy 50; educational 44; institutionalized 38, 41, 50; internalized 29; in schools 38; white liberal 97; white savior 96
racist textbooks 42
Rae, Issa 36–37n6
rape/rape culture: brutalities of 64–65; defined 110; failure to punish male sexual violence 119; *Gabi, A Girl in Pieces* 89–90, 110; rage against 118; rejection of 110; *see also* trauma
Real Women Have Curves (play) 145
representation 144–45
Reynolds, Kimberley 99–100
Rodriguez, Esmeralda 27–28
Rodríguez, R. Joseph 16, 21
Rodriguez, Sarah L. 58–59
Rodríguez, Sonja Alejandra 42, 115, 119
Rodríguez y Gibson, Eliza 25
Román, Elda María 61, 76
Ruiz de García, Tomasa 86
Rulfo, Juan 131

Sáenz, Benjamin Alire 9
Sánchez, Erika 88; *see also I Am Not Your Perfect Mexican Daughter* (Sánchez)
Santana, Patricia 5, 121; *see also Ghosts of El Grullo* (Santana)
Santos, Adrianna 100
scholastic achievement *see* academic achievement
"School Fights" (Rodríguez) 42
schoolgirl 5, 60, 64
school-kid identity 31
schools: gender bias in 34; hindering academic achievement 31; institutionalized racism in 38; racial politics in 73, 75; Students for Fair Admissions 44; *see also* education/educational attainment; teacher/student dynamic
Schreier, Benjamin 22–23
self-acceptance 115, 119, 121
self-discovery 80
self-harm 99–100
self-inflicted violence 91
self-love 111–12, 116–17, 123

sexism: challenging 60; in Chicano Movement 47–48; in Chicanx community 48; fathers and 60, 65, 85, 123–24; feminist critiques of 48, 54n5; good girl ideology and 35; as in the past 32; in publishing world 88, 103; STEM achievement and 58
sexual curiosity 109–11
sexual double standards *see* double standards
sexuality, attitudes on 89–90
sexual promiscuity 114–15
shame 113
silence, as perpetrator of pain 92
smartness, defined 27
smartness trespassing 27–28
social understanding 80
Socolovsky, Maya 92
Soto, Gary 37n8
"Soy Yo" (song) 19
STEM industry 22, 57–59
stereotypes: asexual nerds 109; Chicana identity 3; ChicaNerd texts refusing 3; of Chicanx underachievement 17; coconut (slur) 45, 54n4; computer savviness 21; confrontation with prominent 8; educational 26–31; Google exercise 26–27, 34; of nerds 6, 7, 56; patriarchal-encoded expectations 9; power of 27; sexual availability 66
Stewart, Michelle Pagni 12
Stringer, Sharon A. 100
structural inequality, girl-empowerment rhetoric and 32
Students for Fair Admissions 44
Subtractive Schooling (Valenzuela) 29
Suhr-Sytsma, Mandy 12
suicide 99, 100
systemic oppression 41–43

"talking like a white girl" 98
teachers: Hispanic faculty 142; racist and sexist hostility 141; tenure-track position 141; "white savior" trope 4
teacher/student dynamic: assimilation pressure 71, 77–78; education stereotypes and 29; tense relationship in 117–18; in *Under the Mesquite* 4–5; white savior myth 56–57

Teaching Culturally Sustaining and Inclusive Young Adult Literature (Rodríguez) 16
teen motherhood 66
teen pregnancy 108–9
teen sexuality 108
Tequila Worm, The (Canales) 41–42
Texas landscape 85–86
Titone, Connie 96
Tomás Rivera Mexican American Children's Book Award 38–39
Tovar, Virgie 111–12
trauma: deportations as 50–51; gendered legacies of 100; national identity and 91; white supremacy violence and 50; *see also* rape/rape culture
Trites, Roberta Seelinger 39, 49
"trying to be white" 20, 23–25, 27–28, 75; *see also* acting white

Ugly Betty (television show) 25
unbelonging 126; *see also* outsiderness
underachievement 17
Under the Mesquite (García McCall): assimilation pressure 77–78; linguistic passing 78–79; linguistic terrorism 79; motherlessness 80–82; overview 14, 70; protagonist 3; teacher/student dynamic 4–5; verse genre 71–72
undocumented status 96–97
upward mobility 38, 59, 61, 67
urban spaces of color 31; *see also* smartness trespassing
Urschel, John 36n5

Valenzuela, Angela 29
verse genre 71–72
Vickroy, Laurie 92
Villenas, Sofía 49
visibility 116

Walker, Sheila J. 33
Ward, Janie Victoria 33–34
Weheliye, Alexander 23–24
weight stigmas 118
weirdness, as badge of honor 24
What Can(t) Wait (Pérez): overview 14, 55; protagonist 3; "white savior" trope 4
White Bread Competition (Hernández): bullying by white classmates 43; challenging racist narrative 41–46; community pride 46–49; educational racism 44–45; maternal relationships 49; mother/daughter relationships 49–53; overview 13–14, 38; protagonist 3; racial hierarchy 45–46; school board meeting 43; spelling bee's importance 40, 53
white female teachers 57
White, Jaleel 24–25
white maleness, nerdiness belonging to 6, 9, 16, 21–22
white nerd rule 23–24
whiteness, sexual promiscuity and 114–15
white racism 97
white savior myth: in film 56–57; in *Under the Mesquite* 95–96; white female teachers and 57; white teachers versus 118
white savior racism 96
"white savior" trope 4, 56, 62–63
white shaming 107–8
white supremacist colonization 42
white supremacy: threats to 44; violence of 50
white teachers 4, 29, 95, 118
Whitman, Walt 92
Wickham, Anastasia 100
Wilmore, Larry 16
Wissman, Kelly 80
women nerds of color 25–26
women, role in Mexican/Chicana history 51–52

Yarbro-Bejarano, Yvonne 8, 136
You Have the Right to Remain Fat (Tovar) 111–12
Younger, Beth 113–14

Printed in the United States
By Bookmasters